D0046345

PART
of the
PRIDE

PART
of the
PRIDE

My Life Among the Big Cats of Africa

KEVIN RICHARDSON
with **TONY PARK**

St. Martin's Press ✺ *New York*

PART OF THE PRIDE. Copyright © 2009 by Kevin Richardson with
Tony Park. All rights reserved. Printed in the United States of
America. For information, address St. Martin's Press,
175 Fifth Avenue, New York, N.Y. 10010.

www.stmartins.com

Book design by Rich Arnold

Library of Congress Cataloging-in-Publication Data

Richardson, Kevin.
    Part of the pride : my life among the big cats of Africa / Kevin Richardson.—
1st ed.
        p.   cm.
    ISBN 978-0-312-55674-7
    1. Richardson, Kevin.   2. Zoo keepers—South Africa—Biography.
3. Lions—Behavior—South Africa.   4. Captive Felidae—Behavior—
South Africa.   I. Title.
QL31.R46.A3   2009
599.757092—dc22
[B]

                                                            2009016258

First Edition: September 2009

10 9 8 7 6 5 4 3 2 1

For Mandy, who always trusts and believes in
what I do. Thank you.

CONTENTS

ACKNOWLEDGMENTS

Many people have helped me through my life and given their support to me—sometimes when I might not have deserved it.

I'd like to thank my mother, Patricia Richardson, for putting up with my teenage madness and helping me get through school and university.

Rodney Fuhr gave me opportunities that changed my life, and without him I might never have had the many joyous and inspiring experiences that have shaped my life to date. He and his wife, Ilana, have treated me like a member of their family, and I thank them both.

Thank you to my family and friends for all your support and help, especially Trevor and Corrine.

To Stan, Judy, and the rest of the Schmidt family and the extensions thereof, thanks for always inspiring me to follow my heart and passions.

To the South African Lion Park's and the Kingdom of the White Lion's staff and colleagues, thank you for all your support and understanding during the filming of the documentaries and the feature film *White Lion*. A special thank-you to Ian Melass, Ebrahim Patel, and Ian Fuhr for your continual support and guidance.

To Tony and Nicola Park, thanks for helping me write my story. I know it must have been difficult hearing me waffle on for hours and hours at a time, sometimes politely going without food and drink, when I was on a roll.

I'd also like to thank Michael Flamini and the team at St. Martin's Press for their interest in my story. You have all been such a pleasure to work with.

Even though they can't read this, I have to thank the many other friends I've made on my journey so far. To my "brothers," Tau and Napoleon; my "girls," Meg and Ami; to little Homer; to all my other lions, my hyenas, leopards, and all the other animals and birds who have been a part of my life, I say a humble thank you! I hope that I have enriched your lives as much as you have mine.

PART
of the
PRIDE

PROLOGUE

Tsavo

He was called Tsavo, after the place where man-eating lions devoured scores of workers during the building of the railway from Mombasa, Kenya, into the heart of colonial Africa.

Tsavo had come from a different Lion Park than the one where I was working and he'd had a troublesome upbringing. I felt sorry for him, because he'd been declawed, and a lion without claws is like a human without fingers. It was incredibly hard for him to eat and his paw pads were so scarred and calloused that he walked with an unusual gait. His spoor—the tracks he left in the dust—was almost unrecognizable as a lion's. I used to think it was such a shame, what had happened to him, and I wanted to make a difference in his life.

He was about three years old, but he was a big boy for his age. He must have weighed about a hundred and eighty kilograms, or nearly four hundred pounds, and he had a nice, full mane. Between the ages of two and three, a lion is like a human teenager. They've hit puberty, their hormones are raging, and they think they know everything. They don't want to listen to advice and they're up for a challenge. I was the same at Tsavo's age.

Tsavie, as I sometimes called him, was actually quite a friendly lion. I used to say hi to him through the fence, and when I was in the next enclosure with Tau and Napoleon—two younger lions I'd known from a very early age—Tsavo would run up and down beside us as I played soccer with the other two.

Over the months he was at the Lion Park we became friendly, but even so there was always something not quite right about Tsavo.

My extended family had come to the South African Lion Park, at Muldersdrift on the northern outskirts of Johannesburg, one Sunday for a get-together to celebrate my step-nephew Nicholas's eighth birthday. When I was growing up the Lion Park was out in the countryside, far from the city limits, but the lions now have people living almost on their doorstep. Johannesburg has sprawled outwards, with expensive walled housing estates leapfrogging squatter camps, as humans claim more of the open, grassy veld with each passing year. Wealthy South Africans have fled to the secure estates to escape the city's notoriously violent crime; their maids and gardeners live in makeshift shacks of tin and cardboard in the camps, such as the one across the road from the park.

Visitors to the Lion Park can interact with lion cubs and see hyenas, cheetahs, wild dogs, leopards, and other predators up close, then drive through large enclosures to see lions and other mammals, such as giraffe, wildebeest, and impala, in the open. It's a taste of the African bush, albeit with the hum of traffic noise as a soundtrack and Johannesburg's skyline in the distance. My mom and sister and brother-in-law, nephews and nieces, and various uncles and aunts were all crammed into one of the trucks we used for game drives in the open areas. The trucks were like mobile cages on wheels, with steel mesh on the side to protect the people inside from lions, and vice versa. After stopping for pictures with some cute little cubs we set off for a tour of the rest of the park, with me as the guide.

At that time I had a little bit of knowledge about lions and I suppose I thought I knew a fair amount. Although I wasn't working full time at the park I was trusted enough to go into the enclosures with the lions. Unlike other people who worked with dangerous animals, I didn't go in armed with a stick.

"You're *dorf,* man," other people would say. I didn't think I was crazy, just because I didn't need a stick to form a relationship with an animal. Back then, I was already considered unusual—a bit of a nonconformist—and had a reputation for breaking with convention in the methods I used with the animals. With lions such as Tau and Napoleon, who I considered my brothers, I had developed a relationship based on trust and respect. I'd known them since they were six or seven months old and I had always related to them as one of them, down in the grass at their level, rather than lording it over them with a stick or a whip.

At some point, if you use a stick when you work with an animal, you have to put the stick down. "And anyway," I would say to my detractors, "what use is a stick going to be if a lion really wants to get you?"

It was one of those perfect autumn days on the South African Highveld. The sky was big and blue, stretching away forever, and while the day was sunny, the air was cool and crisp. There was still some green left to the grass, but it would be golden by the end of the long, dry winter. The whole family was enjoying the outing and they watched from the truck while Uncle Kevin went into the enclosure with Tau and Napoleon and interacted with his two favorite lions. I hugged them and we rubbed our heads against each other in greeting, and to give the relatives something more to watch we kicked a soccer ball around for a while. Back in those days I thought it was important to put on a good show for visitors.

When people ask me what it's like to hold a lion, to be up close to it, the first thing that comes to my mind is power. Not my power over an animal, but the sheer strength these creatures exude, particularly now that Tau and Napoleon were fully grown.

It's like when you put your foot down on the accelerator pedal of a car with a V8 engine. You don't have to see the engine in action, you can feel it. You can hear it. When you touch a lion's skin for the most part you are feeling sheer muscle, with not an ounce of fat. When it vocalizes or, even better, roars, you feel the vibration in your body.

Then there's the weight of them. Even as youngsters Tau and Napoleon were pretty heavy, but now they weigh nearly six hundred pounds each. When you see a paw up close and try and lift it, you're also trying to heft the weight of that massive forearm, which is the same width as the paw. It's heavy. It's strong enough to bring down a Cape buffalo.

The smell of a lion depends a great deal on what it's been doing and what it's been eating. The amazing thing about lions is they never bathe. The only time they get clean is when it buckets with rain, yet they don't stink. They have a unique odor that I'm so close to I really find it hard to describe. Mandy, my wife, says I'm desensitized to it, though she is not. I find it's like a mixture of pet smells, though not offensive. Not acrid, like cat urine or that musty wet dog smell.

To keep their hair in tip-top shape they excrete an oily substance from behind their ears. That black hair behind the ears, which you'll see when you look closely at a lion, is actually my favourite part. The hair is very soft, almost silky. The rest of the hair on its body varies, as it does on humans, depending on where it is. On the back it's coarser and denser, like a dog's, while on the underbelly and the underside of its legs the coat is again softer. A male's mane is wiry—it needs to be to stand out.

"How does it feel, being able to interact with a lion like you do?" one of my relatives asked, just as many other people have asked me at the park, or over a drink.

The best answer I can give is that the lions are like my buddies, and at the end of a hard day at work it's nice to just sit with your buddies and have a drink and a chat. When I've had a shitty day and I go and sit with the lions, not saying a word, I walk out feeling recharged—green light, ready to function again. The same goes with the hyenas, leopards, and other animals I live with. Mandy says I'm a new person every time.

When I'd finished the curtain raiser, the show I'd put on with the playful youngsters Tau and Napoleon, I went to the outer fence of the next enclosure, to Tsavo, the bigger, older lion.

"Tsavie! Come, Tsavie," I called. I looked over my shoulder at my family and gave them a wave and a smile.

Instead of responding as he usually did, by trotting up to the fence when I called him, Tsavo stayed at the far end of his yard. Even at that early stage in my career working with lions, I had set some rules for myself when dealing with predators. My rule with Tsavo was that if he didn't come when I called, then I would not enter the enclosure with him. I'd know from his reluctance that he preferred to be left alone.

But my whole family was there, watching and waiting expectantly. I could hardly walk back to the truck and say, "Sorry folks, the show's over." It would have been an anticlimax after my antics with Tau and Napoleon.

"Come, Tsavie."

I felt some unspoken pressure. It was the same when other visitors came to the Lion Park. At that time I wanted to please people, and to show them the relationship I had begun to develop with the lions, and to teach people more about these majestic animals. There were some days when I even felt uncomfortable in front of other people with my close friends Tau and Napoleon, as if the lions were acting differently, as well, because there was an audience present. However, each time I got away with the show without incident.

"Tsavie, Tsavie, Tsavie, come, boy!"

I looked back again and saw the family all still looking at me expectantly. This was going to be the finale of the tour—me with the big male lion. I went through the first fence to the second, then opened the gate and took a bold step inside, even though I was feeling uncomfortable and awkward.

Tsavo stayed at the far end of the enclosure, staring at me. I walked towards him, but stayed close to the fence line. When I was halfway between the gate and the lion, I called him again, in a sterner voice than before. "Tsavo! Come, boy."

His ears went back. The skin on his face went taut as he snarled. He puffed his body up, in the way lions do when they mean business. It was as if he was standing on his tiptoes, trying to make himself look even bigger and grander than he truly was. Then he charged.

Tsavo came at me at such a pace that I wouldn't have had a chance of getting out of the enclosure if I'd run. I just had to stand there and wait for whatever came. My family, I later learned, thought that this was all part of the gig. "Wow, this is so cool," one of the kids on the truck said.

Tsavo stopped a couple of paces from me, raising a cloud of dust and loose grass. He reared up on his hind legs and at that point he stood about seven feet high. I'm not a particularly tall guy and Tsavo dwarfed me as he blocked out my view of the sky. When he swiped at me with his huge calloused paw, he was striking downwards, at my face.

In my troubled teen years I was a bit of a fighter, but that blow from Tsavo was harder than the hardest smack I've ever had in my life. Such was the size of the paw and the weight behind it; the swipe felt like three fists hitting me at once. When he connected, the blood exploded from my nose, spraying all over my shoulder and shirt. The driving force of the hit pushed me backwards, but the fence behind me stopped me from falling.

I don't really remember what happened next—whether he dragged me or I rolled away from what I knew was coming—but we ended up in the middle of the enclosure with me on my back and Tsavo straddling me.

"I think Kevin might be in trouble," my sister Corrine said to my brother-in-law Trevor, on board the truck.

"No, Kev's fine. He knows what he's doing," said Trevor, who later told me he hadn't seen the blood pouring from my face at that point. They thought it was still play time, but this was something I hadn't encountered before, the full fury and strength of an angry male lion.

Tsavo started biting me. He sank his canines into my leg, and when he raised his head for the next strike I reached up and used my fingers to push the skin of his cheek between his teeth so he couldn't bite down again without cutting into himself. I'd never heard of this being done—it was instinctive—but what do you do when a lion is trying to eat you? Anything you can think of.

He weighed so much that I couldn't move, and for a while it was like Tom and Jerry—a cat playing with a mouse. If the mouse moves, the cat strikes, but if the mouse stays still the cat loses interest temporarily. However, even though I kept rigid, Tsavo became restless and attacked me again. He bit me on the leg, calf, and shoulder, but each time he released his hold on me as soon as I pushed the skin of his cheek into his mouth again.

Tsavo's canine teeth were so wide apart that when he grabbed my upper arm the teeth grazed down either side of the muscle. My leg, however, was a bigger target, and the sharp points tore through my trousers and drove into the skin once more.

I was lying bleeding in the dust and my relatives were now climbing down out of the caged truck, running to the fence and screaming. My family knew this was no longer part of any show, and Uncle Kevin was most likely dying in there. It seemed like an eternity that Tsavo had been standing over me, but it may have only been seconds.

The lion lowered his massive, shaggy head to my groin and hooked one of his curved, yellowed teeth under the stout leather belt on my trousers. As he lifted me clear off the ground, my back arched and I thought, "Oh shit! Here we go . . ."

ONE

The Bird Man of Orange Grove

I spent my childhood in stitches—the kind the doctor sews into your skin, not the ones you get from rolling around on the floor in laughter. My mom used to say that I was on a collision course with life. She was a smart one, my mom. There was always a certain wildness in me, that I know. When I look back on my early life, it's easy for me now to see the brave lion, the giggling hyena, and the rogue elephant in the things I did then.

I loved the outdoors, but when I was growing up my piece of Africa was limited to a few blocks in the white middle-class suburb of Orange Grove in the north of Johannesburg. I grew up during the time of apartheid among neatly ordered rows of houses, straight streets, backyard gardens, barking dogs, and meowing cats, not rolling savannahs populated by herds of wildebeest, trumpeting elephants, and stalking lions. It was the suburbs, but it could be just as dangerous as the bush.

My mom was always getting calls from school telling her that I'd been hurt, or else I would simply show up at home, bleeding. I was never one to do anything half-hearted, so if I was going to cut myself I would come close to losing an entire limb. I would fall through glass coffee tables, off bicycles, and out of trees, and generally do all the things mothers like to cry about.

"We had better buy this little Kevin a sewing machine so he can sew himself up, hey, Patricia?" the doctor said to my mom once. The doctor and I saw so much of each other we were like buddies. I laughed, then winced, as the dreaded needle punctured skin again and again and again.

One of the earliest mishaps that I can remember was getting on my neighbor's full-sized racing bicycle when I was only three or four years old. It was, I think, the beginning of a lifelong love affair with dangerous things and two-wheeled transport. I'm into extreme sports, I fly microlights, and I play with lions for a living. I have an old 1969 Triumph Bonneville motorcycle and I love riding super-bikes on the track. My hero is the Italian motorcycle champion Valentino Rossi and while I can't ride as fast as him, I've probably been in as many crashes as he has.

I wanted desperately to ride that bicycle and although I was too small to reach the pedals, my neighbor took pity on me and we went for a spin. I was whooping with joy as we gathered speed down the street, the wind rushing in my face as I clung to the older boy. Another kid from the neighborhood, however, thought it would be good fun to push his little wagon into our path and wipe us out. He did a good job and down we went. No one knows how, but in the process I managed to get my toe caught between the bicycle's sprocket and the chain. The cycle was on its side and I was still attached to it, by a piece of stretched skin that was just barely connected to the top of my toe.

"*Ag,* what are we going to do?" asked the panicked owner of the bike.

"We better pull him free," said the evil little shit who had caused the accident. On the count of three the two other boys grabbed me and pulled. Hard. With a piercing yelp on my part, the top of my toe came free from the sprocket and chain—and from me.

"It's moving!" cried the bad boy, pointing down at my severed digit. Although I couldn't see it, the other boys swore the tip of my toe was jumping and wriggling like a gecko's tail when the lizard sheds it to shake off a predator.

While I lay bleeding, my neighbor ran off looking for help and the wagon driver disappeared from the scene of the crime. The cause of the accident—and my considerable pain—reappeared a short while later with a spade. He raised it over his head with his skinny little arms then slammed it down hard onto the ground, and my missing toe.

"Why are you doing that?" I wailed.

"It's freaking me out. It's alive, man!" He raised the spade and smashed down again and again, as if he were killing a snake. Once he was sure he had killed my toe, he dug a hole and buried the evidence. Shortly after, the man from across the road arrived and bundled me into the back of his brand new BMW. It was a *lekker* car and I bled all over the leather upholstery.

"Okay, where's the toe?" asked the doctor when we arrived at Johannesburg Hospital.

"Um, they buried it," I said to the doctor.

The boys were dispatched back to Orange Grove to exhume the missing digit. South African surgeon Dr. Christiaan Barnard may have made history by performing the first successful heart transplant, but not even the most skilled surgeon in the world could reattach the crushed, earth-encrusted lump of skin that those two boys brought into the operating room.

I was born in downtown Johannesburg in the Nightingale Clinic in 1974, two years before television arrived in South Africa, although my family didn't get a TV until I was eight years old. When we did, we were so excited we'd watch the test pattern, but it was no wonder that I learned early on in life how to get my thrills in the backyard and on the streets, and with my animals.

My mom, Patricia, worked as a trust executive for Barclays Bank. She was born in South Africa, but her parents emigrated from England. I don't know exactly what my father, Peter, did, but he worked for a pharmaceutical company—in quality control, I think. He had moved to South Africa from Reading, in the county of Berkshire in the south of England, early in his life. Our relationship was very formal and separate. He was a quiet man. I didn't have the chance to ask him too many questions, we didn't do father and son things together, and he died when I was twelve or thirteen. Like most of the people in Orange Grove, we lived in quite a small 1940s brick three-bedroom house on a big block. I had an older brother and two older twin sisters. We lived on a busy street, Ninth Avenue, which connected the major suburbs in the area. We had tarred roads and "robots"—what we call traffic lights—and my primary means of transport, until I was old enough to ride a bicycle and, later, steal cars, was my red skateboard.

I didn't have the most privileged upbringing. As kids, we never got pocket money or had many toys. We ran our own jumble sales, finding unwanted clothing and knickknacks and selling them to black African people who were worse off than we were. We'd also do gardening chores for neighbors and wash cars. The little money I made usually went for sweets or small toy cars and my dreams were not very grand. The toy I wished for most was a radio-controlled car, but there was no way I was ever going to be able to afford one. I worked hard and finally saved enough money for a remote-control car—one of those where the car is attached to the control via a cable. I was so disappointed. I saw myself watching the car zoom around the room while I stood still and watched. Not so with this one. The wire from the remote to the car kept on getting tangled on things and I had to follow the car everywhere like a dog on a lead.

It was the poor man's version of a true radio-controlled car and not much fun.

Perhaps because of disappointments like the one with the car or the fact that I didn't have every toy or bike I wanted, I developed a love of animals, reptiles, and insects early on in life. People who know me usually assume that passion came from my mother, but she is not, in fact, a big animal person. It was quiet, reserved Dad who brought our first pet home—that much I can remember. It was a tiny stray kitten called Tiger, which he carried in his lunch box. I was about six years old at the time. Dad said he wanted to give us something that we could nurture. He told us the cat had been left to die at a rubbish dump.

We only went away on holiday as an entire family on one occasion when I was a child, in 1980, to the Drakensburg Mountains in Natal. Money was becoming a problem in our household, so all our school holidays, except for that one to the mountains, were spent at home. My brother Gareth and twin sisters Corrine and Candice and I developed a theory that our parents were giving us pets instead of holidays. After Tiger the cat, there was a procession of parrots, goldfish, and dogs as birthday and Christmas presents. The excuse for not going away somewhere exotic on vacation was that we could not leave the animals behind. My dad probably thought the pets would keep our minds off things at home, which were becoming steadily worse as his grip on his career, and his sobriety, became looser and looser.

At any one time we would have about four dogs, three or four cats, the goldfish, and several species of birds including pigeons, doves, weavers, mouse birds, parrots, and other wild birds. I graduated to brown house snakes, and eventually to anacondas. Until recently I had an anaconda which was more than ten feet long. It even had its own small house on the property where I now live. Even though Dad was more interested in the pets than Mom, I don't remember him being around a lot to share them with us. As I said, he had a drinking problem. He seemed to be away a lot and eventually he was downgraded at work. Even with all his troubles, I do recall him bringing home more stray animals and injured birds, which helped spark my interest in caring for things. He seemed to be trying to make a connection with us, but at the same time always seemed so distant and far away.

One of my schoolmates, Warren Lang, kept homing pigeons—big white fantails—and for whatever reason he was told he had to get rid of them. It seemed natural for me to take them on. Without anyone's permission, we disassembled his pigeon *hok* (the Afrikaans word for cage) and moved it, piece by piece, three blocks away to my house, where we reassembled it. We then shuttled the birds, one at a time.

I started breeding the birds and found that I loved it. I would spend hours with my pigeons in the *hok*. Sometimes I would even sleep in there. My mom wasn't too charmed by this, but I found the whole experience of life in the *hok* to be amazing. I would sit patiently beside a mother while she was sitting on her eggs and calculate the days remaining until the chicks would hatch. I was like an expectant father, although it wasn't enough for me just to watch the females and wait for their eggs to hatch—I wanted to be a part of their lives.

"Come on, kick one out. Let me raise one," I would plead with the nesting mothers. It often happened that when a pigeon had two eggs the mother would favor the stronger and fitter of the two offspring. I would take the frail one and try and bring it up, feeding it and nurturing it to full strength.

Where there are pigeons, of course, there are also mice and rats. The rodents came to the *hok* in search of bird feed and eggs that had been kicked out. The mice bred under the bricks beneath the *hok*, and if I took a brick out of the floor I could look in and see a whole family of mice with their little pinkies—their babies. I had my own mini ecosystem happening in there and it was fascinating.

As my father's drinking worsened and things became tougher inside the house, the pigeon *hok* became my refuge.

If the *hok* was my alternative home, then the backyard was my game reserve. I was always mucking about in the drain or digging up crickets or earthworms—anything I could get my hands on. As a child, you want to catch and collect things and keep everything in a box, and not let anything escape.

One of the few occasions our family escaped Orange Grove was to visit my uncle in Fourways on the northern side of Johannesburg, not far from where I eventually ended up working at the Lion Park. It always seemed like a hell of a trip, for which we'd have to pack, even though it was usually just for a day. I was incredibly jealous of my uncle, because he had a pond and frogs in his garden. I was fascinated by my birds and the other household pets, but frogs—amphibians—represented a whole new subset of the animal kingdom.

On one visit my uncle said I could take a frog home with me and I thought he was the best uncle in the world. I was easily impressed. I named my small frog *Paddatjie*, which is Afrikaans for small frog. Okay, so I was never terribly imaginative with names, although once TV took hold in our house there was a spate of celebrity naming. The American soap opera *Dallas* was the top rated program in South Africa at the time, so our African Grey Parrot was named J.R. after Larry Hagman's character, J.R. Ewing. I also had a gaudy lovebird called Madonna.

Paddatjie was a leopard toad, as common as crap, but I was in awe because I thought I had discovered a totally new species of toads. I made him a little terrarium, decorated with the sorts of accessories I thought a frog would like. I used a cardboard box and even though I covered it, he was able to knock the lid off and jump out. He would leap through the house, and at the time I thought he was a particularly smart and tough guy, being able to avoid being eaten by our pack of dogs and pride of household cats. With the benefit of a bit of education, I now reckon they all probably had a good taste of *Paddatjie* at one time or another, and, finding him thoroughly unpalatable, spat him out.

I was convinced that *Paddatjie* recognized me as his friend and would escape from his box in order to find me and watch *Dallas* with me and my parrot, J.R. Ewing. I think I managed to convince my family of this, too, and they were no doubt impressed with my way with wild creatures from a very early age. I used to catch insects for the frog's dinner and take him for walks in the garden to give him a taste of the great outdoors, rather than spending all his days as a caged, though tough and intelligent, amphibian.

I learned a lot through *Paddatjie*—especially that it wasn't essential for everything I picked or dug up to be kept in a box twenty-four hours a day. Even though I thought it was good for him to experience life as a free-range frog from time to time, I was terribly disappointed when one day he hopped out of his box and disappeared for good.

More rewarding, of course, was when I released my homing pigeons and they actually did come home. However, even in the pigeon *hok* nature could be cruel. One day our Rhodesian Ridgeback, a big, fierce, sandy-colored breed of dog, and our Labrador got into the *hok* and killed all thirty of my pigeons. I think my mother was secretly happy, as I'm sure she had long wanted all the pigeons dead. I just wanted to kill the dogs.

As I got older, my reputation earned me a nickname—The Birdman of Orange Grove. Any bird which was sick or injured would be brought to my house. Some enterprising criminals even began stealing baby pigeons from their nests and asking me for five bob—fifty cents—for them. That was a lot of money for me, but I was usually able to sweet-talk them into giving me the chick for nothing, or for some food from our house. The African people who were taking the birds were doing it because they were hungry.

I couldn't count how many baby birds I rescued, reared, and released. The nicest thing was when a bird I had sent back to the wild returned to the house or sat on my shoulder again. I also found that I was enjoying setting things free far more than trapping them, so I adopted this policy with my collection of parrots, letting them out of their cages. Some flew away and never returned, and although I took to putting up reward posters around the neighborhood, I eventually realized this was part of life. Sometimes things left and never came back.

A couple of birds stick in my mind. Mouse the mouse bird, whose name was about as original as *Paddatjie* the frog, had been kicked out of his nest in the wild because he had a deformed wing. Because he could never fly, he really was like a little mouse. He walked everywhere with me and really touched my life. He depended on me totally, and it gave me a great deal of satisfaction knowing that without my care he wouldn't make it in the world. J.R. the parrot had lived in a cage all his life, and when I released him for the first time he was like a long-term prisoner set free from jail. He didn't know what to do with himself. He would run around the floor in circles acting crazy. It was as if he was panicked by the sudden excess of space around him. J.R. was a vicious bird, who had savaged many a finger in his time, but over time I was able to tame and calm him and he became a gentle companion inside and outside his cage. An African Grey Parrot can live to fifty or sixty years of age, but after having soothed this traumatized jail bird, it was crushing for me when he died of a bird cold. It was always tough for me when one of my pets died. Although I toughened up as I got older, there were some animals that would stay in my heart forever.

From an early age I realized I wouldn't be content just to look at my pets. I wanted to get to know each one, to build a relationship with it and to test the boundaries of how I could react to it, and vice versa. I wasn't cruel to them, just curious. I learned that each bird or animal was an individual. For example, in the pigeon *hok* I discovered the bird in the end box would peck my hand if I tried to take her eggs, but the one at the opposite end would sit aside and tolerate my prying, because I had a better relationship with her and she had a more tolerant nature. From this early age, I became an observer of note, and to this day I am fastidious about keeping notes and records about my animals and every aspect of their lives. I would study my birds and animals for hours on end. I was pretty good at sketching. I could draw a pretty good cheetah from an early age, even though I had never seen one in real life. So I started drawing my animals. I'd draw from life or memory and got help from photos in books. As I drew them, I understood them even more.

My sisters were interested in animals, but not to the same degree as me. My brother liked our pets, but was not as hands on as I was. I have never been one who can look at an animal and say, "That's very pretty." Instead, I'd say, "I wonder what would happen if I touch you? If I could just get to know you a bit better perhaps we could do more together than just look at each other. Do you know me and recognize my voice? If not, I wonder if I could I form a relationship with you?" These were the questions I asked.

I used to talk to my pigeons. They knew my voice and they would come when I called them, which was very nice. I could bounce things off them, as well, and like the dogs and (sometimes) the cats, they gave unconditional love. The pigeons just wanted some food and a scratch on the head. "Kevin, come and get your dinner now," Mom would call. "If you don't come now you can sleep with those pigeons." Sometimes I did, as it was simply better to be with them in the pigeon house than going inside and being witness to the strained relationship that was developing between my parents.

I even tried to develop relationships with the goldfish, which were more my sisters' than mine. I wanted to be interactive with the fish and found the whole concept of keeping them quite amusing. I couldn't believe that anyone would be happy just staring at a fish in a bowl. I used to pat the water and I loved it when the goldfish would come and suck my finger. Eventually I learned that rather than my being able to commune with the fish, they were actually just trying to suck the tiny air bubbles that formed around my finger. I soon realized I'd never be a big keeper or trainer of fish.

I did, however, try and get my animals to do things. I was fascinated with those stories about bird trainers in America who could get their parrots to ride bicycles and perform all sorts of tricks. Before he died, I was able to teach J.R. the parrot how to do bench presses with a pencil.

My career choices as a child included bird trainer, veterinarian, zookeeper, or game ranger. Every young boy in South Africa wants to become a game ranger, but the closest I came to South Africa's national parks and private wildlife reserves in those days was listening to stories from other kids. The Kruger National Park is less than three hundred miles from Johannesburg, but it may as well have been on the other side of the moon as far as I was concerned. Boys would get up in class at show-and-tell and talk about seeing lions and elephants and all sorts of other wild animals in the Kruger National Park, or their family's visit to the pools at Warmbaths, which was considered the height of sophistication as a holiday destination for the people of Orange Grove. I didn't know anything about the wider Africa, with its wide open plains and thorny Bushveld teeming with wild animals, other than what I'd read in a book or seen on television. To me, Africa was my backyard. When it was my turn to get up in front of the class for show and tell, I would say, "Well . . . err, I found a bird's egg."

I changed my mind, though, about wanting to be a zookeeper after a visit to the Johannesburg Zoo when I was in grade one. Zoos in those days were pretty bad. The animals basically lived in concrete cages, and the first time in my life that I saw a lion, pacing from one side of its tiny enclosure to another, it was pretty uninspiring. That visit certainly didn't make me want to abandon my birds and bugs and work with big cats. I stood in front of the concrete pen and looked at the king of the jungle, and all I could think was, "Shame, man, what a way for you to end up." I hated the zoo from that point onwards. It didn't go with what my little animal kingdom in Orange Grove was all about. There was no one, at least that I could see, who was interested in keeping that lion active and alert during his captivity.

While zookeeper was off my list of preferred jobs, I did start thinking that I would quite like to be a vet when I grew up, as I would get to play with animals and make some serious money at the same time. I did well at primary school and I was voted head boy, even though my parents didn't believe it when it happened. I was becoming a naughty child at home, although I maintained an angelic front at school. When I came home, all proud and puffed up, I told my folks the good news, but they accused me of lying. I persisted and they only believed me after they made a point of visiting the school and saw my name inscribed on the big wooden board at the end of the list of all the past head boys. After that, they were very proud of me. I think.

Despite my shiny public persona at school I still managed to get into mischief behind the scenes and out of hours. When I was about ten years old and well into my animal-liberation phase, I became concerned about the plight of some frogs that lived in a terrarium in the science classroom. A mate and I decided that it would be better if we set them free—that is, if we took over their custody until I decided the time was right to return them to the wild.

One Friday at the end of school, we helped close up the classroom, but made a point of leaving one of the windows unlocked in the science room. We hung around until everyone had left, including the cleaners, then climbed up on to the window ledge and into the classroom. The following Monday all hell broke out and everyone was talking about the missing frogs. Some people thought they might have escaped on their own, but in the end the finger of blame was pointed at one or two environmentally conscious teachers, which my mate and I thought was hilarious. Back home we convinced ourselves that the frogs were living a much better life in a shoe box under my bed than in their purpose-designed terrarium in the science room. Unfortunately, I didn't give them nearly enough water and they died. It taught me an important lesson: just because an animal is caged, it doesn't necessarily mean that animal is neglected.

Thanks to the family situation, which was deteriorating, I never really wanted to go home at night. I became so hooked on releasing things that I took it to ridiculous extremes. Not content just to set free our existing stock of birdlife, I took to raiding nests with a friend after school. We'd take out baby birds which I would raise with the sole intent of later releasing them. When I think back on it I realize what I was doing was horrific, but I loved birds so much I wanted to be part of their lives—even the wild ones'. I climbed an aloe and found a common turtledove's nest. There were two babies, and I remember thinking that if I took one then there was no way the mother could reject the other. In my young mind, I was doing good by raising one of the birds and then letting it go. The problem was that my zeal to raise wildlife—indoors—slowly started taking over our suburban home.

My brother and I used to share a bedroom. While his side of the room was always neatly organized and spotlessly clean, mine was a mess. I'm neater these days, but once my brother moved out, my birds, snakes, dogs, cats, bugs, and I took over. Mom and the twins and I came home from a night out and there was an officer from the local security company waiting for us outside the house.

"Your burglar alarm went off. There's been a break-in," the man said. He looked at us and his face was set like granite. "Don't touch anything when you go in as the police are on their way to take fingerprints. Prepare yourself for a shock. The house has been ransacked and one room is far worse than the others."

Nervously, we followed Mom and the guard into the house, expecting the worst.

"It's actually fine," Mom said to the man, trying to hide her embarrassment after a brief inspection of our home and my room, which looked like it had been ransacked. "Everything's just as we left it, including Kevin's room."

My room was a mess, I admit it. Within that mess, I had a growing collection of grasshoppers and locusts, which I kept under my bed. Even though they were right under my bed, the chirping noise of locusts, outside on summer nights, used to terrify me. I could never work out what kind of monster was making this incredible racket just beyond my window. My father found out I was scared of the mystery noise and one night he took me outside and told me it was just a little black cricket that was responsible. We couldn't find one in the dark, and I wasn't completely convinced, but when I heard the same sound screeching from within a box under my bed, I realized my dad wasn't talking rubbish.

Even though he had his problems, I think my dad had a good job, especially when I was much younger and we once went on a holiday to the mountains. I'm sure some people overseas think that everyone who lives in Africa has a small army of servants, and while we had a maid when times were good, when things changed at my father's work we had to let her go. Mom would have to come home and clean the house and as Dad's drinking got worse, she was under increasing stress.

Things might have been going bad for Dad, but he was still our father and he was a strict disciplinarian. When we were naughty we would get lashed with his thick leather belt. It was his tool of choice and it was effective in getting one of us to talk when no one had owned up to a crime. It sounds harsh, but that was the way things worked when I was growing up.

My brother Gareth was a Goody Two-shoes who always had his nose in a book. I used to read books about birds and animals, but he was into everything, including fiction as well as nonfiction. He studied hard, and these days he works as a veterinarian in the UK. Me, I was the naughty little runt of our litter, with a knack for getting up to mischief and bleeding all over the place.

Gareth and I used to fight like cats and dogs. Although he was four years older, I was much more physical and feisty than him. He was always finding ways to show how much smarter he was than me, and how superior he was. He would taunt me, telling me how he was going to end up as a vet, while I was no good at anything and would come to nothing. We'd end up in full-blown fistfights. I don't remember it, but my friend Dave still tells the story about the day he thought I was going to kill Gareth. I can't even recall what started the fight, but it was one of those real Hollywood punch-ups that went from our bedroom into the lounge room, then into the kitchen and finally out into the front garden. There was a heavy old brass weight in our room and apparently I had taken this out of the house with me. Dave said he had to pull me off Gareth as I was about to bash his brains in with the weight. I guess I was in such a rage at the time that I later blanked it out.

I wasn't only curious about animals. I was just as curious about how different mechanical sorts of things worked. One thing that fascinated me was the toilet. I guess all little kids are interested in this funny thing that people make jokes about and I wanted to learn how it worked. One day, when I was still quite small, I decided I would take a peek inside the gurgling thing at the back of the toilet that made all the noise after you flushed. I was able to slide the heavy china lid off, but I wasn't quite strong enough to lift it clear. It slipped from my hands and landed on the bowl. The whole thing, lid and toilet, was smashed into pieces.

When Dad came home from work, my brother, the twins, and I were all lined up and told to drop our pants and bend ourselves forward across the big kitchen table, where we used to eat our meals. My dad unbuckled his belt and slid it from the loops on his trousers. He ran the tap in the kitchen sink until it was half full. We could hear what he was doing, and knew why, though none of us dared to turn and watch as he dipped the leather belt in the sink full of water. Wetting it, we knew from painful experience, made the lash of the belt sting even more. We could hear Dad's footsteps on the kitchen floor as he began parading up and down behind us, while we waited there, quivering.

"Right, who's responsible?" he asked.

"Well, it couldn't have been me, Dad," I piped up. "I mean, I'm not strong enough to even lift the top off the toilet."

My brother and sisters all blamed each other, but in the end I convinced Dad I was too much of a weakling to have destroyed the toilet and the rest of them all ended up in the shit. I was naughty back then, but later I became a monster.

TWO

Rogue Male

At the time of writing this book the South African National Parks service is considering reintroducing the practice of culling elephants in Kruger National Park. Although the park has been expanded across the border into neighboring Mozambique, creating what is now known as the Greater Limpopo Transfrontier Park, it is still a finite area. Elephants were once able to migrate freely over huge swathes of Africa, but these days farming, the growth of cities and towns, and other land uses have confined them mostly to national parks and game reserves. In Kruger National Park, the experts have deemed that unless elephant numbers are managed then the ecosystem will suffer because of overgrazing. Adult elephant bulls eat between a hundred and eighty and two hundred and seventy kilograms—nearly six hundred pounds—of vegetation per day and will knock over fully grown trees to get to roots or leaves out of their reach. While this clearing of the bush has some benefits for the environment, including clearing paths to water for smaller animals and creating microecosystems around the trunks of felled trees, if there are too many elephants in an enclosed area they will destroy their environment faster than it can regrow.

Whatever you might think of culling—the deliberate and planned killing of animals for management purposes—past experience has shown the national parks authorities that the most humane way to control elephant numbers was to take out an entire herd at a time. In the early 1980s, protests from some sectors of the community resulted in the culling teams sparing some young male elephants from targeted herds. These young males were translocated to other national parks such as Pilansberg, near the Sun City hotel and casino complex, and Hluhluwe-Imfolozi in KwaZulu Natal.

Elephants are social creatures and young ones are brought up in a family environment where they learn how to live and how to behave. The practice of relocating individual young bulls, while done with good intentions, proved to be a disaster. The youngsters grew up in their new homes without the benefit of discipline from older males, or being taught life's lessons from their mothers. As a result, they went crazy. They began attacking other animals and vehicles, and there were even examples of elephants sexually assaulting rhinoceroses. In Hluhluwe-Imfolozi alone they killed thirty-eight rhinos. To remedy the situation, older bull elephants had to be introduced into the reserves to knock the youngsters into shape.

When I was in high school I was like one of those young orphan bull elephants.

One Friday, when I was about twelve, I came home late from my school, Highlands North, after visiting a friend's house. This wasn't unusual as I was never all that keen to get home and I'd almost become the adopted extra child in a couple of my friends' families.

Dad was out of work and was spending more and more time at home. Waiting for me outside the house was my uncle, the one who had given me *Paddatjie*. I immediately knew something was not right, as we only saw him two or three times a year. My sisters were both working after school at the Dion retail store. My uncle stopped me as I walked in the gate and said, "Come, we're going to fetch your sisters." On the way to the store he spilled the beans, blunt and to the point. "Kevin, your father's passed away."

I knew my dad had been for a job interview that day and as part of the process he'd had a medical exam that morning, to make sure he was fit. My brother Gareth was at home and Dad had told him that he was just going for a lie-down. Dad apparently asked my brother to make him some soup, and while Gareth was away in the kitchen doing that for him, my dad passed away from a pulmonary embolism as he lay on the couch. On the outside Dad hadn't seemed a sick person, although he smoked like a chimney and we all knew he drank too much.

My first thought when my uncle told me was, "Oh no, what's going to happen now?" But, even though I'm ashamed to say it, then I felt a small sense of relief. Three years before he died, he'd lost his job completely and went on a bit of a drinking binge. When that happened, even though he was our father, my brother, sisters, and I didn't even really want to be around him. I know that sounds a bit strange, terrible even, but I remember thinking that now we could get on with this life of ours, as a family. It was almost like he was a burden rather than one of the household. It was a bit of a relief for my mom, too. My dad was never violent, but things had been strained between them and she'd been the sole breadwinner for a couple of years by the time he died.

When I work with lions I find that if I've known the lion since birth or a very early age, and I've spent plenty of time with him when he's young, then I'll have a much better relationship with him when he matures. As the saying goes, "As you sow, so shall you reap." I think it's the same with fathers and sons. A dad who has spent time with his boy during his childhood will have a better relationship with him later as opposed to, say, one who has been missing from his life until his teens, and shows up late in the piece saying, "How-zit, China, let's go out on the town and be buddies."

Even if my father had not died and there had been a big change in his life—maybe getting another job—and he had decided to pay more attention to us kids, I still think there would have been too much water already under the bridge for him to be able to stop me behaving the way I did over the next few years. The one strong part he had played in my life, that of the strict disciplinarian, was gone forever the day he died.

Things settled down for a while in the family after he died, but the difference for me was that I didn't have anyone controlling me anymore. As time went by and the grieving process ran its course, I started testing the boundaries of the new situation I found my-self in. I'd started off fairly well at high school, but by the age of thirteen I started drinking and going out at nights—*jolling,* as we called it.

My brother's identification book, a document everyone of legal age had to carry in South Africa, had gone through the washing machine, and when he applied for a new one I managed to get my hands on the old, partially ruined one. I took a picture of myself and put that through the washing machine, deliberately, then care-fully placed it on the old one where Gareth's photo had been. I did the same thing with his driving license. Basically, I stole his identify and became Gareth Richardson, aged eighteen, which allowed me to drive, drink alcohol, and get into night clubs.

I was driving from the age of fourteen, and that was partly my mother's fault, though through no intention of hers. I learned early on in my teens how to take advantage of the kindness of others and my mom was a prime target. I wanted to learn to drive so she started by letting me drive the car up and down the driveway, practicing driving forwards and in reverse, and getting used to the stick shift and the clutch, brake, and accelerator. "Mom, if I wash the car, will you take me driving on the street?" I would pester her, even though I still hadn't reached the legal age to start learning to drive on public roads.

When Dad was alive she had taken the bus to work and had never needed to drive, but as the sole parent she now had to learn all over again. She saved her pennies and bought a smart little yellow Mini Clubman. My sisters were old enough to start learning—legally—so all of us would cram into the Mini and go out for driving lessons together. We would find a quiet road or a parking lot, and my sisters and I would teach my mother how to reverse park. It took Mom ten tries to get her license and we all cheered when she finally made it.

Once I learned to drive I realized that it would be a piece of cake for me to take the car out at night, when everyone else in the house was sleeping. I had a couple of mates, Dave and Dino, whom I used to get into trouble with. Dave was Jewish, Dino was Italian, and I'm Anglican, so we were a representative sample of the kids at Highlands North, which was a government-run school. We also had quite a few Lebanese kids, and our school had a richly deserved reputation for fighting with other schools, as well as among ourselves. Dino was a big oke—a six-foot guy who played rugby, and his size and strength came in handy when it was time for me to steal Mom's car. Dave and Dino would come over after dark and wait for me outside. I would creep into Mom's room and make sure she was sound asleep, then tiptoe outside and meet the boys.

"Right. Coast is clear," I would say.

Our driveway was quite steep and it slanted uphill away from the house. We had a heavy steel security gate and the three of us boys had to lift it carefully and slide it along its rails so that it didn't make a screeching noise. I couldn't risk starting the car's engine in the driveway, in case the sound woke my mom or sisters, so Dave, Dino, and I would scrum down, as if we were playing rugby, and push the car up the hill and out onto the street. It would have been impossible without Dino. As we rolled down the street I would start the car on the move once we were out of earshot from my house. After that, it was time to drive and time to party. I used to race that car as fast I could, ramping it up over pavements and pushing my own boundaries as a driver more and more.

"Come shopping with me, Kevin," Mom said to me one Saturday morning as I lay in bed.

Hungover, I rolled over and rubbed my eyes. My mouth tasted like the bottom of J.R.'s cage and my head throbbed from too much cheap brandy. I mumbled, "If I'm going to go shopping with you, then you must give me money to go jolling, Mom."

She gave in, and on the way to the supermarket, she kept glancing down at the dashboard. "Kevin, I think there's something wrong with this car. I filled it up yesterday, but now the gauge is only showing half full."

"*Ja*, Mom, I know all about that." I wound down the window to get some fresh air and burped, hoping she wouldn't smell the booze on my breath. Despite my state I was still thinking fast. "I found a little hole in the fuel tank, but I fixed it for you. Since I did that for you, can we go driving this afternoon?"

Mom believed everything her darling baby boy told her. By nine o'clock she'd be in bed, and by ten my mates and I would be at a club. We'd go to places such as Balalaika in Sandton; Bella Napoli, the Dome, and the Summit, which was a strip club. Back in the late eighties discos were big. It wasn't the whole rave and drug era that goes on today, but we were drinking anything we could get our grubby little paws on. We'd buy the cheapest stuff that would get us drunk the quickest. Our specialty was a two-liter bottle of Coca

Cola topped up with cane spirit—spook and diesel, it was called. We'd fill up on that and then we'd charm girls into buying us beers at the clubs. I've never really been a smoker, though I would take drags just to get a head spin. I tried dope, but it just made me sleepy and hungry. There was no way I wanted to get the munchies and be stuffed full of food and in bed by ten. We just wanted to go out, party, and get laid.

If we weren't going to a club we'd find a house party. Rich kids from Sandton, Parkhurst, and Rosebank would make money while their parents were overseas on holidays by putting on a party and charging an entrance fee. Once inside there was free alcohol and women galore. On nights when I couldn't risk taking the Mini we would walk or hitchhike all over town, and have an all-nighter. I couldn't imagine doing it in Johannesburg these days, because of the crime problem in the city.

We were invincible and not even the cops could stop us. I was pulled over one day by a policeman for no apparent reason while driving a friend to a weekend rugby game. The cop asked to see my license and I produced my fake identification. I told him my driver's license had also gone through the washing machine, but was in even worse shape than my ID and that I was waiting for a new one to arrive. He wasn't satisfied with my excuse and told me that I, Gareth Richardson, would have to report to the local police station the following Monday with a valid driver's license. When I got home I called my brother, who was at vet school at Onderstepoort. As luck would have it, he was coming home for a few days.

"Howzit, *bru*?" I said to him with unusual friendliness. "Guess what? You have to report to the police station on Monday."

"Why?"

"Because you're you, and I'm you, but the real you needs to prove you're the real you . . . to the cops. All right?"

Amazingly, and to his credit, Gareth did this for me. I owed him one, but somehow I doubt I ever repaid the debt. I abused the goodwill of my family, and even took advantage of my sister Corrine, who for some reason would often stick up for me when I got in trouble. I convinced her to give Dave and me a lift in the Mini when she was on her way to work, at a restaurant in Sandton City. I told her we were going to go to the movies. She dropped us at the mall and went to work, but a short time later I went to the restaurant and asked if I could borrow her car keys, telling her I'd left my jumper in the car.

I got in the car and started her up. For the next two hours—the duration of the movie we were supposedly watching—I put the Mini through its paces, driving hard and fast through the suburbs of Johannesburg. I knew I was cutting it fine, to get the car back before she became suspicious, so I was still speeding when we drove up to the shopping center. The tires squealed on the smooth concrete surface of the multi-storied car park and when we hit the speed bumps, all four wheels left the ground.

My brother Gareth had borrowed the Mini and crashed it into a brick wall some time earlier. I had conned Mom into letting me drive the car occasionally in exchange for repairing the vehicle. I didn't have the money for all the proper replacement parts so I had organized for a whole new front end—left and right fenders, hood and grille—to be made out of fiberglass. As Dave and I crested the last speed bump in the car park, the impact of the Mini crashing down on its suspension caused the whole front of the car to come loose and fly off. I put the car into a slide and skidded into the same space where she had been.

Corrine, who had been wondering where we were, walked into the car park as I was slotting the front of the car back into place. "Kevin, what are you doing?"

"Um, just showing Dave the engine, sis."

The Mini was my car of choice to steal for our after hours jolls, but if it was parked in I could also take an old 1979 Toyota Corolla which the family had inherited from my grandmother when she passed away, or dad's 1980 baby blue Mazda 323. We hated being seen in the Mazda. I was used to driving all the other cars, but one night one of my sisters, Candice, who was studying at nursing college at the time, had left her Fiat 131 Mirafiori in the driveway then gone off to stay at her boyfriend's place.

When Dino arrived at my place for our usual nightly departure we slipped outside and started downing our preferred cocktail of spook and diesel. We drank hard and fast, chasing feelings of relaxation, confidence, and euphoria. I pointed to the boxy red Italian car and said, "Come, let's take this one."

It had been raining that night and the roads were slippery, but I hadn't driven the Fiat before and wanted to put it through its paces. As usual, we pushed the vehicle out of the driveway and down the street a bit before starting it. I was still only about eight kilometers from home, on the road to Sandringham, but I was already pushing it to its limits.

With Dino beside me egging me on I floored it. I watched the speedometer climb through seventy, eighty, ninety, and finally a hundred kilometers an hour. The gearbox was automatic, which I hated as I preferred stick shifts. However, I had the engine screaming at full revs as the transmission did its work. I cared for the car about as much as I cared for the feelings of my sister or my mom. I preyed on the innocence and goodwill of my family in those days. I'm not proud of it, but it's the way I was.

"Faster!"

I dropped down a gear and pushed the accelerator into the firewall before ramming it up into drive again. I came to a downhill stretch and I roared with exhilaration as the needle passed the 170-kilometer mark. We were flying at more than a hundred miles an hour down this suburban road and the rainwater hissed like a cobra under the Fiat's wafer thin little wheels.

At the bottom of the hill there was a dip. Even if I'd had time to brake I wouldn't have. The suspension bottomed out as I hit the depression and I lost control. Because of the speed we were traveling at and the slickness of the road, the car spun through three full 360-degree turns. The streetscape was spinning past our eyes at a dizzying speed. We hit the pavement and rolled.

Luck or a guardian angel was on my side, because we missed a light pole by inches. If we'd hit it we would have been dead. The car ended up on the passenger's side. I lay there for a moment, stunned, but Dino climbed up over my lap and out of my window. It was only a small car and he was a strong guy so while I was still inside he pushed the car back over on to its wheels. I looked up, shaking my head and he slammed the open bonnet down with a thud.

He banged on the roof of the car. "Come, let's go, Kevin."

"Dude, the car is stuffed," I replied. "It's come to an end. We're finally going to get busted this time."

Dino climbed in and wouldn't take no for answer. "Let's go!"

As an indication of how drunk we were, Dino convinced me that we could wash the damage off the car, so we found a garage and the owner let us wash the Fiat in the middle of the night. There we were, two drunk teenagers trying to wash scratches off a car. We sobered up pretty quickly.

We managed to limp the vehicle home and I summoned up the courage to tell my mother what had happened. I knocked on the door of her bedroom and opened the door.

"Ma, I've crashed Candice's car."

Still half asleep, she mumbled, "Go back to bed, Kevin, you're dreaming."

"No, Ma, you don't understand. I stole the car and I crashed it."

Mom woke up. "Kevin, I'm going to kill you!"

Even in our moment of shame Dino and I still had a plan. We'd decided in advance that when the shit hit the fan we would start crying. Mom was telling us off and I started pushing the tears out, telling her how sorry I was and how we hadn't meant to cause any damage. My sister Corrine, whom I've always had a great relationship with, stood up for us, though why she did that I don't know.

We were grounded for the rest of our lives and both had to get part-time jobs to pay for the repairs to the car. Dino got a hiding, and his old man wanted to *klap* me, too. God knows, I deserved a hit.

Predictably, my schoolwork took a pounding during those rebellious years. I was out three or even four nights a week on drinking binges and hungover in the mornings. I'd also put my animals to one side. By that stage most had died—because of age, not neglect—or been freed during my release stage, and with Mom struggling to make ends meet, we had scaled down to just a couple of dogs and one or two birds at any one time.

I tried to be a good boy sometimes. I bought my mother a teddy bear for her birthday one year, but I got so drunk the night before that somehow I managed to throw up on the bear. I went to the bathroom, still pissed, and tried to clean it, but needless to say it was in no fit condition to hand over as a present.

My uncle tried sitting me down and counseling me, telling me that since my brother had left for vet school I was the man of the house, and all that sort of stuff. I know that he wanted to hit me, but he couldn't bring himself to do it as he was such a nice guy. I probably needed a beating, but he made no headway with me, and he and Mom thought I would never come right.

If I wasn't bunking off school I was picking fights with other kids. Discipline at school was a joke, and even though we would get six of the best—smacks on our butts with a cane—or be placed on detention, we treated those punishments as a joke. I always knew what was right and wrong, and while I didn't do particularly well at high school, I was able to study enough to scrape through.

We loved playing rugby at school and while the game itself doesn't make people aggressive, we would hype each other up before games and tell each other how we were going to hammer our opponents. Without a father figure to keep me in line, I just continued to play up. My other friends, of course, had fathers and used to be disciplined, so thinking back on it now I was probably a bad influence on them, rather than the other way around.

The only positive outlet I had for my anger was cycling. I would take my cycle out in the afternoons and ride forty or fifty kilometers a day. I used the cycle to visit girls on the other side of the city, and at weekends my friends and I would ride in hundred-kilometer races. I loved going fast—still do. Mom used to insist that I get home by dark, and after visiting a girl who lived near the racetrack at Kyalami I was pushing it to get home by nightfall. As I was tearing along a policeman leapt out from the side of the road and waved me down.

"You were doing eighty kilometers per hour in a sixty zone," the cop said to me. "Do you realize you were speeding?"

"No, officer, I didn't. Anyway, I'm on a bicycle, so what are you going to do about it?"

He shrugged his shoulders and I sped off.

As my friends and I got older we were able to get away from Orange Grove every now and then, if only for the weekend. Dino's family had a holiday place at Bronkhorstspruit Dam about fifty kilometers east of Pretoria. On one visit we found a Grey Heron which had become entangled in fishing lines. Some guys staying at the dam had gone to bed after a big night's drinking and left their rods, baited with balls of corn meal pap, stuck in the riverbed. It was winter, and when I put my fingers in the water it was freezing cold. We could see the bird was alive—just—and I decided that Dino would be the best person to go into the water and free the bird.

"Why me?"

"I know about birds. I'm going to be the one who fixes it and I have to be ready, here on the shore, to take it off your hands when you bring it out of the water." I was, after all, the birdman of Orange Grove.

"Okay."

Dino swam out into the icy dam and was able to free the bird, which was near dead from being trapped in the cold water all night. Dino, teeth chattering and body shivering, was near hypothermic, and the only thing I could think of was for all three of us to go to the shower room and get under a hot shower. Inside we stripped off and crowded into the cubicle. I turned on the hot tap and Dino and I held on to the bird. I had no idea if this was the right thing to do, and just when I thought it might actually die from my extreme treatment the heron came to life.

A grey heron is a big bird that stands about a meter tall, and it looks a hell of a lot bigger when it flares its wings and starts attacking you with its very long beak. Dino and I fought each other to open the shower cubicle door and escape its stabbing pecks. The heron followed us out and chased us around the changing room, flapping its wings and squawking madly. We were trying to chase it outside and the bird was trying to kill us, which I thought was a fine show of gratitude. Eventually we cornered it and, waving and squawking ourselves, shooed it to the door. Sometimes I wonder if there are people in South Africa who tell the story of the time they were camping and saw a Grey Heron running out of a toilet block, being chased by two naked teenage boys.

That wasn't the only time, however, that a few naked teenage boys made an impression on the wildlife of Africa. Once, the three of us went camping in the Retiefskloof of the Magaliesberg Mountains. We were dropped off one weekend and set off to cause mayhem. That sort of unchecked, unauthorized camping doesn't happen in the national park anymore, probably because of what people like us used to get up to.

We decided to go skinny-dipping in a pristine waterhole. It was warm and sunny, and we found that we could slide on our bare bottoms down some water-slicked rocks and splash into the pool. While we were playing we saw a troop of baboons clambering across the rocks high above us.

"*Wah-hoo*," cried one of the baboons, giving a warning call.

"Wah-hoo," we all started yelling back, teasing them.

We thought this was great fun, but the baboons weren't impressed. There was a splash in the water hole next to me.

"What was that?"

"Shit, someone's throwing rocks at us," one of the other guys said.

As we scrambled out of the water, looking for our clothes, there was a minor avalanche of rocks and small boulders raining down on us. As I hopped on the rock while I pulled my shorts on, I looked up again. It was the baboons. They were the ones attacking us and now they were moving down the slope. I'd heard of stories of adult male baboons ripping apart leopards in fights, so I was more than a little worried.

As the baboons closed in on us, two stopped, crouched, and defecated in their hands.

"Oh, no! Shit!" Which was exactly what started pelting at us during round two of the baboons versus the teenagers. I'd heard of primates doing this in zoos, but not in the wild. These baboons were adding insult to injury and we took off, their foul-smelling missiles shattering in the trees behind us. If their lesson to us was to be respectful of others, we forgot it a short time later when we crossed another stream and found a dozen bottles of beer that some Afrikaner campers had sunk in the water to cool. We slipped away with our liquid manna from heaven, and later laughed and drank ourselves stupid.

The car crash had been a wake-up call, but it wasn't until I met my first real father figure that I started to apply myself to my schoolwork and, as it happened, to my animals again. His name was Stan Schmidt, and to my friends and me he was a god. He also had a very pretty daughter, named Lisa, whom I fell in love with. Stan

Schmidt was a renowned South African karate champion and the founder of the South African Japan Karate Association. Every boy knew who he was and we were all in awe of him.

"You can't possibly be going out with Stan Schmidt's daughter," one of my mates said when I told him who Lisa's father was. "Dude, Stan's going to kick your arse big time as soon as you do something wrong to his girl."

However, Stan was so not the person people thought he was. He never threatened me. He and his wife, Judy, would sit me down sometimes and talk to me about the directions I was taking, and life in general. I'd talk for hours with Stan, and started spending more time with Lisa and her family than with my own. As a result of the Schmidts' influence I started studying harder at school, and I even started going to church! It was one of the conditions of going out with Lisa. For some reason they trusted me and I started calming down.

It was all about respect. I don't think I'd had respect for anyone else up until that point. I respected Stan not only for his achievements, but for who he was. When that oke talked, I listened.

Stan and Judy also rekindled my interest in animals. At the time I met Lisa I'd already found another African Grey Parrot, Rebecca, after J.R. died. I convinced the Schmidts that birds could make good pets and they bought a Macaw. Stan had to travel to karate tournaments overseas and the family would take me overseas—a first for me. As well as the karate tournaments, we would go to bird shows. I traveled all over the United States with them and back home in South Africa they took me to places I'd never been, such as Cape Town, the Kruger National Park, and Pilansberg National Park.

As with the baboon and heron incidents, my early encounters with wildlife in the bush gave no indication that I had any natural affinity whatsoever with creatures bigger than parrots and frogs. On one trip to a small game reserve with the Schmidt family,

I decided to take a walk in the bush by myself. I was enjoying the solitude and the sounds and smells of the veld, which made a nice change from suburbia.

Something rustled ahead of me. I froze. I could see the silhouette of a large mammal through the bushes. I heard what sounded like a lion's growl. I turned and ran.

Bushes whipped and scratched at my bare skin and my heart was pounding as I retraced my steps quick time, arms and legs pumping furiously. When I thought I'd covered a safe distance, I stopped and looked back, my chest heaving as I tried to calm my breathing. About a hundred meters away I saw a bull kudu—a large antelope—staring at me. He had covered about the same distance as me, in the opposite direction, after we had both scared the life out of each other.

On another solo hike I came across a dead heron in the shallows of a stream. Curious as ever, I decided I would examine the bird to find out how it had died. I pulled on a wing and it pulled back. Alarmed, I took a step backwards. It must still be alive, I thought, although once again it was lying motionless. Cautiously, I stepped forward and grabbed the wing again. It started to pull back so I tugged harder. I screamed when the crocodile's head broke the surface of the water and it reclaimed, once and for all, the bird it had just killed.

As my own wildness calmed down, my collection of domestic animals started to grow again. A couple of years earlier I'd gone with a mate when he bought an anaconda.

At the time, Annabelle, as he named her, was less than a meter long. When I was sixteen he called me up one day and told me he was moving overseas and asked if I would take Annabelle. I hadn't seen either of them for a while and remembered Annabelle as a small snake. When I got to the guy's house it was a case of, "Annabelle, my, how you've grown." She was three meters long. Annabelle had a big appetite and I found myself searching for a constant supply of chickens and rats.

I regained my reputation as the bird man and a procession of people started arriving with orphaned chicks, cats, and dogs. When the twins left home, Mom and I moved to a town house in Buccleuch north of Johannesburg. Mom and I were like passing ships as I was spending a lot of time with Lisa. I was also spending less time with Dino and David, but that was a good thing for my studies. Lisa was passionate about everything she did—dancing, studying, even fighting with me—but her passion for schoolwork rubbed off on me.

In standard nine, the year before matriculation when we graduated from high school, I went for an interview at Pretoria University. Part of the criteria for acceptance to vet school was your progress up to standard nine, and the interview.

I dressed in my smartest shirt and put on a tie and drove the Mini to Pretoria. Although I still wasn't old enough for a driving license, Mom had given up on me and had started letting me drive. It was about an hour's drive through what was then open farming country that separated Johannesburg and South Africa's capital city.

When I got to the university I had to wait, sitting with other nervous aspiring vets of my own age. When my name was called, I walked into the room and sat down in front of a panel of four faculty deans, three men and a woman.

"How important do you think your school results are to your suitability as a candidate for veterinary college?" one of the male deans asked me.

"I think people place too much emphasis on results," I said. I wasn't being cheeky; I was just saying what I believed. "I don't think people place enough emphasis on a person's ability to work with animals. I think a lot of vets study for five or six years and then work six months in veterinary and discover they're not an animal person and this isn't for them. I really believe your entrance to vet science should involve a practical component so you can see how students work with animals. Obviously study is important, but if you're passionate about what you do you are going to study and you are going to make a good vet."

Well, I didn't get in. Clearly the correct answer should have been, "Yes, results are very important and I'm going to work my damnedest to get straight As."

I also needed a B average in maths and science in my matriculation year, which I didn't get. I wasn't too shattered as I had enough marks to enroll in a Bachelor of Science (BSc), majoring in zoology. As the first years of zoology and veterinary science were quite similar, I knew I would be able to apply again for vet school in my second year.

I loved university life, but I didn't enjoy some of the subjects I had to study, such as chemistry and botany. Also, I worked out pretty soon that even though I was in South Africa, land of the big five and every big, interesting mammal in the world, I wouldn't be studying them. We spent a lot of time learning about sea molluscs and nematodes—worms—but not lions, hyenas, and elephants.

When the time came around for my second interview for Veterinary Science I found myself in front of the deans again. "So," asked one of the deans, "how important do you think your university results are to your suitability as a candidate for veterinary school?"

I couldn't help myself. I gave the same answer again, about the importance of being able to relate to animals. This time the panel seemed quite receptive and nodded and smiled while I was talking. I thought that I'd waxed it, that I had passed. I didn't, and I was pissed off. I ended up dropping out of university altogether.

My brother-in-law had a good job selling real estate and he offered me a position. I thought, "Stuff university, I'm going to go out in the world, get rich, and buy my own game farm with my own animals."

I was quite happy for a while, but Lisa's brother-in-law, Mark, whom I got on well with, sat me down one day and said, "Kev, listen.

You can sell real estate any time in life if that's what you really want to do, but now's your chance to finish your university degree. You've got the brains to do it, but you need to apply yourself."

He was right. If money was my motivator for selling houses and land—which it was—then that wasn't good enough. If you're a real estate agent who loves land, and gets passionate about selling it, then you'll be good at your job. I re-enrolled and eventually completed my BSc.

I finished two years of zoology, but by my third year I'd had enough of studying sea urchins and worms. It seemed one had to put years into this field before the lecturers would let you study an elephant or a lion or something interesting. Since I had no chance of applying for veterinary school again I decided to change my major to physiology and anatomy. Ironically, in second-year physiology I found myself working with the sorts of animals I thought I'd be studying in zoology. We studied vertebrates, everything from rats to baboons to owls, to learn about their skeletons and their musculature. It was fascinating and the lecturer was brilliant.

Mark, who had convinced me to go back to university, owned a gym in Morningside and he was developing a new concept that would suit my qualification. He had a well-founded theory that when someone knew they were going to hospital to have surgery then it would make sense to do some preconditioning on the musculature around the affected area in order to speed the process of rehabilitation after the operation, when the patient would return to the gym. It seemed like a good career choice for me. Animals would still be a part of my life, but I reasoned that as I hadn't needed to make money from my relationships with them as a kid, then I didn't need to make money from working with animals as an adult.

Although I had become great mates with Mark and everyone else in Lisa's family, no one was more surprised than me when our five-and-a-half-year relationship broke up. Lisa was like me, very headstrong, and while we parted as friends, and remain so today,

I think, we worked out that we couldn't spend the rest of our lives together. I finished university and had a promising job to go to, but with my love life in tatters I decided I needed a clean break and a change of scenery. Like a lot of South Africans, I decided I would leave my homeland and go and work and live in England. I left in December 1996, figuring that if I could survive a winter in Britain then I could survive anything.

THREE

Bond of Brothers

England was dire. I hated it.

I did some bar work and some work in a CD warehouse, which I soon discovered wasn't for me. Although I checked out a few of the local gyms, the only work they had on offer was personal training, which was something that did not interest me. It was dark when I woke up in the morning and pitch black in the afternoons. In between it was gray.

I was staying in a crummy little part of London near the Kensington Olympia tube station. I lived in a dark, dingy apartment that you had to walk downstairs from the street to access. When I went to look at the place, the first thing that struck me was the smell of damp. I ended up sharing a bedroom with two other guys, while in the room next to us were three or four Italian girls. There was only one bathroom and a small kitchen for all of us, and to get any space to myself I had to go outside into the cold. My share of the rent to live in this squalor was about eighty British pounds a week and this sapped up most of what I was earning. At first I thought I could get my head around living in London, in that place, but then

I realized it was simply horrific. I wanted out, but my South African mates in the UK urged me to hang in and wait for the summer, which they said would be glorious.

"I don't live my life waiting for summer. I live for now," I told them. They were probably right about me having a change of heart if I waited until the comparatively warmer weather, but after two months I was broke and miserable, so I came home. It's funny how the decisions one makes can change one's life. If I had gone to England in the summer and found that I loved it, I might have stayed and found a job that I liked, but I would never have met Rodney Fuhr, a guy who was to play a huge part in my life.

Stepping out of the terminal at what was then still known as Jan Smuts International Airport, it was good to see the sun again and feel the warm humid cloak of Africa in the summer bringing me back to life. Many South Africans, including my brother, live abroad. Some leave Africa because of the crime problem in our country, which is bad, while others pursue better pay or a better future for their children. I suspect many of them miss Africa, problems and all, and would come back in a heartbeat if they could. I was happy to be home and it was nice to see a blue sky again after the weeks of drab gray and cold winter rain. I'd also taken the space we have in Africa for granted—having room to move and not having to live in other people's pockets was something to savor.

I went back to my job as an exercise physiologist at the gym and things started looking up. Mom had met another guy and moved out of the town house, so I had the place to myself. I had a new girlfriend, Michelle, and with the money I was making I bought my first motorcycle—a Kawasaki ZX7 Ninja superbike—and started riding a lot on the weekends, but I revisited my youth one day on the way to work by riding into a pool of spilled diesel while wearing only a pair of shorts and a T-shirt. I was covered in abrasions and ended up as one big walking scab. It was bloody painful.

Rodney Fuhr had come to the gym for some work on his knee

and I'm sure he wasn't happy about being lumped with me. Rodney is a guy who likes to know he is getting the best when he deals with people. As with my other clients, I started by interviewing Rodney about his knee problem, then weighing him, measuring his height, calculating his body fat, and assessing his fitness. He was five-eight, with graying, curly hair and a moustache, and olive-colored skin. For a man in his late fifties I thought he was in pretty good shape. He seemed a quietly spoken person, perhaps not comfortable around too many strangers, and he may have resented being lumped with a youngster like me, instead of the boss. We didn't talk much at all during his first few sessions, apart from what he was meant to be doing exercise-wise. During this time I developed an exercise regime for him and helped him work his knee and gradually strengthen the muscles around it. I did learn, however, that he was a successful businessman who owned the Supermart chain of clothing and general goods stores in South Africa.

I was hand-raising a Cape White-eye at the time, a tiny little bird which had fallen out of its nest during one of the violent storms that rock the Highveld at the start of the summer wet season. The gym's gardener had brought it in to me.

"*Baas*, I don't know what to do with this thing," the gardener said, cupping the little chick in his big calloused hands and presenting it to me. Even at work and in adulthood, my reputation as the bird man had followed me from Orange Grove. I raised the white-eye until it fledged, and once he was flying he would still come to me, fluttering into the gym from outside when I called him.

As Rodney pushed his leg against my hands, using resistance to strengthen his leg, the barriers between us started to drop. Rodney asked me about the bird and my love of animals, and I found out that he was incredibly passionate about wildlife, especially lions. Rodney had used part of his wealth to sponsor a lion research camp in the Savuti area of Botswana's Chobe National Park in the late seventies and eighties.

Savuti is a starkly barren, scorching, sandy part of Africa that plays host to a seasonal visitation of zebra and wildebeest that provides an annual feast for the area's lions. Because of the prevalence of huge herds of elephant in the area, the lions there have also learned to hunt these huge creatures. I'd seen wildlife documentaries, such as Dereck Joubert's *Eternal Enemies*, about interactions between lions and hyenas in Savuti, without realizing that the man whose knee I was working on had once been Joubert's employer. Rodney had also funded research by Chris McBride, and other well-known figures in the world of African mammal study. Rodney had apparently given Dereck Joubert his first break in filming wildlife documentaries, and while Joubert has gone on to become a famous filmmaker, he and Rodney had fallen out over a difference of opinion about a particular film project which later was to have a huge impact on my life.

Rodney had always wanted to make a dramatic feature film based on the life of a lion, using footage shot in the wild. Some of the people he had funded had also been tasked with filming for documentaries and the feature film project. Rodney had learned, however, that some scenes were simply too difficult to film using wild animals, and he had visited the Lion Park in Johannesburg to organize footage of lion cubs. The research camp was an expensive business and Rodney admitted he had overextended himself by buying more and more equipment—including more than one aircraft—for his researchers and filmmakers. His business had suffered and he had withdrawn from the camp and shelved his movie project.

When I met Rodney, he was rebuilding his business empire. One day in 1998 he walked into the gym with a smile on his face. "Guess what, Kev? The Lion Park has come up for auction and we bid. Guess what? We bought it!" Rodney was looking to start a new research camp in Zambia, to the north of Botswana and Zimbabwe, and was talking about acquiring land there. To complement the footage captured on film in the wild, he now had a handy collection of "extras"—lions and various other mammal species at a well-established tourist attraction on the outskirts of Johannesburg. It turned out that Rodney also had a sentimental attachment to the Lion Park as he had met his wife, Ilana, there.

"You should come visit the lions, anytime," Rodney said to me during our regular session.

I wasn't sure if he was serious, though I know now that even though Rodney is a successful man, he loves sharing his stuff with other people who share his passions. If he has an aircraft and he finds out you love flying then he'll insist you take his plane up. If you enjoy it, he's happy. As it happened, through a mate at the gym I also knew the new manager Rodney had appointed to the park, Richard, whom Rodney had met through a friend of mine in South Africa.

Most of my clients were working people who preferred to schedule their gym appointments for early morning or late afternoon, outside of work hours, so I had most of the day free. I decided to take Rodney up on his offer and one day I took the R512 out of Johannesburg to Muldersdrift. I'd been there once as a kid, and was surprised at how close to the city the park now seemed to be. I'd remembered it back in the day as being in the middle of nowhere. It probably was, back then, but by this time the suburban sprawl was reaching its tentacles around it. Even so, the park was a big chunk of land. From the road I could see wildebeest grazing.

In the car park and reception area was a mix of local families and foreign tourists who had come to interact with the cubs and see Africa's king of the beasts up close through their car windows. I met Richard and he took me away from the main enclosures to show me some lion cubs that Rodney had insisted I visit.

The first were a couple of females, who were still tiny at three weeks. They were in a box and they were incredibly cute. Further along on my private tour we came to another enclosure containing two older cubs. At six or seven months they had reached an age where they could no longer be petted by human visitors to the park, and they were big—much bigger than I had expected. One was called Napoleon and the other, which had yet to be christened, had the most incredible clear eyes.

Conventional wisdom—or perhaps superstition—among lion keepers, I later learned, was that one should never trust a lion with clear eyes. Like a lot of things people told me about lions over the years to come, and conventional wisdom in general, that little gem turned out to be bullshit.

I had no way of knowing it at the time, but these two young lions were to become my best friends—my brothers.

Richard gave me a briefing before I entered the enclosure with Napoleon and his unnamed brother.

"Don't look them in the eye.

"Don't turn your back on them.

"Don't crouch or kneel, or they will climb up on your back.

"Don't run.

"Don't make any sudden movements.

"Don't scream. Talk quietly."

It was a long list of things to remember not to do, but I was going in with Richard and I had confidence in his experience. He's a tall guy, and big, and I didn't really do much during that first visit. I petted them, cautiously, and even though they were young, they were very big and quite intimidating. I suppose I was like most visitors to the Lion Park back then. I thought, "Wow, what an experience," but after it was over my life had to go on. It had been a great day and I was, I think, a little sad to realize that life did, in fact, actually have to go on.

When I next saw Rodney I told him about the visit. "I went to the park and, man, those cubs are so adorable."

Rodney could see that the visit had touched me. "Well, you must go again. Spend more time with them. Go as often as you want, every day if you like."

He was ecstatic simply to learn that I had enjoyed myself by visiting the place he'd just bought. He didn't need to make the offer twice, and I started visiting more often. For the first month I visited about twice a week. I would go and meet up with Richard and he would take me on a different behind-the-scenes visit each time. When I saw the grown lions being fed a horse's leg I had my first close-up view of the feeding frenzy that can overtake a big cat, and the way they rip their prey apart with their claws and use the spiky papillae on their tongues to lick the skin from the meat and separate flesh from bone. It was fascinating.

Richard told me that a fully grown male could weigh between 180 and 250 kilograms—up to 550 pounds. In the wild, young males left their family, or pride, at the age of about two. When they reached maturity they would seek to take on a pride of their own. I learned that contrary to popular belief, male lions often play an active part in hunting and this is not just left to the females. I wondered what it would be like to get close enough to one of these huge beasts to run my hands through its long dark mane.

In Camp One at the Lion Park visitors can drive their own vehicles on a road through the lions' enclosure. At the time I first started visiting the park I was driving an Opel Kadett, a compact little car. I stopped to take a look at some lions lazing under a tree and a huge male got up and wandered slowly towards me through the yellow grass. I swallowed hard and felt my heart start to beat faster as he closed the distance between us. I don't think I had truly realized just how big a lion was until that moment. His beautiful maned head was higher than the roof of my car and he looked down at me through the window.

When he roared, the car vibrated. It was like the scene in the movie *Jurassic Park* where the Tyrannosaurus Rex is breathing on the people in the four-by-four. It was awesome, in the truest sense of the word.

After about a month of my visiting the park on a regular basis, Richard let me go into the enclosure with Napoleon and his clear-eyed brother alone. When I walked in through the gate by myself I thought those two lion cubs were going to kill me. The still-unnamed one was feisty. He would stare at me with his piercing, pitiless eyes and then launch himself at me, biting and mauling me with his claws and paws, which were already the size of saucers. I thought, "Shit, this thing wants to chow me!" Now I know that rather than wanting to eat me, he was simply playing.

If this was play, though, it was roughhouse stuff. When the clear-eyed one locked his jaws on my hand and started biting down with those needle-like teeth of his, it felt like he was going to rip my hand off. I think my attitude towards these two lions was that as much as I loved seeing them and being with them, I didn't want to impose on them. I felt I simply had to wait, and grin and bear their ripping and biting until they tired of it.

"Shit, Richard, is this safe?" I asked him one day as I inspected a fresh set of scratches and my ripped shirt. I had started buying my shirts from the Mr. Price discount shop by this stage, as I was going through about one a week.

"I don't know, Kev," he said.

"Great," I thought, "and you're the expert. Just great." Richard was probably no more expert in the keeping of captive lions than I was at that time.

Richard kept going into the enclosure with the two young lions so I, as someone who can never resist a challenge, kept going in, as well. I have to admit that I was a little concerned, as despite what some of my friends and family say, I don't really have a death wish.

Photograph by Michael Swan, courtesy of Peru Productions

Posing for a publicity still for the press kit of *White Lion*. Thor is a complete natural in front of the camera.

Photograph by Houston Haddon, courtesy of Peru Productions

One of the many adorable white lion cubs used as the hero lion, "Letsatsi," in *White Lion*

Photograph by Mandy Richardson

A quick dental inspection. All looks good, Gandalf, although I would recommend flossing in the future.

Photograph by Mandy Richardson

Has the cat got your tongue…errr, I mean hand!

Photograph by Mandy Richardson

Shy the brown hyena demonstrating that she in fact has a stronger bite force than a lion!

Photograph by Tony Park, courtesy of The Kingdom of the White Lion

It's these moments with the lions that I really love. There's no need for talking, as Tabby and I are perfectly in tune with what each other is thinking.

Photograph by Adrian Wilkins, courtesy of The South African Lion Park

Say aaaaah! Doing the dentist thing again with Shanzi the spotted hyena.

Photograph by Kevin Richardson, courtesy of The South African Lion Park

Accepted into the lions' den. Mom (Maditau) is not even two feet away from these newborn cubs.

She runs…

She jumps…

Photographs by Rodney Nombekana,
courtesy of The Kingdom of the White Lion

She scores!! One of very few lionesses I will let do this to me. Meg and I have a very special relationship, which allows us to play like lions. We have been doing this for seven years now. No jaws, no claws, just unsupervised fun!

Photograph by Kevin Richardson

The animatronic white lion has no idea what's in store for him. Thunder is about to annihilate him. Three cameras were used on a fight scene about to be shot between "Letsatsi" and "Kudzindza" in *White Lion*.

Photograph by Helga Jordaan, courtesy of The South African Lion Park

It's not just the big predators that have stolen my heart. I've never experienced such affection as that which Nandi the black-backed jackal has shown toward me. She thinks I'm her soul mate. Jackals mate for life!

Photograph by Helga Jordaan, courtesy of The South African Lion Park

A few rules are being broken here with my brother Tau. 1) Don't go in with a lion when you're injured (note the moon boot on my right leg, which is broken), 2) Don't sit down with a lion, and 3) Don't try to take possession of something a lion has.

Photograph by Mandy Richardson

Part of the pride

"You'd better give that one with the clear eyes a name," Richard said to me one day as I inspected the rips in my latest cheap shirt. I'd gone through a brief phase of wearing overalls when I was with the lions, but it had been too hot so I'd resigned myself to more trips to Mr. Price.

I wasn't sure if he was serious about naming the lion, so I ran it past Rodney during his next session at the gym. Rodney was clearly pleased that I was enjoying spending time with the lions, but as the cats did, in fact, belong to him, I asked for his permission. He told me it would be his pleasure for me to name the lion.

I didn't want to name him something corny, like Savuti or Serengeti. After many hours of thought I came up with the name Tau, which means lion in the Tswana language. Clearly, I was getting a little more sophisticated than the days when I named my frog. I thought it was a good, strong, original name, and I was proud. Only later did I learn that practically every second safari lodge and camp in southern Africa has the word Tau in its name.

Rodney mentioned to me during a session in the gym that too many of his senior staff at Supermart were unfit, overweight, or out of shape. He asked me if I would be interested in going on the payroll, working part of my day as a private trainer for him and his staff, with the rest of the day free for me to spend at the Lion Park.

I didn't particularly like private training and had deliberately shied away from working in that field when I was England, but the arrangement Rodney proposed was interesting. For a start, it would allow me to give him something back, and to formalize my by now daily visits to his lions. I was spending more and more time with Tau and Napoleon. I now realized I was developing a close relationship with the fast-growing cubs, one of whom I had named. I had also named the two females I'd seen on the day I first met my boys. I called them Maditau and Tabby.

After Tau and Napoleon had tired of biting and scratching me, I would sit in the enclosure with them for two or three hours a day, just watching them. I didn't set out to break the accepted rules of lion keeping, but I found that the rule about not sitting or crouching around the lions was causing problems, not least of all with my wardrobe. It seemed to me that when they jumped up and started clawing me, they were trying to drag me down to their level. After some play closer to the ground they would eventually tire of attacking me and we'd sit calmly in the grass near each other, but not touching.

As we sat there, I began to think about them, how they were alike and how they were different. Napoleon seemed like a long-lost brother trapped in a lion's body, my soul mate. He's regal, confident, and ruggedly good-looking with an extremely compassionate disposition. He's the kind of lion who will do things without putting too much thought into it. Sound familiar? Tau was also a soul mate of a different sort. He's a lion who was not as well liked by people in his younger years because of his tricky personality. I knew that all he needed was some understanding, patience, and love. Tau is a lion unsure of people's intentions, and therefore always a little more reserved. He won't just jump into the fire. His shy nature, contrasted with his crystal clear eyes, is what intrigues people about him. When Tau's in a bad mood, unlike Napeoleon, you can change it. He needs time, just like I do when I'm in a bad mood; I hate nothing more than someone thinking they can fix it for me. Tau takes a while to get his temper up, but when he does, don't get in his way. He'll kill you now and ask questions later.

When Rodney found out exactly how much time I was spending at the park, he offered to pay me for my time there as well as the private training. There were management changes happening at the same time and I think he also needed someone on the staff that he knew. I was employed as an animal welfare and animal enrichment worker, which basically meant my job was to help manage the animals, as well as look for ways to keep them occupied and content in captivity. To be honest, I wasn't totally sure what my job title meant, but I knew it included being around Tau and Napoleon, so I was happy. I'd still been working with my other clients at the gym in the afternoons, but the new arrangement meant I was training Rodney's staff in the mornings and then spending my afternoons at the Lion Park.

I believed then, as I still do today, that it's important to keep animals in captivity stimulated and engaged, and the same thing went for me. I'm an active person and I need to keep myself busy. I could never be a keeper who stood outside an enclosure and opened the gate only when the food truck arrived. I visited all the animals in the park on a daily basis and checked out their enclosures and food and water supplies, and looked for ways that I thought things could be improved.

By the time I started working at the park officially, Richard had left and a new manager, Ian Melass, was settling in at the park. I got on well with the new man. I'm sure a lot of the people at the park didn't know what to make of me. Here I was, the big boss's "informant," who spent a lot of his time in the enclosures with the lions, forming relationships with them. I'm sure there were a few raised eyebrows.

One person who definitely found my methods unorthodox was Alex, a lion trainer from England; Richard had hired him before he left the park. Alex only ever went in with the lions if he was carrying a stick, as this was accepted practice where he was from, and for keepers in general. Tau and Napoleon, however, weren't used to people carrying sticks around them, even if this was the accepted way of working with lions.

Tau didn't respond well to Alex, and Alex preferred not to work with him. His recommendation was that Tau was not a workable lion and that the park should consider selling him. He said Tau couldn't be trusted because of his clear eyes. Tau and Napoleon were getting bigger by this stage and developing their manes. They were no longer cubs and some people were getting concerned about my safety. They were worried about me bending down in front of them, and couldn't believe I had begun hand-feeding them pieces of meat and letting them drink water out of my hands. These were other things one was never supposed to do with lions, but I'd been doing it for months.

Rodney, who by this stage was almost like my father, took me aside one day at the park. "I've heard about some of the things you're doing with the lions, Kevin, and I'm worried. You roll around on the ground with them, playing . . . maybe you're getting too physical with them."

"Rod, I'm just sitting with them, that's all," I said, omitting the bit about how I put my hands in their mouth and grabbed them by the canines, or how I tugged on their tongues.

"What if they jump on you one day for real?"

Others thought I was entirely loopy when they saw me playing with Tau's teeth and pulling his tongue.

To be fair to other trainers, the other difference between them and me was that I was not training Tau and Napoleon, or any of the other animals, to work on film or television commercials or do anything in particular. I was simply establishing relationships with many of the residents of the Lion Park, and in the process Tau, Napoleon, and I were becoming even closer—almost like three brothers. I was doing all this because I wanted to, and because I thought they were enjoying the interaction, as well—not in order to teach them to do tricks in front of a camera.

The Lion Park was approached to help with the filming of a television commercial, and the advertising company wanted a lion with a well-developed mane.

At the time, Tau and Napoleon were our most mature male lions, and Ian, who had been dealing with the clients, asked me if I would like to be involved.

"What do you say?" he said. "You've got a good relationship with Tau and Napoleon. Do you think you could get one of them to walk from left to right in front of a camera?"

It seemed pretty simple. Richard, the former manager, had begun to establish a relationship with Napoleon, but after he had left it had just been me inside the enclosure with the two boys, and Alex, the trainer, had already made it clear he didn't want to work with Tau.

So I found myself working on a film set with Tau and Napoleon as star and stand-in.

When the day arrived I wasn't so sure it was going to be easy, but when the camera crew was set up behind the safety of a lion-proof cage, I called to Tau. He walked from left to right in front of the camera. "Good boy, that's my boy, Tau," I said. I scratched and hugged his big, maned head and fed him a piece of meat.

I hadn't trained the lions to respond to the offer of food—I hadn't trained them at all, in fact. I was never usually around at their feeding time, so it wasn't that Tau had responded to me because he associated me with food. He did it because I asked him to do it; as a bonus, he got a reward. The film crew was happy and the rest of the day went like clockwork. Napoleon got in on the act, as well, and the cameraman shot some scenes of both lions walking together in front of the camera.

People are always trying to pigeonhole me, but I don't fit into any of the stereotypes that people think of in the business of keeping lions. Since that first day I have worked with lions on many other commercials, documentaries, and feature films, but I do not consider myself an animal "wrangler." I am not a *leeu boer*, which is Afrikaans for lion farmer—someone who breeds cats for zoos or hunting—although I have raised lions from cubs. Although I studied zoology for a couple of years, I am not a zoologist, and while I have been a keen student of animals and their behavior all my life, I am not an animal behaviorist. Tau and Napoleon did as I wanted them to on the day of that first commercial shoot, and many others since then, but I am not a lion trainer. My boys did what they did because they wanted to. Sure, they could tell I had a reward in my hand, but I have never used the promise of food to get them to do something that did not come naturally to them.

Eventually, Rodney gave me a full-time job at the Lion Park and I was able to give up the personal training, which I was not sorry about. I had found something I truly loved doing and my life had turned around. It was a complete career and life change, for the better.

At the same time, Rodney Fuhr was looking to set up a new research camp in Zambia. He'd acquired some land at Maziba Bay on the edge of the mighty Zambezi River, but was running into problems there. When the manageress of the camp was shot, Rodney abandoned that site and invested in an alternative camp in the Liuwa Plains area, which had become available.

One of my jobs was to help organize the logistics for its setup. Liuwa Plains is in western Zambia, near the border of Angola. It's a wild, remote place that each year hosts what is considered to be Africa's second largest wildebeest migration, after the Serengeti-Masai Mara migration. Poaching during the years of Angola's protracted civil wars took a heavy toll on the animal population. The area was also well known for its predator species, but these, too, had suffered at the hands of poachers and local villagers who feared for their safety. The researcher Rodney was funding was going to study the migration and the presence of hyenas in the area.

I had to organize supplies and help kit out a Unimog four-by-four truck which would be used to resupply the camp. Rodney also bought an ultra-light aircraft, with the aim of training the researcher to fly, so he could track the wildebeest migration from the air. It was interesting work, and like working with lions, it was a new field for me. At the end of 2000, I reaped the rewards for helping set up the camp when Rodney offered me the chance to visit the plains.

It was staggeringly beautiful wide-open countryside, with grassy emerald floodplains stretching away to the far horizon. It seemed the most isolated spot I'd visited in Africa, yet the reality was that even here animals and humans had problems coexisting. The Lozi people lived on the border of the Liuwa Plains National Park, where they grazed their cattle. Unfortunately, as the park was not fenced, predators were drawn outside the park by the promise of an easy meal. Poachers and villagers had exacted a toll in response and Liuwa Plains's lion population had dwindled to just a handful of animals. One lioness, Lady Liuwa, had taken to living among the tents and tree islands around Rodney's camp, because she knew instinctively that this was probably the last place of safety for her on the plains.

Back in South Africa, I played host to a man Rodney had met in Zambia, who dropped into the Lion Park for a visit at Rodney's invitation. As the unofficial tour guide, I showed the guy around the park and then I went into the enclosure with my buddies Tau and Napoleon. I was doing my usual stuff, rolling around on the ground with the boys, playing with their teeth and tongues and lying on top of them, but I could tell he was not amused.

In the next enclosure I went in with two lionesses I had known since cubs, Maditau and Tabby. The girls always played rough and while I was hugging Maditau, Tabby jumped up on my back. She wasn't meaning to hurt me, but she had her claws out. As well as ripping my shirt she nicked the back of my ear, and although it was not a deep cut, it was a typical head wound—it bled like crazy. Just like Napoleon and Tau have wildly different personalities, so do these two lionesses. Maditau became the best mother lion I have ever met. She's a classic beauty who has never had an unsuccessful litter. Maditau is the responsible one who has no time for fooling around. Tabby, on the other hand, is a lion who's having too much fun in life for kids to ruin it for her. She's boisterous and voluptuous and, if she was a human, I think I would find her extremely sexy. She's sort of the Angelina Jolie of the lion world. She's the kind of lion who's always keen for some fun and games. For her, life's too short to let it pass by lazing under trees.

"Get out, get out!" the visitor started screaming at me. "You're bleeding! That lioness is going to kill you!"

I wiped the blood from the back of my ear and pushed her off me. "Relax, dude. She's not attacking me. This is one of my girls."

The guy didn't believe me and he went to Rodney behind my back, saying, "This guy is crazy and he's going to get himself killed." He asked Rodney if he was prepared to wear the bad publicity if Kevin was eaten by one of his tame lions. I'm sure the visitor from Zambia had the backing of other people at the Lion Park, and Rodney once more had to take me aside for a quiet chat.

"This is kind of hard for me, Kev," Rodney began. "There is something I've been meaning to talk to you about for some time, so I'm just going to come right out and say it. The guy from Zambia says you are too rough with the lions and they are too rough with you. Maybe you should calm it down."

I toned down my play with the lions when other people were around, but when it was just me, with Tau and Napoleon, or Maditau and Tabby, I would roll around on the ground and be a lion with them, the same as always. However, people were still watching me quietly from the wings, and a new debate began at the park about the need for us to carry a weapon, such as a gun or a shock stick, which is like an electric cattle prod. Pepper spray was also discussed, and while it can distract a lion, it's really about as effective as a strong breath freshener when a lion is in a frenzy.

For a while I was ordered to carry a gun, and I was given a monster .44 Magnum—similar to the weapon Clint Eastwood carried in the *Dirty Harry* movies. I felt ridiculous and I looked like a Hollywood parody of a lion tamer. Also, its barrel was so long it started getting in the way when I was rolling around with the lions, sticking into their sides and mine. As an added concern, I genuinely didn't want to be seen walking around or getting into my car with this thing. Johannesburg has a bad enough problem with gun crime and people getting hijacked by car thieves. I didn't want to get stopped by bad guys one night and have them panic and start opening fire on me because they'd checked this cannon I was carrying. For a short while I switched to a snub-nosed .38 to keep everyone happy, but in the end I gradually stopped carrying it. It was a little like going into an enclosure with a stick, as the small caliber pistol would have been about as useful as a lump of wood against a full-grown lion in a feeding frenzy. As a final compromise I agreed to carry pepper spray, and that actually helped me save the lives of both a lion and a human later on in my career.

FOUR

The Clan

I walked into the clinic at Sunninghill in Johannesburg with my shirt covered in blood and my hand held to my nose. When the doctor moved my hand, most of my nose came away from my face

Just as in my childhood, I'm on first-name terms with the medicos and nurses at Sunninghill, and usually their first question when I walk in bleeding is "Lion or hyena, Kev?" More often than not the answer is hyena, as apart from motorcycle accidents (and the incident with the missing toe in the bicycle sprocket) these animals have inflicted the most serious injuries I've suffered in the course of my work. A hyena called Bongo was responsible for me almost losing my nose two months before my wedding to my beautiful wife, Mandy.

"This is going to hurt, Kev," the doctor said to me, as he turned to the gleaming tray of sterile torture devices the nurse had prepared for him.

I don't fear much in life. I've raced superbikes, I fly, and I interact with lions for a living, but there is nothing that scares me quite so much as a hypodermic needle. I hate them like I hate nothing else in the world. Seriously, I know I could never be a drug addict. The thought of sticking a needle in my body is the worst thing I can conjure up if I want to scare myself. I have gotten better with age, but for a guy who gets as many scrapes, cuts, and bites as I do, this is not a good phobia to have.

"Thanks for that, Doc," I said, trying to be brave but wincing from the pain talking caused in my nose. I was assuming that he was making it sound worse than it really would be, so that when the hideous, sharpened point entered the torn flesh of my face, it wouldn't be quite as bad as I feared.

"It's going to sting like hell and hurt for at least five minutes," the doctor said, taking the syringe in his gloved hands and pushing the plunger a little to clear the air bubble.

"I thought that maybe the nose is, like, not the most sensitive part of the body," I snuffled through a mouthful of blood and mucous.

He smiled a little. "Kev, this is going to burn like someone has poured acid into the wound, and then it's going to feel like I've pulled your entire nose off your face."

"Thanks, Doc." He was right. On all counts.

Later, after I had stopped crying and the doctor had stitched my now numb nose back to my face, I answered the casualty nurse's "lion or hyena" question.

"Neither."

I explained that I'd gone into the hyena enclosure and slid the gate closed. My hyena friends, as usual, came loping up to greet me. Hyenas love having their chins scratched, like dogs, and Bongo was first in line for the special treatment. I was sitting on the ground with him when one of the others came up behind me, out of sight. While I was talking to Bongo, the other hyena—I'm not sure which one it was—touched the side of my face with his nose. I got a fright, and as I turned my head I caught my nose on a sharp piece of steel that was protruding from the security gate. As I whipped my head around, the skin tore down to the septum.

It's a myth that tame hyenas will savage you if they scent blood. As I held one hand to my bleeding nose and staggered to my feet, Bongo was licking my free hand as if to say, "Kev, why are you leaving me, buddy? We were having such fun."

Rodney Fuhr decided early on in my time at the Lion Park that he wanted to expand the range of animals we were keeping and turn the facility from a Lion Park into a predator park. Eventually our species tally included cheetah, caracal, jackals, wild dogs, leopards, and black leopards, and even a South American jaguar, but the first acquisition on his list was spotted hyena.

Hyenas have a bad reputation as marauding scavengers and this has been perpetuated by Hollywood, documentary makers, and even local African tradition. In parts of the continent people believe that witches ride on the backs of hyenas in the dead of night. The truth about hyenas is that they are intelligent predators who hunt as well as scavenge. They live in strictly ordered clans where the females rule supreme. The highest ranking male in a hyena clan is still subservient to the lowest ranking female. It's a little like marriage.

To be honest, I thought Rodney was a little mad, but he was the boss. None of us at the park knew very much about hyenas, but we hit the phones and eventually found a guy who was breeding spotted hyenas in captivity. He offered to sell us two cubs, for what I thought was an astronomical price. However, Rodney paid, and the baby hyenas, named Ed and Shanzi, were delivered to us.

These little guys were aggressive as hornets, and even though I hadn't been a hundred per cent convinced of Rodney's logic in buying them, I was fascinated by them. To start off, we had to try and work out what sex they were. This is not as easy as it sounds, particularly when you have never seen a hyena up close. Female hyenas have external sex organs—that is, an organ like a penis. We were all trying to work out the difference—assuming these two hyenas were different sexes—and it was my job to tickle them in the crotch to produce a reaction. I felt like a hyena pervert. These two looked pretty similar down there and we decided they were both probably males.

Right from the start people started telling me that hyenas were not lions, and there was no way I could carry on with them in the same way I did with my buddies Tau and Napoleon.

"These are display animals, not relationship animals," someone who probably knew even less about hyenas than I did told me. "You might be able to play with them when they're small, but after a year they'll rip you to pieces."

As usual, I wanted to see for myself, and I got bitten to shreds by those two little animals. I was like Kev the Hyena Punching Bag and Pin Cushion. I'd go into the enclosure with Ed and Shanzi and they would wreak havoc on my ankles. My shins would be covered with bruises, and if they ever locked on to my arm it felt like they were about to bite it off. I was petrified of those baby hyenas, far more so than I'd ever been with young Tau and Napoleon.

I still never went in with a stick and I tried using the same tactics I had with the lions. Eventually the babies would tire of biting me and sit down a distance away from me. Even though they caused me pain and people continued to say I was wasting my time, I felt sorry for them in their small enclosure. I thought they needed stimulation and if that came in the form of my ankles and shins, then so be it. Also, I didn't want to admit defeat.

The hyenas proved popular with visitors and we expanded the numbers to five, with Trelli, Bonnie, and Chucky. We were convinced Trelli was a girl, but when Bonnie really displayed her phallus one day in all its glory, we could all see how different it was from the others so, in fact, we had one girl and four boys. It had been a very confusing process.

"Howzit, Kevin, it's Maureen here."

I rubbed the sleep from my eyes as I mumbled a return greeting into my mobile phone. It was early morning and I wondered why Maureen, a local tour operator who often visited the Lion Park, was calling me at home.

"Kevin, I just thought I'd let you know, there are a couple of spotted hyenas walking down the N14 and I thought they might belong to you."

I nearly tripped over in my rush to get dressed. I jumped in my four-by-four and set off for the Lion Park. The N14 is a busy motorway that links Krugersdorp with Pretoria and in the morning it is thick with commuter traffic. I called Ian at the park and he confirmed Bonnie and Chucky had done it again.

Hyenas, I have learned, are very clever animals, and Bonnie and Chucky were our two top escape artists. At six months they could escape from just about any enclosure we could find or build for them. They knew where the lock was on the sliding gate and if a careless attendant had forgotten to close the padlock, Bonnie and Chucky could knock the lock out of its latch and use their noses to slide the gate open. They had already broken out three or four times, but up until now their wanderings had been confined to within the Lion Park's outer perimeter. I was picturing the news headlines as I crisscrossed the roads around Muldersdrift and tore up and down the main N14 motorway looking for our two escaped inmates.

The phone rang and I snatched it up, still driving and scanning the roadside. "Kev, it's Ian. Come quick, the hyenas are back in the park."

When I arrived, a cloud of dust following my vehicle as I roared up the dirt road to the park, I found Bonnie and Chucky waiting for me outside their enclosure, waiting to be let back in. They had apparently escaped sometime during the night, gone out for a wander, and returned at nine A.M. the next morning. Relieved, I gave them a gentle scolding then picked each of them up and plonked them back in their home.

There is a small office at the Lion Park where Ian and I have shared many an interesting story or engaged in debates. We were in the office laughing about our close call when Ian's phone rang. As I sipped a cup of coffee I began to worry about the frown on his face as he spoke to the caller.

"Yes," he said. "Oh, no. I see."

Ian was still not smiling. "No, okay. Look, I'm very sorry about that. How about we give you three thousand rand, and we call it quits?"

"Give me the bad news," I said when Ian ended the call.

"Bonnie and Chucky broke into a house down the road last night, terrorized the guy's dogs, and destroyed his lounge suite."

Forget Bonnie and Chucky—these two were Bonnie and Clyde.

We moved Bonnie and Chucky to the Lion Park's equivalent of a maximum security prison cell, an enclosure with double-locked electrified fences. They still managed to get out a few more times, but in the process they taught me some lessons about hyena behavior.

After they escaped from Fort Knox yet again, I found them wandering in the park. Bonnie came peaceably and I put her back first, but when I carried Chucky into the enclosure he was squealing like a pig. Clearly he wasn't ready to come home. Bonnie started biting me on the ankles and legs. When I put Chucky down, he and Bonnie ganged up on me and now they were both biting me. This was weird because I thought I had a really good relationship with both of them. I realized they were not little kids anymore, but I wasn't ready for my first truly serious bite from a hyena. Bonnie reared up and grabbed my arm in her mouth and clamped down. Her teeth penetrated both sides of my arm and I felt the terrible crushing force of a hyena's jaws, which is equivalent to seven hundred pounds per square inch of pressure, so the experts say. I needed stitches and my skin was black and blue.

I figured that either I had been taught a lesson or I'd had a lucky escape. Then I started to think about hyena society in the wild. When the hyenas ganged up on me, I think they were telling me my place in the hierarchy. I was the lowest of the low. They tolerated me, but that was about it, which was why they were biting me.

I discussed the hyenas with Rodney, and when I told him Ian and I were considering the idea of forming them into a clan, he was very enthusiastic, as he wanted them to start breeding. Up until now we had kept the hyenas singly or in pairs. Bonnie was at the right age for breeding, so we got an expert, Lawrence Frank, who had done a lot of research on hyenas to come to the park and advise us. I think Lawrence, like many other people, was surprised that I was able to interact with these three- and four-year-old hyenas and that I still had both my arms and legs—even if they were a bit scarred by now.

He agreed with us that forming a clan would give Bonnie more choice about who she wanted to mate with. Space was also becoming an issue, so from a management point of view it would be much better for us at the park if all the hyenas could live together in one of the larger enclosures. Even though Lawrence was an expert on hyenas in the wild, he admitted that we were probably in a better position to make decisions about the animals' future than he was.

To begin the process we decided to divide an enclosure into sections and allow the various hyenas to get to know each other through the common fence. That seemed to work, but when we started putting different animals together they became really violent with each other. It was painful to watch. They would latch on to each others' ears and start ripping and biting. We took a chance and let them get on with it, even though I winced when I heard cartilage tearing. What we learned was that this was part of hyena life. As the group slowly started coming together they would fight to establish a pecking order. If there was a fight, it would continue until one of the animals decided to submit to the other, and this was repeated each time we introduced a new hyena to the group. They were really violent, but we had to let them sort themselves into a clan.

We added another female, Geena, to the mix, and she and Bonnie used to fight like crazy for the top position. Female hyenas are generally bigger and more aggressive than the males and they have high levels of testosterone coursing through their bodies. It might sound cruel to some people, what we were doing, but in fact we were watching the establishment of a whole society.

One of our male hyenas, Trelli, was a good friend of mine. He was rough and tough, and while the other keepers at the park were scared of him, I used to play with him and even take him for rides in my car, which he loved. When I took him for a drive we would have to travel through the lion enclosure and that used to drive the lions crazy, but Trelli loved it.

His love of cars proved a bonus because one day a request came through from an advertising company that wanted to organize a photo shoot of a spotted hyena that didn't mind posing in a car. I had just the man for the job and Trelli performed like a star. There is a beautiful shot of him with his head out the back window of an estate car, like a dog. During the filming of *Dangerous Companions,* which was about me and my relations with the animals at the Lion Park, we shot a lovely scene in which Gambit, our resident tame giraffe, came up to my pickup to check out Trelli. They touched noses together and Trelli, thankfully, resisted the temptation to rip Gambit's face off while the camera rolled.

I put Trelli in with the clan, but the other hyenas hammered him. Around people he was dominant, but with his own kind he was the lowest of the low. Ironically, Geena, who became the dominant female after winning against Bonnie, mated with Trelli, behind the backs of all the other superior males! When the other males caught him and Geena going at it, they gave him an even worse time. I used to take Trelli out and give him pep talks, telling him to go back in and assert himself over the others, but of course that didn't work. In time we formed another clan, made out of rejects, who couldn't cut it with Geena and her family, but even they picked on poor Trelli and I was worried they were going to kill him. In the end I had to take Trelli out and put him back in an enclosure by himself, even though he had done his duty with Geena.

When Geena gave birth to her second litter of cubs she became very protective. When I tried to approach her and the cubs she started giving me low growling calls, which told me not to come any closer, and I respected that. Interestingly, when Bonnie later gave birth to a single cub, it was a different situation. I arrived at the enclosure one morning and the clan was all very excited. All of them, except for Bonnie, rushed up to the fence to greet me, and when I walked in it was like they were all smiling. They had their tails up, which meant they were excited, and it seemed as though they were busting to tell me something. I walked in and found Bonnie in one of the concrete pipes the hyenas used as shelters. Nestled between her front paws was a cute little chocolate brown cub. She was quite relaxed and I was able to walk right up to them, slowly, and check it out. It was a first for me, and a touching moment.

As the clan became established, the hyenas started changing the way they interacted with people, as well as each other. When the animals were in separate enclosures, there were about five of us humans at the park who could go in with them and interact with them to varying degrees. The hyenas knew us by sight, smell, touch, the sound of our voices, and how we tasted—especially how we tasted. Slowly, the clan started asserting their dominance over us.

The hyenas were all getting older and stronger by this time, and one by one they started rejecting the people who had worked with them. Keepers who had patted and tickled the hyenas when they were younger started coming in for rough treatment, and one by one they began refusing to go in with the clan. The people who liked to carry sticks around the animals fared no better than the touchy-feely people. Hyenas eat bones, so a stick is nothing to them, and if you hit them with something to teach them a lesson it just makes them crazier. You can't enforce or reinforce a relationship with a stick. They'd raise their tails and start giggling, getting themselves into an attacking frenzy, and another keeper would call it a day. With the clan already developed and functioning as a unit, if the dominant female decided she wanted to attack a human then the rest of her family would back her up.

With my lions I try to be part of the pride, although even then there are differing degrees to which I am accepted by individual members of the pride. I am like a brother—sometimes even a father—to some, a friend to others, and an acquaintance to the rest. Not all of my acquaintances like me, but they know me, and we respect each other. I've never gone into a lion enclosure thinking I must dominate them, but the situation was different with the hyenas. I needed to assert and maintain my dominance over the clan, but I couldn't do that with a stick or a shock stick or a can of pepper spray, as that would just infuriate them. I had to be a hyena.

I was tough with them and I used to rough them up, in the same way one hyena would assert dominance over another. I would tackle them to the ground and roll them around; I would lift them up off the ground under their arms and swing them around, and I would bite them on the ears. I had to do this with all the hyenas, to assert my position in the clan, because they all wanted to challenge me. I also had to be down at their level, and it was a battle of wills as much as teeth.

If something happens to me there is one guy who could continue to do the work I do with lions and hyenas, in the same way that I do. His name is Rodney Nombekana and he is a fantastic guy.

Rodney was in his early twenties when he came to the Lion Park several years ago, from his home in Port St. Johns, in the Transkei region of the Eastern Cape. We call that part of South Africa the wild coast, because of its stark, spectacular beauty.

Rodney was one of several young black African gentlemen who were being sponsored by a private body, the Endangered Wildlife Trust, to study for a Field Guides Association of South Africa (FGASA) qualification. I imagine he pictured himself becoming a game ranger or guide for a private game reserve, or working for the national parks board when he qualified, but as part of his training he and some others visited us at the Lion Park.

Rodney stood out from the rest of the group from the first day. He was enthusiastic and excited and, like me, he would always ask questions. He didn't take things at face value—he always wanted to know why I did what I did, and how I did it. He reminded me a bit of myself. He was a hard worker and a good listener, with an analytical mind. Unlike some young people, he didn't expect to get to the top position in five minutes. He knew he would have to work hard, but that didn't mean he had to do things the same way as they had always been done, simply because that was the norm. The feedback from tourist visitors to the park was excellent and many people took the time to tell us what a knowledgeable and polite guy he was. In time, the other trainees fell by the wayside, but Rodney attained his FGASA level one qualification and was offered a full-time job at the Lion Park. Although I have since left the Johannesburg Lion Park, Rodney followed me and still works with me to this day.

Rodney had a soft spot for hyenas and took the time to research the various African cultural beliefs, insights, and misunderstandings about these fascinating animals. We were in with the clan one

day and I noticed that Agip, one of the males, was trying to dominate Rodney, who was backing away from the menacing animal.

"Hold your ground, Rodney," I said. "If you turn away from him
now you'll be finished with the rest of the clan."

"I'm not sure, Kev," he said to me. "He's going to bite me!" Agip
had lowered his body and raised his tail. A hyena's back and head
are tough as nails, but their underbelly is their weakest point, so
when they crouch you know they mean business. He was closing on
Rodney.

"Push him, Rodney. Get your hands on him and push him back."
Rodney grabbed Agip and dug his feet into the dirt. Agip kept coming at him, snarling, and he started to whoop and giggle, a sure sign
that he was upping the ante with Rodney and trying to intimidate
him.

Although I do it often, it was exciting to see Rodney standing his
ground against this powerful animal. Agip backed down and Rodney kept his place in the clan. It was great to watch and just rein-
forced my own respect for Rodney.

To this day the hyenas are excellent around Rodney. However, if
I'm there at the same time, there are a couple of individuals who
will try and gang up on Rodney in front of me. It's an interesting
dynamic; we all have our place in the clan.

We bought another hyena, Peggy, who was on her last legs. She
was a real hand-me-down, in poor shape and with bad teeth. Amazingly, she gave us our first cubs, before Geena's, but we had to hand-
raise them because Peggy rejected them.

Spotted hyena cubs aren't born with spots; they are a chocolate
brown color. They are extremely cute and extremely vicious and
they come into the world kicking and screaming and fighting. Hyenas are born fully mobile, with their eyes open, and with a full set of
deciduous canine teeth, which they know how to use. They run around
like little rats trying to bite each other and anything else that crosses
their path. When a hyena baby clings on to your finger, believe me,

it feels like your digit has been put in a vise grip lined with needles. They scream like little pigs, so loudly that people think you're trying to murder them, when in reality the opposite is true. For some reason, hyenas also seem to pick the worst possible days to have their cubs, such as sub-zero days in the middle of winter, or during torrential rainfall in summer. Their babies come into the world either freezing their asses off or nearly drowning in mud and water.

So, raising our first cubs was difficult. They didn't take easily to the feeding bottle like lion cubs; they would try to bite through the rubber teat. Sometimes they would not feed for four or five days, which initially worried me. I started researching baby hyenas, reading anything I could get my hands on in books and on the Internet, and I found out that this was normal, as in the wild, hyena mothers often have to leave their cubs in the den for long periods while they go out hunting and foraging. The reason the cubs can last so long without losing condition, I learned, was that their mother's milk is very high in fat—much more, in fact, than the puppy milk formula that we usually fed to lion cubs. As a result, their diet consisted of a mixture of egg, cream, full-strength milk, and anything else we could think of that was high in fat and protein.

By this stage I was living with my then girlfriend Mandy and we had some hectic nights looking after Peggy's cubs, who were like two little devils. Mandy has had to endure all sorts of predator cubs around the house but the hyenas were without doubt the most destructive. I learned the two best places to keep baby animals were the kitchen or bathroom because of the amount of cleaning involved, and because those rooms generally had fewer things that could be chewed. Even so, the hyena cubs savaged my toilet brush and loved jumping up and pulling all the toilet paper off the roll.

In the wild, cubs fight with each other for dominance. A brother and sister will fight until the female asserts her dominance and same-sex cubs will sometimes fight to the death. We had a boy and girl, and Mandy and I would have to separate them sometimes for their own good. I've had other cubs who have been so seriously injured by their siblings that we have had to take them to the vet. In the wild, if one is killed outright, or dies of an infected wound, the mother will take it out of the den for the other clan members to eat, or consume it herself.

Some people might think it's fun to raise a predator cub, and while it has its moments there are many unpleasant chores that have to be done. Lionesses stimulate bowel movements in their cubs by licking their bottoms. I don't do that, but I do have to rub them vigorously to make them defecate. The same went for the hyena cubs. When I noticed the hyena cubs weren't urinating, I had to stimulate their organs. It worked and they started peeing in every direction— all over me.

Uno was a wild hyena, a stock raider, which meant she had been killing cattle. She was captured by the government nature conservation people. They called the Lion Park and offered her to us, rather than releasing her into the wild, as they knew she would return to the farms and wreak havoc all over again.

So, this wild animal was dumped on our doorstep and we didn't know what to do with it. We didn't even know what sex it was. We put her—as it turned out—in the hyena enclosure's night pen, a solid room at the end of the compound, so she could recover from being captured. When she came around—I will never forget this— she was crapping all over her legs and cowering and running like crazy right at the brick walls. She had rubbed her head raw against the pen's walls, to the extent that you could see the white of her skull. She was in a complete frenzy, and I actually thought at one point that it might have been kinder to put her down. She had never known life in captivity and it was clearly freaking her out.

After thinking about it, we decided that if we were going to keep her we should try introducing her to the clan, so she could be part of a new social system. I'd seen the ear biting and fighting that went on when we introduced hand-reared hyenas to each other, so I was more than a little concerned about how this wild creature would associate with the others.

My first thought, when the nature conservation people arrived with her, was that we would introduce the newcomer to the others in the clan in the same way that we had brought the rest of them together, putting her in an enclosure within or next to the clan's so they could start off by getting to know each other through the fence. We never got that far. Uno was under so much stress that if we left her in her night enclosure for too much longer she would kill herself, so we just opened the gate and let her out with the rest of the hyenas.

Uno shot out of the pen like a bat out of hell. She couldn't wait to escape and when she emerged into the sunlight, she was confronted by a bunch of other hyenas. She annihilated them! Our captive animals were completed frazzled by the onslaught they received from Uno and they just fell into line immediately. It was right then that we decided to name her because she was, without a doubt, and in a matter of minutes, Numero Uno.

This was a high-ranking woman, and she knew how to fight. The trouble was that Geena was not in the enclosure at the time we released Uno, and we knew that when the girls got together the fur was most definitely going to fly. We ended up putting Geena and Uno in an enclosure together—just the two of them—to let them sort things out. The two girls took one look at each other and battle commenced. They tore at each other's ears and jostled and rolled and charged at each other as each tried to get the better of her opponent. They were whooping and giggling and biting and pawing. Geena went down a few times, but she just would not submit to Uno. Their thick necks were covered in a froth of saliva, and blood poured from their ears. There were puncture marks everywhere, but they kept on going ballistic. At times we thought we might have to intervene, but I knew that if Uno was ever going to join the larger clan then this fight had to happen. Slowly, Uno gained the better of Geena, but our original female would not back down easily.

Eventually we decided to release the rest of the clan, to take some of the heat off Geena, and maybe give her a chance to muster support. It didn't help. Uno not only kept the pressure on Geena, she also sorted out every single one of the other hyenas and still had energy and attitude to spare. At that point, Numero Uno took over the clan.

Having introduced Uno to the clan, I wanted to see how she would react to me. I didn't want to lose contact with the rest of the clan simply because there was a new hyena in charge, so I went into the enclosure, just as I always had.

Uno stared at me, but kept her distance. It seemed that she tolerated this weird two-legged creature interacting with the rest of what was by now her clan—just. I didn't chase her or even walk up to her, but as the months went by she started approaching me, and came a little closer each time. She would sit and watch the way I tickled and played with the others and I think she made a decision that I was not a threat to them—or her—and that she might like some attention. If I did stray too close to her, she would circle me and the hairs on her back would rise as she displayed her aggression, and let me know that if I came closer she would have a piece of me. That was fine, and I kept a respectful distance of about five meters from her.

I will never forget the day that Uno came up to me and offered me her nose, stretching it toward my hand. She had come close a few times, standing just out of reach and bobbing her head up and down. This time, I extended my hand and she came right up to me and sniffed it. She had broken the barrier that she had imposed up to that time. It was her decision.

She sniffed my hand a second time. I held my breath, not knowing what would happen next. Then Uno gave my hand a lick. She was trusting me, big time, and I was trusting her right back. After that, when I approached Uno I did so on all fours, down at her level. In time, I was able to scratch her under the chin and behind the ear, but I knew I would never be able to pick her up under the arms and carry her around like I do with some of the others.

My experience with Uno got me thinking about the intelligence of a hyena. I could never have done what I did with her with a wild lion that had been captured by humans. This wild hyena, however, had the ability to sit there and rationalize the situation. For my part, I learned that I could form a bond with Uno—a relationship that allowed me to interact with the rest of her clan without threatening her. I did not seek to break her or dominate her, although I was dominant to the other clan members. Uno had had a terrible experience at the hands of the humans who had taken her from the wild and placed her in captivity, yet she could learn to trust me.

I have heard of a guy making contact with a clan of hyenas in the wild, but that was done over a long period of time. My experience with Uno happened in a compressed timeframe and I think it highlights how intelligent these animals are—intelligent, but naughty.

As the guy in charge of animals, I pushed for the clan, which was growing all the time, to be moved to one of the much larger fenced camps in the park, where tourists could drive their cars through, simulating the experience of a big game park. I thought it would be cool for people to see a clan operating in its element.

Ian and Rodney Fuhr approved the idea and we set to building a hyena den. We dug a pit and roofed it with a half-moon of concrete pipe, some tin, and some wooden poles. In the wild hyenas make dens in disused termite mounds, and in some of South Africa's national parks they take up residence in concrete drainage culverts under the roads, so this new home was perfect for them. They loved it.

Everything was going well and the hyenas loved the additional space. Also, the tourists were enjoying seeing the clan interacting with each other and I felt good about striking a blow for hyenas, and giving people a chance to see what interesting animals they really were. What happened next, however, was that the hyenas started interacting with the tourists' cars.

First it was a fender, then a rearview mirror, then a door handle, and finally a tire. They loved eating tires. The hyenas became better than a Johannesburg chop shop at dismantling cars, even while they were moving. People were driving around in circles, in panic, with the clan, led by Uno, chasing them around trying to tear pieces off the cars. Maybe Uno saw this as a chance to get some payback against the humans who had taken her out of the wild, or maybe she just liked the taste of car parts. Sadly, the cost of repairing damage to visitors' cars signaled the end of that experiment, but the hyenas had enjoyed themselves immensely.

FIVE

Tsavo the Teacher

People sometimes ask me if I think I have been born with a gift for working with so-called dangerous animals. If I have a gift, I think it is knowing when and how far to push barriers.

I believe I know instinctively when a situation is bad or otherwise. I know, for example, if I walk up to a parrot in a pet shop whether it is going to bite me or not. Of course, a lot of what I do has been learned, but I also believe that animals pick up on your intent, your fear, and your innocence. They can tell, instinctively, if you intend to harm them. They can tell if you are weak or strong, or arrogant or genuine. Too often, people have an agenda when they enter an animal's space. They may wish to control it, probably by asserting their dominance, or they may need to get an animal to behave in a certain way for their own ends.

What I do has taken me ten years to understand and learn. I'm amazed when, as often happens, people contact me or come to visit me and my animals and say they want to go into an enclosure and have their picture taken with an adult male lion. They want to use this animal, who is a friend of mine, for a photo opportunity. They don't care about it or understand it or know its moods or its feelings, but they see me rolling around on the ground with it and think, therefore, the animal must be as tame as a pet.

There was a lion researcher who had worked for Rodney Fuhr, and her dream was to have her picture taken with an adult lion. In the past, I was more blasé about letting people have contact with the animals in my care. There were two very good lions at the park, Thunder, a male, and Rain, a lioness. Thunder was so friendly that at Rodney Fuhr's step-daughter's twenty-first birthday, which was held at the Lion Park, all the party guests were allowed to pat him. This big-maned lion was like a pussycat. About six months later the researcher contacted Rodney and I said I thought it would probably be okay if she had her picture taken with Thunder. As I've said, I was more cooperative in the past.

It was a cold winter's day, which turned out to be fortunate. To be safe there were three of us with the researcher and we all went into the enclosure, which Thunder shared with Rain. The woman's husband, who had also researched wild lions, said he preferred to stay outside.

"Hello, Thunder, my boy," I said, pleased that he had trotted up to us, as friendly as usual. The woman was already loving it, getting up close to the lion.

I looked around the enclosure for Rain and I saw her. Lions usually have golden colored eyes but Rain's are the most amazing red-brown. They're quite eerie at the best of times but when she fixed me with them I knew something was wrong. Her tail started to swish.

"We'd better get out," I said to one of the other guys.

"What?"

"Get her out!"

Rain charged and went straight for the researcher. Because of the weather the woman was wearing a big bulky jumper and a pair of jeans. Her clothes may have saved her life. Rain bit down but only succeeded in grabbing the folds of the woman's jumper. The lioness clawed her around her waist and shredded the jeans, but the thickness of the denim prevented the injuries from being worse than they might have been.

I reached for my pepper spray and gave Rain a blast. I hated doing it, but it caused Rain to let go and take three steps back. She sniffled and then wheeled and came straight back again for another attack, but by that time we had bustled the woman out of the enclosure and just managed to shut the gate in time.

Rain was in the two-to-three-year-old age group, which I've learned the hard way is when a lion is at its most dangerous, in my opinion. They're big enough to kill and young enough to want to try. Rain didn't like us being in her territory. She gave me a warning—not quite enough for me to get the woman out before the attack—but long enough for us to be ready to react. I didn't blame Rain for acting the way she did. If a strange lion had come into that enclosure, Thunder and Rain would have killed it in a heartbeat. The woman who entered the enclosure was not part of their pride. That was the last time we let a stranger in an enclosure with an almost adult lion.

My guiding concern in the way I do my work is that I care about the animals I live with. It started with two little lion cubs, Tau and Napoleon, and before I knew it I was responsible for an entire family of extreme creatures. They are not my pets or my employees, they are my companions. If I was doing what I do with dogs, no one would find it unusual, yet a dog can kill a person.

Lions are perceived as killers, and they certainly have the ability to take a human's life in a heartbeat, but so can another human. A lot of what I do is based on respect. The way I work with my animals is to get down to their level. I'm not the tallest of guys and that helps me. If I stand with my feet quite far apart I'm basically at an adult lion's eye line. I don't walk in carrying a stick or a gun and then expect them to love me or relate to me because I have the means to hurt them.

To use a human analogy, if I go to Japan and walk into someone's house, I take my shoes off. I don't take my shoes off at home, but I do it in Japan because I can see the world through their eyes and I want to show some respect and be accepted on their terms. Like I say, it's all about respect.

I hadn't shown Rain the respect she deserved when I brought the researcher in, and I didn't show Tsavo respect when my family came to visit the Lion Park.

The rear edges of a lion's canine teeth are serrated. I don't think this little known fact saved my life, but it probably had something to do with the story that starts this book.

When Tsavo hooked one of his fangs under my belt and lifted me off the ground, I was only suspended for a couple of seconds. Even as he hoisted me, with my family watching and screaming for help, the serrations had begun sawing through the leather. My belt snapped and I landed on my back in a cloud of dust. My step-nephew, Nicholas, still has the two pieces of my belt as a reminder of a birthday he could hardly forget.

What did save me from worse injury that day was the fact that Tsavo had been declawed. If he hadn't been then that first mighty swipe of his arm might have ripped me to shreds. So much of a lion's power is in his claws, and when they attack their prey they fillet them with the sharpness of their claws and the power of their blows.

My family's screams alerted Alex, the lion trainer who had come to us from England. He was at the far end of the Lion Park, but when he heard the commotion he came running, with two sticks in hand. Alex ran in through the gate in the inner fence of the enclosure just as my belt snapped.

Alex charged fearlessly at the lion. Tsavo left me and turned on the other man, as if to say, "Right, I'm going to have a piece of you now." Alex squared off against Tsavo and started banging the sticks together and beating the ground in front of the lion. I later learned that by this stage my brother-in-law, Trevor, was at the fence whistling to try and distract Tsavo. Needless to say, Tsavo wasn't one to respond to whistling. I was on my feet and moving and was out of that enclosure in quick time while Alex kept Tsavo at bay.

My clothes were covered in blood and my nose was bleeding.

When I got outside the enclosure I was thinking, oh no, my arm is probably half hanging off, but when I checked I found that Tsavo's two canines had actually passed either side of my arm. I'd been lacerated and my shirt was torn, but Tsavo hadn't bitten into the skin of my arm. When I checked my leg I found that while he had punctured me, it was nothing fatal. If he had bitten down harder he might have severed the femoral artery and I could have bled to death.

Tsavo had always seen me playing with Tau and Napoleon in the next-door enclosure, and I think that for me and Tsavo our clash may have been a territorial dispute. It was about him teaching me who was the boss, and who was in charge of the piece of land where he lived. I know now that lion never meant to kill me, though if he'd had claws that may well have been the outcome. He wanted to give me a slap around, which he did, in the same way that male lions do to each other in the wild.

Perhaps my running up and down the fence with the younger lions was irritating, or possibly he was simply telling me—as deep down I think I knew on the day of my family's visit to the Lion Park—that he didn't want me in his territory.

However, when Tsavo bit me, it wasn't a case of me being lucky or fortunate that he missed an artery—it was him deciding to teach me a lesson rather than kill me. He was in total control, and every action he took, everything he did, was calculated.

I also don't believe now that pressing my fingers into his cheeks and forcing his skin between his teeth was what stopped him from going further. I have seen lions over the years since then in a frenzy of feeding or fighting, and I know that Tsavo would have bitten through his own flesh and severed my finger without hesitation if he was intent on finishing me off and feeding on me. He was playing with me as he moved his teeth from my shoulder to my calf and to my leg. Lions have incredible control over their jaws and the pressure they want to exert.

People have often asked me if my life flashed before my eyes when Tsavo attacked me. It didn't. I knew that I had to try and survive this incident one step at a time. When I asked my family how I reacted, they said I was cool and collected and that they didn't know how I managed to stay as calm as I did during the attack.

I've been in situations with leopards and a jaguar when I've thought to myself, "How did I get myself into this situation—*again?*" I used the knowledge and experience I'd gained to get back in control, but mostly these days I try to not get into those situations in the first place.

Deep down inside I think I was hoping that Tsavo would just leave me alone. I didn't think I was going to die—that didn't cross my mind—or that I should have told my mom I loved her. One thing I do remember was that when he started charging towards me, I thought, "Kevin, you should have listened to your instincts, boy." I look back now, though, and realize that Tsavo was an example of how a person's childhood, or a lion's "cubhood," can influence the way that person or lion behaves as an adult. Initially, I think Tsavo was a well-loved animal who eventually got tossed aside like a used oil rag. He reminds me of one of those Hollywood child actors who never quite cracked it as an adult actor. Even though he tried to kill me, I knew that Tsavo's behavior stemmed from the fact that his spirit was conflicted and broken. I could only guess at what a very sad place that is for an animal to find himself in. Given half the chance, if Tsavo were human, I would guess he would've committed suicide by now. And that makes me all the sadder for him.

The first thing I took away from my experience with Tsavo was to obey my sixth sense.

Everyone has this sense and I think I've merely had to develop mine over the years, working as I do with big animals. The trick is to know the difference between the hair rising on the back of your neck and excitement or adrenaline. There's a fine line between your instincts trying to tell you something and your body reacting to the exhilaration of the moment.

The second thing I learned was not to succumb to peer pressure, as I had in front of my family. It was about me, not them, just as it was with letting the researcher into the enclosure with Thunder and Rain. I had the power to say no in both of these cases, and the ability to concentrate and listen to my sixth sense, but I didn't exercise it.

I've also learned, through Tsavo and during other incidents, that animals can react differently to you if there are other people around. I was messing around with Shanzi the hyena one day, carrying him around and scratching under his chin, when some tourists drove up to the enclosure and tooted their car's horn. Shanzi panicked and his first reaction was to bite down. Unfortunately, my arm was in the way and his teeth passed right through me. "Come closer, we want to get a picture," this woman was calling, while I was bleeding. Shanzi ran off in a panic, but returned a few seconds later. Hyenas have a switch in their brain that can flick on and off very quickly, taking them from peaceful and cuddly one second to extremely crazy the next.

Even with Tau and Napoleon now I play differently when we're alone, compared to, say, if Rodney Fuhr or some volunteers are visiting. Animals pick up on the fear or excitement of bystanders, and I'm even more conscious these days that when I interact with my animals, it's for my benefit and theirs—not for the purpose of putting on a show for visitors.

Pressure comes in different forms. On the night after Tsavo attacked me, I was sitting in a bath, bruised and battered and inspecting my wounds while having a calming glass of red wine. I remember thinking that I must have a guardian angel, and that there were still many things I wanted to do in life. I am a glass-half-full person, even though my red wine needed topping up.

My girlfriend at the time, Michelle, walked in to the bathroom and said, "Kev, I love you with or without the lions, but you've got to give it up."

My hero Valentino Rossi doesn't give up motorcycle racing every time he has a crash. Presumably he thinks about what went wrong and learns from it. That's what I did. Michelle and I eventually split up and I later met and married Mandy.

Mandy works at the Lion Park and she loves animals, though perhaps not in the same way as me. Certainly she wasn't crazy about the hyena cubs that peed all over the house. However, she accepts me for who I am, and she accepts my lions, hyenas, dogs, motorcycles, and flying. She even accepted my anaconda while we still had it. That acceptance is just one of the reasons I love her so much. She has never tried to pressure me into being something I'm not, or doing something I don't want to.

My philosophy has always been to live life to its fullest, as I could be dead tomorrow. I could put myself in a cupboard and wrap myself in cotton wool and live to the age of a hundred and one, but it wouldn't be fun. What you think is crazy may be okay for me and what I think is insane may be fine by you. Look at base jumping, for example—that's crazy.

The day after Tsavo attacked me I went to work at the Lion Park and all of us who worked there had a debrief about what had happened to me the day before. I thanked Alex for intervening when he did.

I was downplaying the seriousness of the attack because the last thing I wanted was for someone to ban me from going into the enclosures. I hated the thought that I might be banned from seeing Tau and Napoleon again. Ian and Alex and I were sitting around, and everyone was surmising what might have gone wrong and what might have motivated Tsavo.

I stood up, cutting the meeting short. "You know what, guys,

I've just got to go and check on a few things." I left the office and headed to Tsavo's enclosure. I knew that talking would solve nothing and that I needed to confront Tsavo.

"Here, Tsavie. Come, boy," I called when I reached the same spot where I had stood in front of my expectant family.

Tsavo ran up to the gate like normal, as though nothing had happened the day before, and stood there expectantly, waiting for me to enter. I started to wonder again if it was my fault, for running up and down the fence with Tau and Napoleon before entering Tsavo's enclosure, and if that had annoyed him.

I know now that wasn't the case. I run up and down with the hyenas, playing with them in full sight of the lions all the time. The lions hate the hyenas and would kill them given half a chance, but they don't take out their hatred on me when I enter their enclosure, so that couldn't have been the problem with Tsavo.

I slid open the gate and walked in. When lions talk to each other, they go, "*Wuh-oow, wuh-oow,*" quite softly and it's a good sign. Tsavo started talking to me, so I thought I must just get back in the saddle. I didn't have a stick or a gun with me, and there was no one inside the enclosure with me. Tsavo was fine and he showed no sign of aggression towards me. That's the difference between us and animals—they have no hidden agenda. They act on instinct and don't necessarily hold grudges in the way that humans do.

He was the same Tsavo he had been up until the attack. Of course, he had never changed. He'd sent me a signal in front of my family and I had ignored it. But I felt different around him, no doubt because of the kicking he had given me. Right then I felt as though I had two left feet, and that if someone had asked me a question I would have started stammering and stuttering. I found myself acting differently around him. We interacted, but I found myself staying very close to the gate. Lions like to rub their heads on each other, just like house cats, and when Tsavo presented his big head to me, I moved to one side, just like other people had told me in the past.

"Always stay to the side of the lion . . . don't touch its head or tail . . ."

I wasn't confident enough to confront him head-on and I was drawing on the words of others, rather than my gut instincts. This wasn't me. Tsavo hadn't changed, but I had, as far as our relationship was concerned. I had confronted him, and in doing so had confronted any residual fear I might have had as a result of the previous day, but I was being more cautious than usual around him and that is no basis for a relationship. I think my own insecurities stopped me from continuing to work with Tsavo.

Also, I realized then that I didn't really know Tsavo. Tau and Napoleon and I have an intimate relationship because we've grown together as friends and brothers over the years. I know exactly what they like and what they don't like. We can read each other's moods. I had come into Tsavo's life when he was three and I didn't know what he had been through, or really very much about him at all. How would I know, for example, that if I raised my hand to pat him one day, he would know I was being kind and not about to beat him? I just didn't know.

I have walked away from my relationships with some animals, as I have walked away from some of my human relationships. If the trust and respect is not there I can't pretend as though it is, or that it might come back or develop again. If I'm not getting on with an animal, I don't want to break it or train it until it does what I want. I want to be its friend and to have it accept me for who I am. If lions have done things for me, for example on film or commercial shoots, they have done it because it was easy for them and they enjoyed it, not because I forced them.

As I've said, some of my lions are like family, some are like friends, and some are acquaintances. On that day, in that enclosure, Tsavo went back to being what he probably was and should have been all along—an acquaintance.

SIX

Slowly . . .

I'm always very wary when I receive an e-mail from someone who wants to come and work or volunteer with me and the message starts with something like this:

"Dear Kevin, I think I would be a perfect addition to your team because I have a natural affinity with animals. Some people say I have a gift and . . . "

At that point I usually hit delete, or Mandy sends a polite, "Thanks, but no thanks." It's like someone telling you they're a people person, and that they get on with everyone. Forming a relationship with another person—even a business relationship—takes time. The same goes with animals.

I've based a lot of how I work with animals on watching them, and learning how they behave. This goes for how I relate to individuals, as well as species. As a child I liked observing and keeping records about my pigeons and other birds and animals. I was watching and learning not just for the sake of learning, but because I wanted to work out how I could relate to my pets. It was never enough for me to just look at them.

It was the same with Tau and Napoleon, the young lions I met at the Lion Park when I first started visiting. I was allowed to enter the enclosure with them, so the interaction started with them from day one. Like any new relationship there was a bit of trepidation and some nerves. I didn't know them and they didn't know me. As I've said, in those early days I thought that what Tau and Napoleon wanted from me was a couple of pounds of meat off my lower legs, but I later worked out I was wrong.

Although Richard had given me the basic ground rules, about not crouching or sitting or bending over in front of the lions, or showing them my back, or running, or this and that, I was on my own for much of the time with Tau and Napoleon, so I was free to experiment and test some boundaries with them.

As I started to get more confident with Tau and Napoleon and understand more about how they behaved, I learned what was play and what wasn't. Sometimes something I thought was quite serious was actually play, and vice versa. For example, some lions are very possessive. If Tau grabbed my jersey and growled, I wasn't sure whether it was because he wanted to take it, or if he was just enjoying playing with it. I had to learn which actions and noises meant he was serious, and which meant he was having fun.

The way he looks, the way he acts, the way he behaves, the way he talks, the way his hair stands up or his tail flicks can all tell you something about what's going through a lion's mind. Behavior also needs to be taken into context. A lion locking eyes with you doesn't mean he's going to challenge you, although it can mean that he's challenging you for possession of something. During filming I've stared at Tau confrontationally to try and make him growl at me, and while it works sometimes, at other times he knows it's not for real and he calls my bluff.

To live and work with animals you have to get to know them, and understand that an individual's behavior will change from time to time, in the same way that people change from day to day. I've known Maditau the lioness since she was a baby, and over the past nine years she's raised several litters in my presence. She knows me well and she's never been particularly possessive about her cubs, but her current litter is different. It could be because it's probably going to be her last litter, but whatever the reason she doesn't like anyone— not Tau or Napoleon (either of whom could be the father) or me— going near them. I think she thinks we're going to eat her babies.

While Maditau has made it clear to me that she doesn't want me approaching her cubs this time around, sometimes the cubs will come to me when I'm sitting in the enclosure with the rest of the pride. When I can, I spend two or three hours a day just lying around with my lions, snoozing in the midday heat or checking e-mails on my PDA. Cubs are curious and one time when they walked over to me, Maditau watched them like a hawk. She tolerated them approaching me and checking me out, and when they returned to her she looked at me and I looked back at her. She curled her lip and growled at me, so I looked away. When I looked back at her she growled again, so I knew that while she was putting up with me, she really didn't want me in the enclosure near her babies this time around. I have to respect her wishes, so I got on all fours and slowly crawled away from her, the way another lion would if she was giving him the same signal. I didn't stand up and back away, because that might have aggravated her even more—she might have construed standing as me challenging her. What she did and how I responded constituted normal behavior for lions, but other lion trainers and wranglers would probably have a heart attack if you told them to, one: be near a lioness's cubs in the same enclosure; two: turn your back on a lion; three: get down on all fours in front of one; and, four: crawl away in the opposite direction with your back to her.

My lions aren't used to me acting like a lion tamer or zookeeper would, they're used to me acting like a lion.

There are plenty of so-called experts on lions in South Africa and I've heard a few interesting theories on how it is that I can do what I do with my lions. One of the most common theories is that my lions are so well fed that they would never consider eating me, or that they are declawed (Tsavo was the only declawed lion I've ever interacted with). Other theories are that I carry a concealed weapon or a shock stick, or that there is always another handler outside the enclosure armed with an AK-47 assault rifle who is there to step in when things go wrong. All of this is rubbish. Some people can't understand that I can have a relationship with lions and that's their prerogative. I'm not going to get upset if someone doesn't believe me. If people want to believe that I need a cattle prod or gun-toting guard to work with my lions, then good for them.

There are some milestones in life that you never forget.

When I was visiting Tau and Napoleon in the early days, I used to go into the enclosure walking fully upright, like a human being—naturally. The lions would nip and bite at my ankles and legs and try to leap up on me, hooking their claws into my pants and shirts. Eventually they would tire of greeting me in this way and they would go and sit down. Even though I had been told not to sit down or crouch around the lions, I wanted to spend time with them and I couldn't very well stand up for two or three hours. I could have gone to the far end of the enclosure and sat down and watched them from a distance, but that would have been the same as sitting outside the enclosure and I wanted to be closer. Eventually I decided to sit down about two meters away from Napoleon, as back then I thought I could trust him more than the clear-eyed Tau.

I remember sitting there one day, the warm sun on my back, just watching the pair of them and thinking to myself how lucky I was just to be there, sharing time with these two amazing, fast-growing cats. Napoleon got up. He was about fourteen months old by this stage so he was getting tall, with a grizzly fringe of hair under his chest that would later become his magnificent mane. He stretched and yawned, showing off his lengthening canines, and then started walking towards me.

Normally, when he stood up I would stand up, but this time I remember thinking, I wonder what would happen if I just sit here? Napoleon came closer, entering my space, and he just flopped down beside me. He wanted to be near me.

What I've found out about lions since then is that they love to touch. Even in the middle of the day in the heat of summer, you'll see lions in the wild and captivity lying all over each other. They love it. These days, Tau, Napoleon, and I will often sleep in the grass together and they need to be touching me. If I roll over and break contact with one, I'll feel a massive paw reaching blindly for me, or the twitch of a tail as it snaps over and lands across my leg. It's so cute—I love it. If I have to get up, they'll both wake up, looking at me as if to say, "What's wrong Kev, why do we have to get up?"

I'm not into spiritual mumbo jumbo but I do believe that every-one, every person and every animal, has an aura—an energy around them. Sometimes we don't like having our space invaded and at other times we do. Personally, I don't like being crowded unless you're my wife, my lion, my hyena, or my dog.

When Napoleon flopped down beside me that first time, I knew he had come into my space so I thought it was okay for me to do the same. I leaned over and put my arm on him and he did nothing at all. It was a memorable moment. The next time I sat next to him, I was confident enough to touch his paw and hold it. After that it was me tickling him on the belly then him interacting with me when I lay rather than sat, or crawled through the grass. I would still give the lions time to release their energy at the start of our sessions to-gether, and try the experimental stuff once they had calmed down.

Sometimes the experimentation was unpredictable or scary, mostly because of what other people had told me not to do and the preconceptions they had drummed into my head. The first time Tau jumped on my back set my heart racing. I was crawling and he pounced and landed on top of me. He was a heavy boy. I waited to see what he would do, but he just lay there, hugging me. I was starting to realize that my inhibitions about these lions were simply in my mind. In the back of my mind was the guy saying, "Don't trust the lion with the clear eyes." These days I listen to my own senses and instincts, not the words of people.

Touching and playing and rolling around on the ground led to hugging, but I found things were always easier when I was down on the lions' level. I wondered if the boisterous play at the start of each visit was not so much about them being excited and full of energy, but rather just them trying to pull me down to their level. The next time I entered their enclosure I did so on all fours, and then lay flat on the ground. When I was down in the grass on my belly, they didn't jump on me because there was no need to—I was already at their level.

I started taking meat into the enclosure with me to feed Tau and Napoleon. Not knowing any different, I fed them from my hand. That, I soon learned, was a definite no-no in the world of lion handling. Meat should always be given to a lion from the tip of a stick, as a lot of people believe that a lion can't tell the difference between the meat and your hand. As well as not crouching or crawling or lying around a lion, I wasn't supposed to approach it head-on, or put my hands near its mouth. I let my lions drink water out of my cupped hands and that, like most things I do, is also forbidden in the world of lion-keeping. I'd already broken all these rules before I even knew they existed.

Rubbing heads with each other is a form of greeting for lions, so that's what I started to do with my boys. Even though they are full-grown adults we still greet each other the same way. In the wild, lions also have to clean each other. After devouring a buffalo or wildebeest carcass in the bush, lions' faces are covered in blood and gore. Like house cats, they rely on their siblings or parents to clean the parts of their face they can't reach. My lions love to lick me, and while it's an important part of the bonding process, it can also be quite painful.

A lion's tongue is covered in scores of spiky papillae. A house cat's tongue is the same, though in miniature. When feeding, this allows them to literally lick the skin from their prey, and to loosen the meat from the bones of the carcass. A few good licks from Tau and Napoleon on the same part of my arm will start to draw tiny beads of blood—it's like rubbing fifty-grade sandpaper against your skin. They lick me because they want to groom me, and as I can't return the same favor I carry a round plastic hairbrush with me with stiff but flexible plastic bristles. I comb them with it, particularly their faces and manes, not just to remove stray burrs and twigs, but to bond with them.

Later, my "unorthodox" methods started to come to the attention of people outside of the park, when we started filming commercials. When it was time for a break, I would have to take the lions back to their enclosure and call out, "Lions back in enclosure—safe!"

Instead, I would call out, "Lions and handler back in enclosure—safe!" Then I would lie down with my boys in the shade of a tree and have a sleep with them. One of my favorite positions with Napoleon is to lie down at right angles to him with my head on his belly and one of my arms on his forelegs and the other on his hind legs, as though he's a big hairy armchair. He loves it, too.

What was becoming clear to more and more people as time progressed at the Lion Park was that I actually did know what I was doing, even if my methods seemed a bit unusual. Workers on the film and commercial sets started taking happy snaps of me with the lions so people began seeing what I was doing without knowing the full story of how I was doing it. This is probably what started to give rise to the stories about full-bellied and declawed lions, cattle prods and guys in the background with AK-47s.

I'm not on a one-man crusade to change the way people work

with tame lions. While I believe, naturally, that my way of relating to predators is good for me and good for them, I cannot write a textbook for lion-keepers on how to form relationships with their animals. It doesn't work that way.

I learned about animals slowly, over a number of years, and I'm still learning. As I've said, I love motorcycle racing, so I'll use an analogy from that world. People have asked me how I learned or developed my methods. It's the same as asking me how I was able to break the one-minute, fifty-second barrier for a lap around Johannesburg's Kyalami racetrack on a motorcycle.

When I first got my bike, the best time I could do was two-minutes-twenty and I thought I was going to crash as I went into every single corner. Over several years I was able to reduce that time to one-minute-fifty. There are superbike schools that I could have gone to, but I already knew how to ride my bike. One-minute-fifty was a good time for a recreational racer like me, but I wanted to push the limit. I realized pretty early on that when I was trying very hard to better my time, it wasn't happening, and I probably stood more chance of having an accident than when I was riding for fun and not really concentrating on what I was doing. Reducing my time from two-twenty to one-fifty happened over time, not overnight. I shaved half a second off my time here, a tenth of a second there, and little by little those savings added up.

I learned to do what I do with big animals the same way that I bettered my racing times—in increments. I started when they were young and it took us years to get to the place where we are now. A lion—any animal—will often allow you the opportunity to explore something.

Swimming is an example. One day I was walking in one of the open areas of the Lion Park with the lionesses Meg and Ami. Meg's the athlete. Like Napoleon, she has oodles of confidence and will try almost anything, although don't be fooled—she has an extremely sensitive side and can sulk for weeks. Then it's up to you to figure out why! She knows she's special and knows she holds a huge chunk of my heart, therefore gets away with murder because she tugs on my heart strings.

Ami is slighter than Meg and built in a more slender way. She'll follow what Meg does more often than not, but always seems less boisterous and not as confident in her own abilities. Ami's like that child who just needs a bit of reassurance every now and again.

It was summer, the grass was long and green, and we were passing a dam, filled to the brim and surrounded by thick reeds. I noticed that Meg was quite interested in the water and was padding around in the shallows, experimenting tentatively by splashing the water with her big paw. It was a warm day, and I thought, what the hell, I'll get in the water and see what happens. I took off my sandals and waded in, wearing my cargo shorts and T-shirt. It might have been sunny, but the water was chilly. I carried on regardless, wading out into the middle, and once there I lowered my body fully into the water and started doing an imitation of what I thought a lion would look like swimming—kind of an exaggerated dog paddle.

"Come, Meggie. Do you want to swim, my girl? *Wuh-ooow, wuh-ooow*," I called to her as I swam.

Meg looked at me, puzzled, as if to say, "Kev, what you doing there, boy?"

I kept calling and swimming and, one tentative step at time, Meg started to enter the water. She looked left and right and then walked in until her front legs were wet. She lunged away from the bank and swam out to me. Once she reached me she was relieved, but maybe a little nervous, too, as she clung to me like I was a human raft, with her big front paws up on my shoulders. I had some meat in the pocket of my cargo pants, so I fished some out and fed her from my hand while we swam. She loved it, and afterwards we sat on the grassy earthen wall of the dam together in the sunshine and dried ourselves off before continuing on with the walk.

I've also been told that lions hate water and that it's virtually impossible to teach one to swim. I didn't even try to teach my lioness to swim—she saw me doing it and decided she would try it, as well. Someone called out to me to be careful in the dam; they thought Meg would claw me to death when she swam over to me, with her paws slapping the surface of the water. We played and she climbed on my back, but she didn't hurt me. Meg and Ami are a joy to work with because they don't automatically bring their claws out when they paw you. In my experience maybe one in forty lions can play like that.

All we did on the day Meg went swimming was to explore an opportunity. With captive lions there are only so many opportunities to explore, so I believe Meg was enjoying trying something different.

I think of my lions as tame, but not trained. However, just because they are tame for me does not mean they won't try and kill a stranger, and just because they're not trained does not mean they won't do what I ask them to do.

My lions respond to me the same way as my dog Valentino (named after my hero) does. If I call him, he comes for one of two reasons—because he wants food or attention. My lions respond to me for the same reasons, and because we have an established relationship.

Sometimes it doesn't work out as planned. I received a request for two male lions to be filmed for a short sunset shot that was needed for a television commercial. It sounded simple, but if there is one thing I've learned in the world of film and television, it is that there is no such thing as simple. While the crew set up, I went to check on my boys. They had clearly been fighting the night before the shoot because as soon as I walked in, I saw Tau was limping. He had received a gash in his paw from his placid, chilled brother. Napoleon almost couldn't wait to get up in the truck which was going to transport them to the more open, savannah-like area of the park for the filming. A cage was being erected around the film crew and everything was progressing except for the second lion. Tau was not keen on getting into the truck and for a while I thought I might have to call off the shoot.

In the end I took Napoleon out of the truck and Tau seemed a little more relaxed about going up to the back of it on his own. I fed him some meat and took my time with him. Another wrangler might have bullied him into getting into the truck, using a shock stick or cattle prod, but there was no way I would do something like that. The shoot was delayed for a couple of hours as a summer storm was brewing over Johannesburg. Ominous black clouds were rising like towers in the sky, obscuring the setting sun so the crew had to set up artificial lighting.

Tau got up into the truck and I gently closed the door on him. He'd done it of his own accord. Napoleon, of course, leapt in eagerly with his brother and we trundled off to the other side of the park. My boys behaved impeccably and the film crew got the thirty seconds they needed of two majestic, maned male lions looking out into the distance while the (artificial) golden light bathed their faces. At the end of the shoot, Napoleon obediently hopped back into the truck, but Tau decided he was going nowhere.

Tau is stubborn, but that's one of the reasons I like him. He's like me. We do things at our own pace, and of our own choosing. While the crew packed up their gear and Napoleon was driven home, I sat beside Tau, resting against him, as the light faded to darkness. His paw was probably still a bit sore and once he decided it was rested enough—when he was good and ready—we called it a night.

I am not advocating my way of working with lions to anyone else—it's simply what works for me. I don't think there is anything special about me. As I've already said, if I have a "gift" it is simply my ability to follow my sixth sense. My wife doesn't think I'm anything special—she knows I am just an ordinary guy. I think it's arrogant to say, as some people do, that they have a special way of working with animals or a special talent, and that no one can do what they do.

When I started interacting with Tau and Napoleon, it wasn't because I hoped that one day they'd be able to star in television commercials or films, or that one day I would get the opportunity to make documentaries about wildlife and a feature film. I'm just pleased that people took an interest in my animals and the way I've worked with them. We've certainly all received a good deal of publicity. I'm pleased if people see one of my documentaries and it changes the way they perceive hyenas, not as scavenging vermin, but as intelligent, sociable animals. I'm pleased if someone sees me on television with Tau and Napoleon, and they learn that lions are sociable animals that can show love to each other—and me—and that they're not the mindless, man-eating killers they're sometimes made out to be.

The positive things about documentaries, film, and television is that it allows me to get out important messages about animals and conservation to many more people than I could if I was showing groups of tourists and South African schoolchildren through the Lion Park. I'm not the first person to say this, but as human beings we need a wake-up call to start getting serious about conservation and the environment. The number of lions in Africa has dropped from about 350,000 to between 23,000 and 25,000 in less than twenty years, so anything I can do to educate people about the importance of conserving these animals is worthwhile. In fifty years time there might be no lions.

I think the Australian conservationist and documentary-maker Steve Irwin was a great guy. He brought simple messages about conservation to a huge number of people around the world. What I particularly admired about Steve was that he put his money where his mouth was. Some other wildlife presenters are just TV personalities who don't give a damn about the beaver or polar bear they're talking about. Steve was different. He bought up large tracts of land to be set aside as wildlife areas. If I could buy up some land and convert it to a national park, I would do it, but I can't. So I keep making the films and the documentaries. If all the filmmaking and television and publicity went away tomorrow, though, I wouldn't shed a single tear for myself because it would give me more time to spend with my animal friends and my wife. I would shed a lot of tears, however, for the animals and the environment. They would be the ones losing out if the message of conservation couldn't be spread any longer.

Often, when people ask me how I work with the animals, they usually want to know why I do what I do. It's not for money. I didn't start spending half my days at the Lion Park, or take a full-time job there, because the money was good or I thought that we might make a movie one day. I formed relationships with those animals and sometimes those relationships have allowed me to get my friends to work with me. In the early days I did what I did out of a sense of obligation. My job as the animal enrichment, or animal welfare officer, at the Lion Park was to make sure the lions and hyenas and other predators at the park had the best possible quality of life for enclosed animals. Part of my job was to provide them with stimulation, but what I quickly found was that this was a two-way street. I got as much, if not more, enjoyment from the burgeoning relationships I was forming with the animals as they did.

One day I approached the enclosure of another lion, Siam. I was surprised to see him by the fence and calling me. "*Wuh-ooow, wuh-ooow,*" he said to me.

"Hello, my boy. This is a surprise." What was surprising for me about this little encounter was that Siam was sharing his area with a female and was mating. I'd always been told to stay away from mating lions, and that they would not want me near them. I went in and spent some time with Siam, rubbing his head against mine, grooming him, scratching him, and generally hanging out while his female companion lazed nearby. At the end of our time together, I said, "Thanks, Siam." For whatever reason, he had invited me in. I got a huge kick out of that.

I've found that Napoleon is happy to have me around him when he's mating, but other people who work with lions don't believe me when I tell them about Siam and Napoleon. The funny thing is that even though he doesn't mind me being there, Napoleon won't let Tau near him when he's mating. Tau won't have any other male around him when he's mating.

So where do I fit in—what's my place in the lives of these animals, and how do they perceive me? The short answer is that I don't know. Napoleon and I have a better relationship than Tau and I do when it comes to women. Don't get me wrong, Tau and I have a good relationship, but he doesn't trust me with his chicks. The human world's the same; there are some of my friends I trust around my wife, and others I wouldn't. Could the relationship between Tau and me sour one day to the point where he sinks his teeth into me and kills me? I don't think so, but you can never say never. What drives one human to kill another? Women, possibly. Even if one of my lions killed me, I'm sure that, given the chance to live my life over again, I wouldn't do a thing differently. I've learned so much from the various relationships in my life, including my animal relationships. I was defiant to the point of insolence earlier in my life, but in that respect I was probably like a two- or three-year-old lion, finding my way in the world and relishing any opportunity to challenge authority.

My relationships with lions and other animals have put me in very good stead for my relationships with people. When working with predators, you have to be more aware of behavior and behavioral patterns. I've found I've become more attuned to human body language, as well, able to determine if people are agitated, paying attention, or cross. With people, sometimes you don't want to accept the behavior they're exhibiting and so you might push some buttons to get a different response. You don't do that with lions as you will get a response you really don't want.

I've changed in the ten years I've known Tau and Napoleon. We've grown together and our relationship has changed. I don't go in with them now because I feel sorry for them, because they live in an enclosure instead of the wild, and I think it's my job to enrich their lives. If the truth be told, Tau and Napoleon have flipping good lives, for lions, and even for people, considering the conditions some humans have to endure in Africa. I spend time with my brothers Tau and Napoleon now because I want to, and because I get something out of it. I am part of their lives now and they are part of mine.

I miss them when I have to go away. In a way, it limits me, but not more than any other relationship with a close family member or a pet. I couldn't leave them for six months, and even after three weeks away from them Mandy says I am like a bear with a sore head. I worry about what will happen to them if they outlive me, but I suppose that is a normal element of a family relationship. Who is to say what's normal in any family?

So, will there be a Kevin Richardson text book on how to keep lions in captivity? The answer is a definite no.

I'm happy to share my rules for working around lions with people, but they're mostly common sense. Rule one is don't wake me when I'm sleeping. Rule two is don't come near me when I'm eating (unless I'm feeding a lion from my hand, and I'm not advocating anyone try that, simply because it works for me). Rule three is don't surprise me (make sure I know you're coming closer), and rule four is when I tell you I've had enough of you, I mean it. Any lion keeper would say pretty much the same thing, but could I teach someone else to do what I do in the way that I do it?

I could teach someone how to ride a motorcycle, but I couldn't teach them to do a lap of Kyalami in one minute, forty-nine seconds. You have to learn that for yourself, and the only way to learn how to go fast is to take it slow.

SEVEN

―――――――

Managing the Lives of Others

When I visited the zoo as a kid I worked out that I didn't like zoos. Today, some people would say that the Lion Park, and the facility where my lions now live, the Kingdom of the White Lion, are little more than zoos with large enclosures. I would disagree with that analysis.

There are some people who think that no wild animal should ever be enclosed, anywhere, no matter what the conditions, and that all animals should live in the wild. That's a nice theory, but it becomes unworkable if you challenge the definitions of "enclosure," "conditions," and "the wild."

In South Africa "the wild" doesn't exist anymore. We have some fantastic national parks—the best in the world, I would say—yet they are finite areas that are either fenced or surrounded by physical features or human development that prevents the animals that live there from straying into the wider world.

The Kruger National Park, South Africa's flagship reserve, is huge. It covers an area the size of Israel, and even though it has recently been extended across the border into Mozambique, forming what is now known as the Greater Limpopo Transfrontier Park, it is still an enclosure—albeit a big one. As soon as you enclose animals, and deny them traditional migration routes and the ability to roam endlessly, you have to start managing them. If you have too many animals in a lush part of the park with year-round water and good rainfall then you may have to lure some of those animals to drier parts of the park by building pumped waterholes. All of a sudden you start changing the natural makeup of an ecosystem.

As I have already mentioned, Kruger has a problem with elephants. As a finite area, the park can only sustain so many of these huge creatures, which consume huge amounts of food and water each day. Relocation of elephants to other reserves was tried, but proved not to be extremely successful. About six hundred elephants were transported across the border into the new Mozambican extension of the park, but most of them simply walked back to South Africa. Darting female elephants with contraceptives has proved to be a difficult management option. While numbers of elephants on the Mozambican side of the border have subsequently increased, culling, which was out of vogue because of local and international objections, is now back on the agenda as a part of the elephant management strategy.

Some people are against the domestication or training of animals. If everyone had always followed that line of thought, we wouldn't have domestic cats or dogs today, or be farming sheep or cattle, or chickens, or goats, or riding horses. Some people say I shouldn't be domesticating my lions, but I say that is rubbish. I enrich their lives and they do the same for me. In fact, every lion I've ever worked with has been domesticated in that it was conceived in captivity and born into captivity. I don't support the capturing of wild lions and placing them in captivity, nor do I believe all the captive lions should be prevented from breeding and allowed to die out.

What angers me about the debate over animals in captivity is that it's been hijacked by a small number of people at the extreme ends of the spectrum. The die-hard greenies want to end any form of captivity, and at the other end of the spectrum unethical hunters and keepers who are cruel to their animals have given anyone who keeps an animal captive a bad name. You can't set all the captive animals free or eradicate everything in captivity—that's a crock of shit. As I've said already, my contention is that there is no "wild" area in South Africa anyway, as even in the national parks animals have to be managed to suit the physical constraints.

Does a captive lion long to be roaming free in the wilds of the Serengeti or the Kruger National Park? This is a human perception, and in my opinion the answer is no. A lion knows what it knows. If you take a lion out of a hundred-acre enclosure and put him in a small cage, he may adapt to his new environment, but it will have a negative impact on him. The same goes for putting a human in jail.

On the other hand, I take my dog Valentino for drives and for walks in areas much bigger than the yard around my house and I do the same thing for my lions. Does exposing Valentino or the lions to bigger areas make them long to run wild? From what I can see, the answer to that, too, is no.

Lions exist in captivity for a number of reasons. Firstly, there is education. Even if I stopped working in television and film, I would still want to bring school groups to see my animals because I believe firmly in educating young people about the beauty and wonder of wildlife, and the problems facing animals in the wild. Some people would find it ironic that captive lions are needed to highlight the plight of wild ones, but many of the schoolchildren I've seen come through the Lion Park over the years would probably never get to see a lion in the wild in their lifetime. Despite its reputation as a wildlife Eden, South Africa is a very urbanized country with most poor people aspiring to a job and decent housing in a city or large town.

Lions are kept in captivity at facilities such as the Lion Park for tourism purposes. Not everyone who comes to Africa will have the time, the money, or the inclination to go to the bush, but they will probably want to see a lion. Zoos, too, keep lions as exhibits for educational and tourism reasons.

I see no problem with any of the above reasons for keeping lions in captivity as long as the lions are well cared for and happy. Of course, "happy" and "cared for" are subjective terms. I formed my views on these areas out of my experience first as a visitor, then as someone whose job it was to stimulate and enrich the lives of predators which, no matter your views on this, were destined to live their lives in captivity. What I have found is that my so-called unorthodox ways of relating to and working with lions and other predators have helped me come up with some new, different, and I believe better ways of managing captive animals.

I've noticed over the years that if visitors perceive your animals are happy then they probably are happy.

Take space, for example. The perception in most people's minds is that an animal in a small enclosure is going to be unhappy, which may or may not be true. For me, if I see an animal pacing up and down the fence of its enclosure, whether his cage is four meters by four meters or twenty-five hectares, then I believe there is something wrong.

Lions are funny creatures. A male lion is happy if he has water, food, and sex. If he's happy, it's also highly likely that he will spend most of his time sitting in one spot. One of my white lions, Thor, has a twenty-five-hectare enclosure and he sits in one spot, day after day, under his favorite tree. When the sun shifts and he starts to get hot, he gets up and moves to the shady side of the tree. This is similar behavior to a wild male lion, although they have work to do, patrolling their territory. To simulate this, and to give them some exercise, I rotate the animals between different enclosures. When I move a lion into an enclosure that's been occupied by hyenas, or even other lions, he will spend time running around marking his territory and sniffing about. It's something to keep him interested. Once he's satisfied that he's staked his claim, he'll sit under a tree quite happily.

We also exercise the lions and take them for walks in the open areas of the park. Once, the lions got more exercise than we expected. Three of us, Helga, a fantastic keeper from the Lion Park whom I call the mother of all cubs because of the number she has raised; Alex the trainer; and I took Thunder and Rain for a walk one day. We left their enclosure and went out in the greater fenced area, where there were wildebeest, zebras, giraffes, impalas, and other harmless game.

This was a new initiative and I suppose some of the others at the park were a bit wary. However, I wanted to enrich the lions by showing them new and bigger areas.

Thunder was talking to me and I was answering him back in lion and in human. "Hello, my boy. You're loving this, aren't you?"

Thunder stopped and raised his nose. He started sniffing. I looked in the direction from which the breeze was coming, across the open plain of gently waving golden grass. On the horizon was a small herd of grazing wildebeest. Thunder was staring intently at them.

"Check," I said to Helga and Alex, nodding to the lion and the strange creatures that had caught his interest.

Alex shook his head. "No way. These two will never catch a wildebeest. Look at Thunder, he's unfit, and those wildebeest will take off before these two get anywhere near them."

People—these people who know all about lions—say you can't reintroduce a tame lion in to the wild and teach it to hunt. I looked back at Thunder and he had gone into stealth mode, lowering his tawny body into the matching grass. He was slinking forward. Who had taught him to behave like this? He'd been raised in captivity and never hunted a single thing in his life. Nor had his mother or father, for that matter. This was innate, instinctive behavior.

"Look at Rain," Helga said.

She seemed to be getting in on the act, as well, and had speared off in a classic flanking maneuver, or so we thought.

"Zebra," I said, following Rain's path and eyes. "It's got a foal with it." Rain clearly had her sights set on different prey and the foal was, I thought, an easier target.

"Thunder!" I hissed. "What are you doing, boy?" He moved a hundred meters ahead of us, through the grass, then broke cover. Breathless, we watched as he charged into the group of unsuspecting wildebeest. They, too, had led a very sheltered life, but they scattered as though their lives depended on it—and they did. Thunder carved a path across the veld as he charged. Through the dust cloud thrown up by galloping hooves, we saw Thunder again. He leapt on to the back of a hapless wildebeest and pulled it down. Within seconds he had his jaws clamped hard around its throat as its hooves flailed at the air.

Thunder killed that thing as though he had done it every day of his life.

Perhaps emboldened by her mate, Rain charged after the zebra. She closed in on the foal, but at the last minute some instinct of its own made the young zebra turn suddenly. Rain tried to follow its track and reached out one massive paw to hook the zebra's hind leg with her claw, but she missed—just. She lost her balance and fell, but was on her feet and crankily shaking the grass and dust from her coat straight after.

The area we were walking in was huge—about two hundred hectares—and the wildebeest and zebra are wild (that is, they have not been hand-reared) so they had a fair chance of escaping Thunder and Rain. I do believe that if we had let Rain try again she would have caught something, but the Lion Park does not work that way, and that was the end of the experiment of walking lions in the greater park with other game.

Food is an important part of the management of any animal in captivity. At the Lion Park, and in The Kingdom of the White Lion, where my lions now live, we rely heavily on donations from farmers who have lost large animals through natural causes.

We collect dead cows, horses, and pigs, and will shoot animals that need to be euthanized. We don't take animals that have been put down with drugs by a vet because the Lion Park learned the hard way early on that residual chemicals in the flesh of a euthanized animal can kill a cub. Adult lions just get stoned, but it's not good for them. We provide a good service for farmers, who would otherwise have to pay significant sums of money to dispose of dead livestock.

One school of thought in keeping captive lions is that they should be overfed. Some owners believe that a lion with a full belly will be happy and less likely to try and eat a keeper, or escape in search of human or animal prey. I always believed that this was nonsense, and set out to prove that contentment had little to do with being stuffed with food.

Different people I spoke to had different theories about how much lions ate. The most common blanket statement was that a male lion ate 35 kilograms (77 pounds) of meat per week, and a female between 15 and 20 kilograms.

I have always been an astute observer and a meticulous record-keeper. I find I can never have too much information about the animals in my care. No one at the Lion Park could tell me exactly how much the lions were eating. People were guessing and various numbers kept coming up, but no one knew for sure. This was like a red rag to a bull to me.

I began a strict regime of observation and record-keeping. Over the course of a year, I worked out that a large male lion, such as Thor the white lion, was eating an average total of about 20 kilograms (44 pounds) per week, usually in two sittings. We were feeding twice a week because it would have been quite a chore to cut and prepare meals for all the lions on a daily basis, and because this mimics the frequency with which a lion would feed in the wild.

Over the next year I began experimenting with Thor's food intake, sometimes increasing it and sometimes decreasing it. What I was trying to work out was the correct average intake of food that would allow Thor to maintain a healthy, stable, average weight without losing condition and without detrimental changes to his behavior. It's quite easy to tell when lions are losing weight and condition, as it shows quickly on their hips and ribs, and their hair starts taking on a fuzzy feel and look.

What I found was that Thor needed 17 kilograms (37.4 pounds) of meat per week, which was less than what we had been feeding him and well short of the 35-kilogram minimum portion per week that other people had talked about. I don't think that lions should be kept overweight simply because some people think this makes them less dangerous. No one wants to see a fat lion on a film set, but that wasn't my motivation for experimenting with Thor's diet. I wanted a content, healthy lion in top condition, and that's what I got. I hope that this fact, at least, puts an end to the claims that the only reason I can go into my lions' enclosures and interact with them is because they are overfed. I'll also quite happily go in and play with a lion a minute before he is due to receive his regular feeding. They do not see me as food and their contentment has little to do with being stuffed.

My special relationships with my animals means that managing them on a day-to-day basis is much easier for me than any zookeeper trying to care for his charges anywhere else in the world.

Keeping an enclosure clean is very important, and when it's time for cleaners to come in, I can call my lions and move them all into their night pen. I know from experience that when you try to move a pride of "wild" lions—ones that you can't approach up close—into a cage, one will always resist. Cleaner enclosures mean less flies and disease, but if my lions do develop a problem with flies, I can put ointment straight onto their ears. Not many other keepers could do that without darting the lions.

If my lions get worms, I can walk up to them and give them deworming medicine. Likewise, to prevent ticks I pour the treatment onto their shoulders individually. If I do find a stray tick, I can just pick it off. De-ticking lions that are not used to people walking up close to them is difficult. The cats have to be driven into a type of crush and then sprayed, which they hate. If one of my lions needs antibiotics, I can give it to him personally, out of my hand, and make sure he has taken it.

Once Napoleon and Tau had a fight, as lions do, and Tau gave Napoleon a really nasty gash in the pad on one of his paws. I called the vet, and when she came to the enclosure she asked if I could show her the wound while Napoleon was still conscious. Because of the relationship I have with Napoleon, I was able to lead him, hobbling, to the gate, pick up his paw, and show it to the doctor while she stood on the other side of the fence.

"It's bad, but I can't stitch it," the vet said. "It's not like we can put a bandage on it and say, 'Hey, Napoleon, be sure and stay off the paw for a few days.' He'll chew the bandage off as soon as we put it on him."

Instead, she asked me if I could dip his paw twice a day in a bucket of water and Hibiscrub, the anti-bacterial soap that surgeons use to wash their hands before operating. After that, I should put cream on the wound and give him an antibiotic pill.

"Sure. No problem," I said, wondering if she believed me.

Napoleon was in pain, but he let me do exactly as the doctor ordered, and even I thought, "Wow, this is special." It got to the stage where he would come hobbling down to the gate when he saw me coming. It must have hurt him each time he put his paw in the bucket, but he knew it was doing him good and that I wasn't trying to cause him pain. That's the relationship I have with Napoleon, but I don't know if Tau would have been as patient a patient.

As I've said before, Tau is a different lion. It is not as though I have a better relationship with Napoleon, it's just different. Tau is just a less trusting and more skittish individual than Napoleon. Napoleon is relaxed and chilled and very confident. Just like two human brothers can be different, so too can lion brothers be different, one from the other. And, of course, this can cause problems. Tau and Napoleon needed to be microchipped for identification purposes, and while I can do a lot with those two lions without anesthetic or the need for other people to be around, sticking a big fat needle loaded with a microchip into either of their shoulders would have earned me a bite. In some cases, even with my special lions, there is sometimes no alternative to sedating them so that certain procedures and treatments can be done.

I had to get a vet involved. I arranged for Dr. Paul Bartells to come and do the chipping, and to get some DNA samples from the two lions while he was there. Dr. Bartells is a well-respected veterinary surgeon who has compiled a DNA bank of lions across South Africa for research purposes. The plan was for him to take a small tissue sample from each lion's ear while they were under.

Paul prepared a couple of tranquilizer darts and loaded the dart guns. I don't like putting my lions to sleep, but sometimes it has to be done. He took aim at Napoleon from outside the fence of the enclosure, took a breath, and squeezed the trigger. The dart hit him in the rump and he went down like a sack of potatoes. Paul reloaded and fired at my other lion. While the dart found its mark, Tau seemed very resilient to the drug. He staggered, walked around a bit, sat down, but then got up again. For some reason the dose just wasn't taking effect.

"I'll give him another shot," said Paul.

I nodded, my concern growing. He fired another dart and said, "That should do it, but let's go start working on Napoleon or else he's going to wake up soon."

I agreed, against my better judgment. Tau was woozy, but he still looked too alert for my liking. He was probably pissed off, as well, as he had just had two darts in his butt. However, as luck would have it, Tau was at the far end of the enclosure and Napoleon had dropped right by us, near the gate. We decided to go in—Paul, his female assistant, and me.

No sooner had we slid open the gate, kneeled down by Napoleon, and started to work on him than a couple of onlookers outside the enclosure began shouting.

"Look out!" one cried. "Tau's getting up!"

All three of us turned. Tau had seen us messing with his brother and he was not happy. He charged and we got up and ran for the gate. Tau was about fifty yards from us and we were about five from the gate.

Paul and I bundled his assistant through the gate and she made it to safety. Paul was next at the gate and I was behind him, but Tau was still bounding towards us. Although he had received two doses of tranquilizing drug, Tau covered the distance between us quicker than Paul and I could get through the gate.

Tau reared up and lunged at Paul. Tau had bypassed me, even though I was the closer target, but he locked his jaws around the vet's arm and all I could hear was a crunch, like someone biting into a crisp, juicy apple.

Tau hooked his claws into Paul's buttocks and started trying to drag him down and back into the enclosure. At the same time, the doctor's assistant and the other people outside the enclosure had hold of Paul and were trying to drag him to safety. Poor Paul was at risk of being pulled apart, and I was terrified that Tau was going to tear Paul's arm off.

I didn't have pepper spray with me on that day, so I did all I could think of to make Tau release the vet. I reached around Tau's huge head and jammed two fingers of one hand into the lion's nostrils. I drove the fingers of my other hand up under Tau's jaw and pressed hard, blocking his airway.

Tau gasped, and that momentary pause, during which he released his bite on Paul's arm, allowed the people outside to drag the bleeding man to safety. I, however, was still in the enclosure with an enraged, drugged lion. He didn't know who I was anymore, or what I was doing to him, or why I was doing it. He started coming after me so I ran back inside the enclosure. I must have looked like a rodeo clown being chased by an enraged bull, though I was running at the same pace as an Olympic sprinter doing the one hundred meters. I ran in a complete circuit of the enclosure with Tau bounding after me.

I was heading towards the exit, but blocking my way was a waterhole which must have been about two meters wide. With Tau gaining on me I decided to try and jump the waterhole, but as I left the bank I tripped and landed face-first in the water.

The funny thing was that as I tripped, Tau also stumbled, in perfect synchronicity with me. I guess the drug was finally starting to take effect on his coordination. If he hadn't fallen when he did, then my beloved, stoned lion probably would have munched and clawed me. The difference between Tau and Tsavo was that my boy had a full set of claws. I splashed through the water, thoroughly soaked, and made it back to the gate in quick time while Tau, finally, passed out behind me.

Paul was airlifted to hospital by a medical evacuation helicopter, and he received somewhere between a hundred and two hundred stitches to repair his mangled arm. It took him more than a year to recover and to this day he still can't extend his arm fully. He's quite a guy, though, and certainly hasn't let that stop him. He flies micro-light aircraft, like me, is the head of the National Zoo's Wildlife Biological Resource Center, and won the National Science and Technology Forum Award. To this day, though, I think he might be secretly proudest of the fact that one day he was mangled by a lion and lived to tell the story.

I saw a saying above a guy's computer one day which read: "Engage brain before putting mouth into gear." I think that's a good philosophy to follow with humans. I've found that it's an even better philosophy to follow when I look at a lion and think about how he's being treated. Before I make an assumption about a lion or take a step towards him, I try to take all the facts I know into account. For instance, I have seen lions in captivity that appeared to me to be unhappy. However, I don't really know what's in that lion's head, as he lives behind the bars of his cage and I don't know the relationship that lion has to its keeper. By the same token, most people don't really understand the relationship I have with my lions and that creates disagreements among us. Both that keeper and I have different relationships with our lions. Maybe I can explain how I think about a lion, and in doing so give you an idea of how I approach and manage all the big cats I work with.

First off, I don't have the same relationship with all of my lions that I do with Napoleon, and I constantly try to keep in mind that all animals are individuals. Tau and Napoleon, for instance, are brothers, but like all brothers they fight sometimes, and that affects the way that they interact with me. Like people, we must understand that even animals related through birth can have very different personalities, and we must also remember that they go through different stages in their lives. Just like us, they can have good days and bad days. Many factors can affect the relationship, such as the way I happened to be getting on with one or more of the pride males at the time, or the way that a mom with a new litter of cubs eyes me.

Second, the amount of time that I know a lion can also affect my relationship with it. For instance, there is a group of lions that I call "acquaintance lions," lions that I don't know as well as my own lions. I will work with them, but I am more careful. Things can change with time, though. An acquaintance lion can become a good friend. Problems that might have existed between us might just have been related to age, for instance.

That brings up a third point: the age of the lion. As Tsavo and others have taught me, relationships with lions can become a bit sticky between the ages of two and three. Lions that I don't see eye to eye with at this age can become great friends of mine at five. By the same token, some animals I've been friendly with at that earlier age don't get on with me as they get older. When lions hit the equivalent of puberty, they change, and that can manifest itself in their behavior with lions younger and older than them. Just like I ran wild when I was a young man, so can they, and I keep that in mind when I'm with them. From a management point of view, it's about understanding these changes, and being aware of what else is going on around the animals. For instance, if I move some sexy young lady lions in next door to Thor, he might not want to know me for a while. It's not rocket science. When I was an adolescent, if a sexy young girl had moved in next door to me, I pretty much would have wanted my mom, say, to keep her distance, if I ever got the chance to talk to the new neighbor. Some keepers, though, wouldn't consider their own human experiences to understand a change in a lion's behavior. And that, I think, is a big mistake.

It must be terrible, I think, for lions introduced into a zoo to hear the strange calls of all the other animals around them and not be able to see or interact with others of their species. Think of how you might feel, dropped down in the middle of a country where you didn't speak the language and were all alone. You'd be just like those lions. They're the ones you see pacing up and down in their cages. They're "wild" animals that are being kept in captivity. By wild, I mean they are unable to interact with humans, and only see them as something either to fear or to hate. They don't know whether to be aggressive or submissive towards their keepers. My lions aren't wild. They know me, they know their surroundings, and it makes life easier for all of us.

Part of the problem with a troubled captive lion is that it may have been hand-raised as a cub and exposed to humans when it was little and cute. I believe that cubs that get this sort of attention are enriched and contented animals. They play until they get tired and then they fall asleep. In the wild, they get similar attention from the rest of the pride and are allowed to exhaust themselves with play. In captivity, there usually comes a point when the cub is withdrawn from public contact, because it has reached a certain size, and never interacts with a human again on friendly terms for the rest of its life. It's no wonder they seem troubled. I wish it was different. I wish that those people who cared for the cubs would keep up the relationship, even in a different form, when those cubs grew. Staff in zoos and other Lion Parks come and go, but just as I try to understand my lions as individuals, so have I made a commitment to them that they will be looked after, even if I am not around.

Starting at birth, there are two ways to manage captive lion cubs—they can either be left with their mothers or taken away and hand-raised.

Leaving a lioness to raise her cubs, in the presence of the pride males, means visitors can see a whole pride together, which is a nice experience. It also saves money, because hand-raising a cub costs about R6000 ($800) per animal. You can tell the difference when a cub is fed on mother's milk—it grows faster, it's more solid, and its fur is in great condition.

Traditionally, though, the problem with leaving a lioness to raise her cubs is that the young ones grow up "wild"—that is, not exposed to humans from a young age. This is because conventional wisdom had it that a human could never go anywhere near a lioness and her cubs. Lionesses were so fiercely protective that they would kill anyone who tried to spend time with their cubs. In the wild, young males are forced to leave the pride once they reach an age of between eighteen and twenty-six months. If they stayed, they would be killed by the dominant pride male. The same thing happens in captivity, but the downside is that if the males have been raised "wild" then humans can never work with them.

Removing cubs at birth means that they could be raised around humans, meaning they might be available for, say, film work later in life. However, a lioness who loses her cubs goes straight back into estrus, so taking them away may mean more cubs to deal with—at more cost—a little more than three months later. Space becomes a factor, as well, because creating more and more lion enclosures is a costly business.

A better model for raising cubs was staring me in the face, but people said it couldn't be done. What if we could have the best of both worlds—cubs being raised by their mother, but with me allowed to go in with them while they were still small, to habituate them to humans and form relationships with them? I thought that if Tau or Napoleon could mate with Maditau, one of the female cubs who had been born about six months after my boys, and I could get Maditau to accept me around her babies, then we would solve a number of issues. The cubs would grow up healthy and strong; they would get used to me from the start of their lives; the Lion Park would save on hand-raising costs; Maditau would not go into estrus and breed again; and visitors would get to see a whole pride in action.

Further down the track, the male cubs could be separated from the pride once they came of age—and I had already formed a relationship with them—and the female cubs could stay with the pride, on the contraceptive pill, so Tau and Napoleon would be unable to mate with them, as these lions would be their daughters.

In the wild, the problem of fathers mating with daughters is usually solved by the fact that by the time female cubs are sexually mature, the pride males have been kicked out by new, unrelated males. However, in areas that are over-hunted or heavily poached, dominant males may stay in charge longer, and eventually mate with their daughters, causing problems with interbreeding. Likewise, if the dominant male is killed off too soon by a hunter, younger males can end up mating with their siblings and even mothers and aunts.

The idea of interacting with cubs while they were still with their mothers sounded good in theory, but would a lioness let me get near her cubs? And, more important, would even I be crazy enough to try?

EIGHT

The Lion Farmer

Mandy and I were having dinner in a restaurant one night with some people we knew and others we'd met for the first time.

A woman I'd just been introduced to said to me across the table, "I know you work with lions and I think it's wrong to keep them in captivity."

I could have been upset that someone I'd just met felt entitled to make such a sweeping statement, but I'm used to it. "What about cows?"

"Excuse me?" she said.

"Do you think it's wrong to keep cows enclosed on a farm? They're descended, way back, from wild animals, and were domesticated."

She raised her nose a little, and took on a look of understanding where I was coming from, mixed with superiority. "I'm a vegetarian and I don't agree with keeping animals for meat."

"That's a very nice leather strap you have on your watch," I said to her, then lifted the tablecloth and took a peek underneath. "And you have nice leather shoes, as well. I bet you have leather seats in your car. Do you think it's wrong to farm cows for meat, but right to kill them for their skins?"

"That's irrelevant," she said, as people do when they know they're losing an argument. "Cows are kept for consumption, and even though I don't like it I can understand it, but lions aren't kept for consumption, they're kept to be shot by trophy hunters."

Certainly, no one is going to shoot any of my lions for sport, but I wanted to keep playing devil's advocate—at least until the main course arrived. "Okay," I continued, "if people ate lions would that make it okay to keep them?"

"No."

"Why not? People farm crocodiles for their meat and their leather. If that's okay, why couldn't you farm a lion if you ate the meat and used its skin? That's consumption. Wouldn't that make it all right?"

"No."

"Oh," I said, leaning back in the chair, "so it's okay to keep and kill cows and crocodiles for meat and leather, but not lions. Is a cow worth less than a lion?"

She couldn't answer me. It's an argument that goes around and around in circles, and one in which people have very set opinions which don't always hold up to close scrutiny. People always like to categorize things and other people, and this process usually involves a line they won't cross. Consciously or unconsciously, the woman in the restaurant had drawn a line between meat and leather. She thought it wrong to kill an animal for its meat, but okay to execute it for its skin. Odd. Following on from her logic, people who kept cows were all right, but people like me, who kept lions, were horrible.

When I thought about it, I realized that like everyone else in the world I had my lines when it came to lions.

Like many other people in South Africa and subsequently around the world, I was shocked when our local *Carte Blanche* television current affairs program showed images of a lioness in a cage being shot during a "canned" hunt. I was working in the Lion Park at the time, developing my close bond with Tau and Napoleon. Canned hunting is a term for shooting an animal which has been bred for the sole purpose of being killed as a trophy, for money. In the case in point, the lioness had been lured closer to the hunter by placing one of her cubs in a neighboring cage.

I cannot understand why someone would pick up a gun and shoot a lion simply because the animal has a big black mane. Nor can I understand why someone would shoot a magnificent kudu bull just because the antelope has a nice pair of long curly horns. I can, however, understand why someone would kill an antelope for its meat. To me, that is the same as killing a cow for steak.

As someone who keeps lions and knows a thing or two about them, I started thinking about lion hunting, in the wild and on farms where the so-called canned hunts take place. This is an emotional issue, especially in Africa, but outside it, as well. I'm not the sort of person who listens to conventional wisdom and takes the views of others as gospel. I never have been and so I decided the best way for me to make an informed judgment about lion hunting, and farms where lions were bred to be shot, was to go and see one of these places for myself.

I contacted the owner of a hunting lodge where they bred lions and he agreed to show me around. I won't say where in South Africa it was, but it was far enough from my home for me to justify flying myself there in a light aircraft.

I love flying, and I fly the way I interact with my lions. When there is someone else in the aircraft—just like when there are visitors watching me with my lions—I keep it toned down and conservative. I don't show off for people in front of my lions, or push their limits, and I take the same approach when I'm piloting an airplane. When I'm alone, however, it's a different story. When I'm flying solo I'm never unsafe and I don't break the law, but I do enjoy myself. It was good to be airborne again, and the sun streamed into the cock-pit as I passed over open plains of golden grass and the neat geo-metric circles and rectangles of cultivated fields. As my course took me farther into the heart of the country, the farmland gave way to more rugged country, hills and valleys covered in the gray-greens and khakis of the bush. Away from the tarred highways, graded dirt roads ran like red arteries back into the heart of Africa.

I checked the GPS and found the remote airstrip. Banking, I executed a low-level pass over the airstrip to make sure there was no game grazing on the close-cropped grass.

The farmer who had agreed to host me was waiting for me, lean-ing against the warm side of his dusty Land Cruiser pickup, his eyes shaded by the brim of his bush hat, arms folded. I climbed down from the plane, took off my sunglasses, and walked over. He was a young guy—younger than he'd sounded on the phone—but like most farmers I've met, his face and arms and legs were tanned from a life outdoors in the sun. His handshake was firm.

I threw my bag in the back of the Cruiser, and as he drove me to the farm I asked Dirk, as I'll call him, how long he had been run-ning the hunting farm.

"All my life. I was born to be a *leeu boer*," Dirk said, using the Afrikaans term for lion farmer as he navigated along the corru-gated road. "My father farmed lions and so did my grandfather. My father bought this farm many years ago. This is the only place I have ever lived."

"Why lions?" I asked him.

He shrugged and looked at me. "Why not? Like the man down the road on the next property breeds cows, my family breeds lions. We don't see them like your Tau and Napoleon at the Lion Park. For us the lions are commodities, not pets."

"Are you a hunter?" Dirk asked me.

"I like fly fishing," I said.

"Do you eat what you catch, or do you have the fish stuffed and mounted?"

"I mostly catch and release," I said honestly, "and besides, the big ones taste like crap." He smiled. "Hunting's not for me, but I can understand why some people want to do it. A lot of people tell me it's not right for me to go into the enclosures with my lions or to domesticate them, but that just makes me want to do it even more."

"I thought that since you love the lions so much you must be one of those bunny-huggers that think they know everything," Dirk said as we neared the farm buildings.

"I'm not a hunter and I'm not a bunny-hugger," I assured him. "I'm probably somewhere in the middle."

"What we do is not illegal, you know? This four-by-four *bakkie* that we're driving in was paid for by lion farming and lion hunting. I pay my taxes like every other honest person."

Dirk stopped near a high electrified fence, got out, and unlocked the gate, which he slid open. I got out and closed it behind the Land Cruiser as he drove through. Once inside the perimeter fence, we walked to the cages and I saw his lions.

At first I was horrified, and then I became angry. In cage after cage there were lions and lions and lions—more than I had ever seen in one place. I can't remember how many there were—scores or maybe hundreds. They were mostly males, and of varying ages, as this was obviously where the money was for trophies. I saw tiny cubs still squeaking and squawking; youngsters that reminded me of Tau and Napoleon when I'd first met them; and two- and three-year-olds that did nothing to hide their anger and resentment as we walked past them. The biggest males, with dark manes, would be the next to die. The females were breeders, pure and simple, no different than hens on an egg farm. What a life these poor cats must lead, I thought to myself.

We left the cages and drove back to the farmhouse. On the drive

I thought about what I'd seen. I am an observer, and I had taken note of the conditions in the cages. The lions were well fed and watered and their cages were kept clean. I suppose the lion farmer kept things clean and orderly for the same reason I do—to keep my lions healthy and prevent the spread of flies. The adult males were in good health, and I imagined that a rich professional hunter from overseas would not want to shoot a mangy lion with his ribs showing, any more than a film or documentary-maker would want to see one of my lions in less than top condition,

As we drove through the gate to Dirk's home, I realized that if I had been looking at pigs or cows or chickens or goats instead of lions, I wouldn't have found anything wrong with this farm. These lions were not "free range" but neither were they being mistreated. Once I stopped thinking about how Tau and Napoleon would feel if they were penned in like Dirk's lions, with no enrichment or stimulation, and started thinking of these animals in the same way as I might judge domestic cows, my anger abated.

I wondered if Dirk might ever be persuaded to take up some other form of farming, but then I saw his two small sons playing in the garden. Each had a toy rifle and they were playing at shooting big game, stalking imaginary lions and leopards and buffalo.

"I've organized for you to go on a hunt, Kev. Are you still keen?" Dirk asked.

"Sure." I didn't know if I would have the nerve to watch a lion being shot, but Dirk's client, a wealthy American businessman, would also be hunting other game on the farm.

That afternoon I climbed into the Land Cruiser and was introduced to Dirk's client. I looked around for a rifle, but didn't see one. "What are you going to shoot with?" The American drew a .44 Magnum pistol from a hand-tooled leather holster and proudly held it up for my inspection, its nickel-plated barrel glinting in the afternoon sun.

We left the farm and drove out into the bush. Dirk slowed the four-by-four and pointed off to the left. "Sable," he said quietly.

"Where?" the American asked.

While Dirk gave an indication of where it was, I looked at the majestic creature. The sable is one of the most beautiful antelopes on the planet. The males have a jet black coat with white markings on their faces and are quite striking, while the females are a rich red-brown. What makes the sable—the males in particular—so attractive to trophy hunters are their long curved horns. A sable can kill a lion with a backwards thrust of his head, piercing his attacker with the sharp points.

"How much for that boy, Dirk?"

Dirk quoted a hefty figure in U.S. dollars and the deal was sealed.

Dirk drove closer, which surprised me, as I thought the hunter would want to get out of the vehicle and stalk the antelope on foot. Instead, we drove right up to the sable, which seemed accustomed to the sight of the vehicle. It had had a better life than the lions, roaming about in the bush of Dirk's farm, but its time was about to come.

The hunter—and I now use the term loosely—leaned back in his seat in the open rear of the vehicle, drew his pistol, took aim, and fired. *Blam, blam, blam, blam.*

He fired four shots into the black skin, and although he hit the sable with at least one, it wasn't dead. The sable started to run, though it was clearly in agony, thrashing about as it tried to escape the sudden terrible pain. Dirk took up his rifle, took aim through the telescopic sights, and squeezed the trigger. Mercifully, the sable dropped to the ground. Dirk, at least, knew what he was doing.

We drove to where it had fallen and the hunter lowered himself awkwardly to the ground, setting foot in the African dust for the first time that day. He waddled over to the sable, knelt by it, and lifted its head, posing for photographs as he proudly displayed his latest trophy.

As I watched this spectacle, I thought to myself, "You, sir, are not a hunter. You are a wanker."

After that little display I decided to give the lion "hunt" a miss, although Dirk explained to me how it was going to work.

This wasn't your archetypal cruel canned hunt, as Dirk was not the sort of farmer who would let the hunter shoot one of his lions through the wire of its cage. By lion farmer standards he had acted ethically, releasing a large male lion into an area of a thousand hectares, forty-eight hours before the hunt was due to take place. These were the regulations in force at the time.

While this sounds like the lion might have a sporting chance, it doesn't work that way. If you release a lion that has lived in a small cage all its life into what is in effect just a larger enclosure, it is going to panic. He will run to the fence, and once he reaches it he will keep running along the fence line. I suspect this is the reason why the media has been able to get film of lions being shot through fences. Whether the cage is four meters by four, or a thousand hectares, the lion will probably still be on the fence when it gets shot. In other cases, farmers put a carcass deeper inside the enclosure, and once they know the lion has found it and started feeding, they drive or walk their client to where the action is happening, and say something like, "Check! This lion has made a kill! That shows you how wild it is. Let's kill it now while it's feeding!"

The same, I'm afraid, is true for a truly wild lion that has grown up in a finite area, such as a private game reserve. If the lion has been identified by the owners as suitable for hunting, it is tracked and figuratively marked with an X. The reserve's owners will know where to find it, and when the hunter arrives from overseas that lion doesn't stand a sporting chance of escaping its fate. One must realize that lion hunts cost a lot of money, and if the hunter doesn't get his trophy, the farmer or land owner doesn't get paid, so it's in everyone's interest—except the lion's—that the cat is marked, tracked, and offered for slaughter.

The problem I have with lion farmers releasing a caged lion into a larger area is that the lion might not be killed with the first or even second shot. The quickest and most humane way of killing an animal with a bullet, to my way of thinking, is a brain shot. However, lion hunters don't want to shoot their quarry in the head because it ruins the trophy. Instead, they aim for the heart-lung area, which is also an efficient way to kill the animal, but is a difficult target to hit. Sometimes they need two or three shots to end it quickly. If the hunter makes a mess of the shot then the wounded lion could easily hide himself inside the thousand-hectare enclosure and lie, in pain, for a couple of days until someone eventually finds him and finishes him off.

If I were a captive lion, bred on a lion farm to be killed, I think I would actually rather face my maker—or a rich American hunter—inside a four-meter by four-meter cage. At least it would be hard for him to miss at that range. Besides, no matter the size of the enclosure, the lion doesn't stand a chance anyway.

After the media and public outcry over canned hunting, the government considered stopping the industry, but money got in the way of a decision being made.

Lion farming and hunting is big business. A trophy hunter will pay about $35,000 for a lion, so if a farmer only runs five hunts a year he is still making serious money. The lion farm I visited probably employed about forty African people. When the government announced it was considering banning hunting, there was an outcry from African farmers who were breeding donkeys for slaughter as food for the lion farms. A whole industry was under threat.

The debate about lion hunting is related to the management of lion populations on private game reserves. In many parts of South

Africa wealthy individuals are buying up former farmland and re-habilitating it as private nature reserves. Even if the owners of a game farm are opposed to hunting, the reality of managing animal numbers eventually confronts them. In an enclosed reserve there is only enough room for a finite number of animals. The people who have a problem with lion hunting rarely seem to have an issue with the culling of species such as impala or kudu or wildebeest. How-ever, as the debate about elephant culling stirs the passionate emo-tions of environmentalists, so too does the issue of lion hunting. What happens, for example, on a private game reserve where too many lion cubs are surviving to adulthood? Even a land owner who is opposed to hunting may be faced with the reality that it is far easier to shoot some of their lions—or have someone pay them for the privilege—than to go through the complicated processes of ad-ministering contraceptives to wild lions or darting and selling them to other reserves as live animals. Besides, there are few reserves that would purchase these lions, other than for hunting.

If you asked seven different people in South Africa to define canned hunting you would get seven different answers. Some people say it comes down to the size of the enclosure, but whether it's four, ten, or twenty square meters, or two hundred, fifteen hundred, or two thousand hectares, a finite space is a finite space. Other people will tell you that a lion is not canned if it is allowed to feed off wild prey. My reply to that is that if a farmer is buying wildebeest or al-lowing them to breed to provide food for his lions—and probably culling a few wildebeest when there are too many—then that lion is farmed and, by extension, canned if it is offered to hunters.

What if a lion has been hand-raised and then released into the "wild" of a finite private reserve? As I said, we all have the place where we draw our line in the sand, and this is mine. I have a prob-lem with any lion that has been hand-raised by human beings shot as a trophy later in life, rather than with arguing about the size of the enclosure in which it is hunted. My dog, Valentino, is a beautiful example of a Staffordshire terrier, but if one day hunters decided they wanted to hunt Staffies as trophy animals, there is no way I would accept any amount of money, no matter how large, to let someone shoot him. Why? Because I raised him from a pup. I couldn't live with myself if I allowed someone to hunt and kill him. That would be taking blood money.

It's the same with Tau and Napoleon, and I have had offers for their heads. They're getting old now and in a year or two their teeth will be falling out, but that doesn't mean that I could or would suddenly decide to make money out of someone killing them. They are a part of my family and I am a part of theirs. I have shared things with those two lions that I haven't shared with people. I've ridden with them in the back of a truck most of the way from Johannesburg to Cape Town—something else I was told lion keepers shouldn't do—just to make sure they were all right.

On the other hand, I don't have a problem with people such as Dirk, the professional lion farmer and hunter, breeding lions for hunting. It is his constitutional right in this country to make a living that way, and as long as he is not being cruel to his lions and is keeping them in decent, clean enclosures and feeding them correctly, I cannot think of his lions as more important than any other farm animal.

I do have a problem with some facilities that are using their lions for dual purposes. On one hand, they operate as a petting zoo where young cubs are exposed to the public and begin to develop relationships with their keepers. Later in life those lions are sold off as trophies for slaughter. That's an example of where a lion hunting farm starts to come into my territory, and I don't like it.

When it comes to hunting lions in the wild, some people may be surprised to learn that I have no problem with this concept, as long as it is done professionally.

In Botswana, truly professional and ethical hunters have had long-term projects in place that involve monitoring prides of lions in the wild. Using identification charts, they can track the fortunes of individual lions and know their ages and positions in the pride. For example, when one or two pride males are ousted by younger lions then these animals' days alive in the wild will be numbered. Shooting these lions, who are near the end of their lives, would not impact the viability of the prides in the area. At the same time, they would provide much more of a challenge to a hunter and, unlike in a canned hunt, there is no guarantee they would be taken, so each animal has a sporting chance.

This is an example of sustainable hunting, but sadly there are plenty of examples of unethical hunting in the wild. Shooting dominant males that have not yet been ousted from the pride can have disastrous consequences. If a younger male is able to take over a pride without challenging, then the natural order is distorted. For a start, he will kill cubs sired by the original pride male, and those cubs may have had a chance to grow to adulthood if the original male had been allowed to live until his time was over. Alternatively, as I've already mentioned, you can also have a situation where a male cub grows to adulthood and takes over his own pride, mating with the other females in his family.

In a way, hunting is like any other farming business. You have a commodity, and you make money out of it by selling it to someone else. In this case, the commodity is a living creature's life.

I don't begrudge an ethical lion hunter making money out of lions, any more than I would think it wrong for a fair cattle farmer to sell his animals for slaughter. Where things start to go wrong is when greed and money, in the absence of ethics, become the motivating factor for hunting. A cattle farmer who treats his animals poorly in order to cut his margins is as bad as a lion hunter who shoots a male lion in its prime. An unethical lion hunter's not worse than a poor cattle farmer—despite what the media might say. They're each as bad as the other.

Flying home from Dirk's farm by myself, I had time to think about what I had seen and what I had learned. In turn, it made me think a little bit more deeply about my own spiritual beliefs and how they related to the animals I knew and worked with every day.

As a teenager I had been an altar boy for a while in the Anglican Church. Mom wanted me to be one, and I told her I would as long as she let me drive the Mini. She agreed, so it wasn't a bad deal, but I let my religion slip until Lisa and her family persuaded me to start going back to church. Even then I think I was doing it to impress her, in part. In my life I've always known, in my heart, the difference between right and wrong. Sometimes, when I was younger, I chose wrong. These days, however, I still have my faith, and Mandy and I go to church most weeks for the right reasons, and not because I'm trying to impress someone or get something in return.

The evening before I left, Dirk and his family invited me to have dinner with them. Before we started eating we all joined hands and bowed our heads. "Thank you, Lord, for everything we have on this farm and thank you for the food we are about to eat. Amen," said Dirk. For a moment I thought to myself, "This is so wrong. How can these people slaughter lions and yet maintain their Christian faith." In the peaceful solitude of the airplane's cockpit I realized that if I had sat down to dinner with a cattle or sheep farming family, I would have had no such reservations and I was embarrassed to have been such a hypocrite and so wrong in using my faith to judge them.

I pray about things in my life and for guidance about what I do with my animals. If it is the will of God, I hope to continue doing what I do for a very long time. I find that having spiritual beliefs helps with my decision-making—being able to know or make a judgment on what is right or wrong—and with my personal ethics. My "faith" in terms of how I live with my animals and how I work with them is the same as my faith in the church. I am not an evangelist, and I do not seek to force my methods of working with animals on to other lion keepers any more than I would try and convert someone to Christianity. I'm more than happy to help someone on the right path, whether it be in life, faith, or animal-keeping, if they are minded to ask for my help, but I am not someone who will sit in judgment on others.

Who was I, I thought as I looked out over the wild beauty of Africa from above, to say that the life of a lion was more important than that of a cow?

NINE

Cheeky Cheetahs and Jealous Jackals

Voluptuousness is a quality prized in some African cultures. A woman who is well rounded—all around—is considered attractive to many African men. Lenny the cheetah was an all-African male.

When I finished my morning coffee at the Lion Park I met up with the latest crop of volunteers. The park, like several other African wildlife, educational, and charitable organizations, accepts volunteer workers from abroad. They tend to be backpackers who have a bit of extra time to spend on the continent, and want to contribute something.

This group was pretty typical. There were about half a dozen of them and they hailed from all around the world. Holland, Germany, and Italy were represented, and there was an Australian and a New Zealander. This group was all pretty young, and mostly women, but the age range varied enormously, from kids just out of school on their gap year through to people in their seventies.

After I took them in with the lion cubs, I made them wait outside the big lions' enclosure while I went in and did my stuff with Tau and Napoleon. As usual, I toned down my play in the presence of strangers, as I had learned from Tsavo that animals can react very differently when there is an audience at hand. I went in with a plastic atomizer bottle and I sprayed some of the liquid near the lions' huge, hairy faces. The boys sniffed the air and rubbed against me, urging me to spray more.

"What's that spray?" the Aussie girl asked, preempting my explanation.

"It's a mix of water, citronella, and other goodies. Cats love scents and this stuff is like catnip for lions. They like to sniff it and rub it." To further demonstrate, I sprayed some on the grass and Napoleon lowered his massive body to the ground and began rolling in it. We left the boys and I went in with some of my other lions—Siam, Kaiser, and Gandalf, one of my white lions. Kaiser loves the spray, and was pushing his shaggy head against me to get some more of it while the volunteers watched and took photos from outside the enclosure fence.

"What would happen if one of us went in there with you?" asked a young German guy.

It's a good question, and it always comes up. "I don't know," I answered truthfully. "Lions can smell fear and the adrenaline coursing through your body. If you walked in confidently and showed no sign of fear, you might be okay. Or this lion could decide he didn't like you and he could charge into you, go for your stomach or throat, put you on the ground, and kill you."

Now that I was sure I had their attention, I continued the explanation. "I've known all these lions since they were born. I haven't hand-raised them all, but I've spent time with them, and I have a relationship with them. They're between two and three years old—roughly equivalent to the teen years in humans, so some of them have an attitude. I know them, so I can relate to them, but if a stranger comes in with them, it's like, say, if your parents had split up when you were young. If your father suddenly reappears in your

down on his mouthful of butt, but eventually I managed to prize his jaws from the tender, succulent flesh. The poor girl was screaming as I ushered her out of the enclosure.

"Give us some privacy, please," I said to the others. The girl unzipped her jeans and lowered them. There on the pale white skin of her bottom were four neat red puncture marks. "I'll have to clean them," I said.

The girl groaned. "Will I need a tetanus shot?" she wailed.

"I'm afraid so," I said to her. I pitied her, as I myself would have been a lot more worried about the needle than Lenny's bite, but he had drawn blood.

That was the last time we let volunteers in with an adult cheetah. It was the third time Lenny had tried to bite a volunteer, though the first time he had successfully sunk his teeth into his target. With some groups Lenny was fine, but on each of the three occasions when he had caused trouble, there was a young lady in the group with what I can only describe as a derriere that pushed Lenny's particular button. And it was only girls he was interested in. There had been amply padded men in the enclosure and Lenny had ignored them.

I was in a difficult position. I could hardly say to one member of a group of volunteers, "Sorry, you can't go in with Lenny because Lenny likes booty."

Even old Ricksey, who was a far better behaved cheetah than Lenny, could be unpredictable.

Ricksey was the first cheetah we bought for the Lion Park and Ian had scoured the zoos and parks of South Africa to find him. There were plenty of places breeding cheetahs, for tourism or release into the wild, but they were reluctant to sell their cats and when they did offer us one, they would invariably ask for a huge amount of money.

Eventually an Afrikaner farmer from the Free State returned Ian's call, saying he would sell us a cheetah for a reasonable price.

"Is it tame?" Ian asked the farmer over the phone.

"Tame, man? This thing is *hondmak*," he replied, meaning his cheetah was "dog tame." He assured us that Ricksey was a brilliant cheetah, in top condition, who was also very good with people. Someone went to the Free State to fetch him. I was so excited about working with our first cheetah, but when I first saw Ricksey he looked like he had been dragged out of his death bed.

One ear was half moth-eaten; his eyes were glazed over; his breath stank; and his fur was in poor condition, like the fuzz that lions get when they're old and nearly dead. With the benefit of some knowledge I'd now say that Ricksey was probably twelve years old, as he lived another couple of years, and even in captivity cheetah only reach about fifteen or so.

He was a nice boy, though. He was friendly, although he wasn't exactly *hondmak*, because he used to have little attacks of aggression now and then. I would be scratching him under the chin and he'd be purring loudly, and then all of a sudden he would rear up in a frenzied ball of yellow and black fur like he'd been shocked with ten thousand volts and try to attack me. Eventually he would calm down, and he was very good with the volunteers, unlike his successor, Lenny.

I met my wife, Mandy, at a very rough bar. It was called Tempos and was the kind of place that would have strippers at lunchtime to cater to the working crowd. Mandy was a personal assistant at an insurance company at the time. Tempos is on the R512, not far from the Lion Park and near where I lived. On the weekends there was a slightly better, mixed crowd, and a mate of mine invited me to drinks there on a Sunday.

I had a black eye, as two weeks before I had been at Tempos on

the Monday of a long weekend, and I had been in a fight. I had been chatting to girl and we were getting on quite well, but she had neglected to mention that she had a boyfriend. When her boyfriend showed up, I said; "Howzit," and he head-butted me.

"I'm never going back to that place," I said to my mate.

"No, come. It'll be fun."

So I walked into Tempos with my mate. As soon as he was inside he was scanning the bar for girls. "Check, over there," he said, pointing to two attractive females.

I fingered my eye and told him I'd go to the bar and order the drinks. When I had paid for our drinks, I saw my friend had already struck up a conversation with the two girls, and was focusing on one in particular. Her friend was blonde—at the time—and very pretty. I smiled as I approached.

"This is the guy," my mate said. "Kevin works at the Lion Park, with the lions. Serious. You must come to the park and see him in action. Kevin will put on his show for you and wrestle with the lions—won't you, Kev?"

I groaned inwardly. It's embarrassing when your mates use you as their pickup line. It wasn't the first time it had happened, so I agreed to show the girls around the park and my mate got busy organizing dates and times and sourcing phone numbers.

A week later I was at the Lion Park with my mate, who was waiting expectantly to see "his" girl again. Instead, Mandy, the blonde-haired girl, showed up with a girl neither of us guys had seen before. My mate was devastated, as he had packed a picnic and planned to make some serious moves. Undeterred, I set off, giving everyone the grand tour of the Lion Park.

Tau and Napoleon, as usual, were as good as gold with me, and we moved on to Ricksey's enclosure. "Ricksey's tame. We can all go in with him, Come," I said to the girls and my mate.

No sooner had I stepped into the enclosure than Ricksey charged me and started smacking me with his paws. "Calm down, my boy,"

I said, as his running claws scratched my arms and legs. I was smiling and laughing, putting on a brave face as the expert lion keeper, but Ricksey was in the midst of one of his psycho attacks. "Good boy, Ricksy," I said as he ripped my pants. "Don't you want to come in, guys?" I called to the others, who had stopped near the gate of the enclosure.

"Um, no, I don't think so," Mandy said.

I emerged with a torn shirt and pants and several scratches, laughing off Ricksey's little incident as nothing. Mandy clearly thought I was an idiot. I could hear her saying later that day to her friend, "They say this guy's got a gift, but it's more like a death wish."

Despite Ricksey's fits, he was a fantastic animal and we wanted more cheetah. We managed to buy Lenny and Arusha when they were still cubs, at about six months, but they were a step away from heaven's gates when we got them. Our vet was not impressed with our purchase. She looked at us like kids who had gone to a pet shop and bought the runt because we felt sorry for it, or who had picked up a mangy stray on their way home from school. Arusha was slightly better off than her brother, but Lenny was riddled with problems.

Anyway, we didn't really have a choice. We could have walked away from the deal, but we wanted cheetahs desperately, so we took what we could get. Lenny and Arusha needed twenty-four-seven care and I took them on.

Despite my "impressive" performance in front of her with Ricksey, Mandy had agreed to go out with me after our picnic at the Lion Park, and by the time Lenny and Arusha came along we had moved in together, in a town house in Lone Hill.

Mandy has been an inspiration to me, as well as a pillar of support during the tough times in my life. I'm able to bounce ideas off her and she is forthright and honest in coming back at me with her opinions. She believes firmly in what I do, how I do it, and why I do it. It's fantastic for me to have a partner who doesn't see herself as being in competition with the animals in my life. Mandy loves animals, though fortunately not in the same hands-on way that I relate to them. We're different people, and while we have both worked together at the Lion Park and around animals, there has never been competition between us on the work front, which I think is important. Mandy works in public relations and marketing, so she is great with people, while I am less into socializing with humans. I prefer my animals.

Mandy had already had some exposure to raising baby animals, so she knew that the novelty of bottle-feeding a cute little ball of fluff soon wore off. We had raised a leopard cub in a house we lived in for a while on Rodney Fuhr's property. The leopard was called Sabrina, and boy, was she a little witch. She bit and she scratched and she tore us and the house to shreds. We'd been told she'd been born in captivity and had been partially hand-raised, but I'm convinced now that she was taken from the wild, a practice I don't agree with. She was a feisty little thing but Mandy and I finally managed to tame her down. She was fine around us, but unfortunately, uh, she tore up some other people who went into her enclosure, and she now lives with a male leopard at another park.

When I told Mandy I was bringing two cheetah cubs to our nice town house, she rolled her eyes. Rodney Fuhr was happy for me to raise Lenny and Arusha because he knew I had the patience and experience to do the job. Some people would try and hand-raise baby animals because they thought they were cute, but few of them had the patience or commitment to see the job through. Helga, the mother of all cubs, was an exception. People who think they have what it takes to raise an animal soon learn the truth about themselves when they realize they have to miss birthdays, parties, public holidays, and Saturday nights out with friends because a cub needs feeding in the middle of the night. I made those sacrifices, but I enjoyed the experience, as well. As always, I kept records, and I knew that if a cub needed 92.3 milliliters of formula, then that's what it got—not ninety or a hundred.

Lenny and Arusha looked like skinny rats. No pets were allowed in the complex where Mandy and I lived, so needless to say some of our neighbors would have freaked at the thought of us raising two cheetahs. Smuggling Lenny and Arusha inside, in a cardboard box, was a minor military operation.

"All clear," Mandy hissed from the darkness.

"Coming in now," I replied, carrying the two squawking cubs. "Hush!"

Lenny and Arusha did it tough. They required constant attention and it took us quite a while to get them on the bottle. When we finally did get them used to formula, they didn't want to be weaned. They both had a problem digesting solid food, which gave them diarrhea and made them throw up. After that they became dehydrated and we had to put them on an electrolyte replacement fluid and other liquids to protect their intestines and rehydrate them.

After weeks of hard work and sleepless nights on our part, Lenny and Arusha were finally picking up. They were getting cute and fluffy and developing cheeky personalities. We thought they were just about ready to move back to the Lion Park. As the cubs were so full of beans, Mandy and I thought we should resurrect our social lives with a well-earned Saturday night out. We decided to go out for a meal and see a movie. Things an ordinary couple might take for granted were a special treat for us. I fed the cheetahs and closed them in the kitchen. As we grabbed our jackets I peeked over the kitchen counter to make sure they were okay. They had their box to sleep in and enough room to play. As I'd learned with the baby hyenas, the only place to safely pen cubs is the bathroom or kitchen, as they're the easiest to clean. Lenny and Arusha looked up at me, a picture of innocence. "Be good now."

The meal was great and the film a nice distraction after all our time cooped up inside with the cheetahs. I was feeling pretty happy, until I opened the door and a sickening stench just about overpowered me.

In the wild, cheetahs like to sit on the highest vantage point available. It allows them to survey their territory and scan for prey. In captivity, ours sit up on top of their night houses during the day. The highest points in our town house were the backrests of two lovely new cream-colored sofas that Mandy and I had bought just a few days earlier to replace the beanbags we'd been sitting on up until then.

With one hand over my mouth and nose, I groped for the light switch with the other. When the lights came on I saw Lenny and Arusha sleeping on our new couches. So full of life had the cubs become, they had managed to jump from the kitchen floor up on to the bench tops and serving areas, knocking everything off the counters in the process. From there the rest of the house was just a few bounds away in any direction.

Unfortunately, as I also learned that night, cheetahs like to crap on their high perches, and our two cute little cubs had done just that—all over our cream-colored furniture.

"*I did not sign up for this!*" Mandy wailed.

"Yes, you did, my love, the moment you met me."

Jackals are incredibly intelligent animals, but they are perceived as vermin on livestock and game farms in South Africa.

Farmers are concerned that jackals will linger around antelope and other animals about to give birth, and kill their offspring as soon as they are born. Research has found, however, that older, experienced jackals don't bother with killing calves or foals, but rather clean up the mother's placenta, or afterbirth.

A problem occurs, however, if an experienced jackal is trapped and killed. If younger jackals move into an area previously dominated by a lone animal, more animals will die. These newcomers kill the domestic livestock, and as their territories get smaller and they start to breed, there are more hungry mouths to feed. It's better, in my opinion, for a farmer to live with one smart old jackal in an area, and risk losing the odd animal, rather than take out a territorial male and virtually invite more jackals to come and have a go at his game or livestock. It's a hard concept to convey and jackals are up against generations of prejudice.

Nandi was a young, female, black-backed jackal who was brought into the Lion Park by a farmer. The farmer had shot her parents, and Nandi had been wounded in the attack. I found it amazing that the man had no qualms about taking out Nandi's mother and father, but had felt compassion towards their baby.

Nandi had been hit in the back and her little body was full of shotgun pellets. We fixed her up at the Lion Park and a few of us there took on the task of raising her to adulthood. I hoped that by showing Nandi to visitors and explaining her plight, we might be able to change some of the preconceptions people have about jackals. In my lifetime the African Wild Dog, one of the continent's most endangered mammals, has gone from being classed as vermin to one of the most popular animals people can hope to see during a visit to a game reserve or national park, so perhaps there was hope for Nandi and her kind. I wasn't the only person who cared for Nandi, but I believed we were forming a close relationship.

As Nandi got older she started turning on some of the people who had raised her, biting them when they came into her enclosure. One of the keepers, Cara, started going in with her, as did Helga, however neither of them had the same relationship with Nandi that I did. Nandi would tolerate Cara and was friendly with Helga, but that was about as far as it went. One by one, over a period of months, she began eliminating humans from her life until it became clear that I was the only person she accepted fully inside her domain.

We decided it would be nice for Nandi to have some company of her own kind, especially as she had rejected almost all her human friends. We were given another jackal called Wilbur, from the Johannesburg Zoo. I really hoped that Nandi and Wilbur would mate as I thought it would be cool for us to have some baby jackals to show off at the park. From everything I had learned about jackals, I was fairly sure that Nandi and Wilbur would hit it off immediately, but that wasn't to be. Nandi tolerated Wilbur and occasionally they would squabble and snap at each other, but there was no way she was going to let Wilbur mate with her.

Whenever I entered Nandi's enclosure she would jump up and run across to me, then leap up into my arms. Wilbur, I could see, was quite irritated by this, and occasionally he would sneak around behind me while I cradled Nandi, and nip me on the bum with his sharp little teeth.

"I don't get it," I said to Cara one day.

Care smiled. "I do. Jackals mate for life."

"Yeah, I know," I said, still not seeing what had been staring me in the eyes from the animal in my arms. "So why won't she mate with Wilbur?"

"You're the only one for Nandi, Kev. She thinks you're her man and she's not interested in anyone else."

TEN

___

Part of the Pride

The Lion Park pitched to provide the lions and one of the locations for a French film called *Le Lion*—The Lion. It was a big deal for the park, and we won the contract to do the film shoot, but the most important thing in my life at that time was an imminent birth.

There was a rumor going around the park at the time that Mandy was pregnant, and that I was going to be a first-time dad. The rumormongers got the first part wrong. Mandy was definitely not expecting, but my girl Maditau definitely was.

Maditau and Tabby, the two female cubs who were only a few weeks old when I first met Tau and Napoleon, had been living in the same enclosure for a while with my two favorite male lions. My boys had been living the life of a pair of bachelors for their formative years, and this was perfectly natural for lions, as it had been for me until I met Mandy. It had given Tau and Napoleon time to grow and learn some discipline, and basically how to be a lion. It also meant they wouldn't go all stupid the first time they come into contact with a lioness in estrus. My boys had earned their stripes, and they were eventually put in with Maditau and Tabby, my two girls.

We learned from the French film company that they wanted to shoot in June, in the middle of the South African winter. This is standard for filming in southern Africa as our winter is long and dry. We would be assured—as far as one can make assurances about the weather—of clear blue skies and spectacular blood red sunrises and sunsets through the dust and smoke and smog that coats Johannesburg at that time of year.

Two weeks before shooting began, Maditau gave birth to three male cubs and I was over the moon. A few days later—to the surprise of me and everyone else—Maditau's sister Tabby gave birth to two female cubs. We didn't even know she was pregnant. If Tau and Napoleon were my brothers, then I was now uncle to three boys and two girls. I didn't know which of the lions had fathered which of the cubs, but that didn't matter, as we were all happy.

As first-time moms, however, Maditau and Tabby were poles apart. Maditau did a fantastic job raising her litter, taking the cubs to her teats straight away and licking their tiny bottoms to help them defecate. She was proud and protective, as a lioness should be. Tabby, however, left her two cubs for dead. She wanted nothing to do with them.

I'd read that lionesses in the wild would sometimes adopt a sister's cubs if something happened to the other mother, and I have since had some success in staging adoptions in captivity. I gave it a try with Maditau, thinking she might not be able to tell the difference between three cubs and five. I carried the two little females into Maditau's night enclosure, when she was a safe distance away, and left them there. I sat down outside to watch what happened.

Maditau sauntered inside, walked over to one of the new arrivals, and picked it up in her mouth by the scruff of the neck. I felt a moment of hope. She had identified the cub, but had not savaged it or ignored it. Maditau carried the tiny bundle to her water bowl and dropped it in with a splash.

While the helpless cub squealed and thrashed in the water,

Maditau calmly walked over to the other little female, picked her up, walked back to the bowl, and dropped her in with her sister. I couldn't believe it. The cubs were yelling their heads off, but Maditau just walked back to her three male young, sat down beside them, and went back to sleep.

I thought, "This is not on!" I got up and went into her enclosure. Everyone had always told me to stay away from a lioness with newborn cubs, but I couldn't let those two little girls drown. Maditau opened her eyes as I entered, but she was as calm, cool, and collected with me as she had been while going about her business a few moments before, trying to drown her nieces. I fished the wet, panicked cubs out of the water bowl and hurried them back to the nursery.

The hapless youngsters were named Meg, after the actress Meg Ryan, and Ally, after Calista Flockhart's character Ally McBeal in the television show of the same name, which was a hit at the time. Some of the staff, however, couldn't pronounce Ally too well, so she ended up being called Ami.

Meg and Ami, who had been sired by my brothers Tau and Napoleon, became like foster children to me. If I was uncle to Maditau's boys then I was dad to Meg and Ami. I have been with them all of their lives. I was angry, though, at Maditau for not accepting them, and at Tabby for rejecting them. My girls had put me in a difficult position. With filming about to start I was going to be bottle-feeding two cubs at night after long, hectic days on the set. Also, with no cubs to suckle, Tabby would come back into estrus straight away so our leading lions, Tau and Napoleon, would be distracted while they were supposed to be working.

It was a busy time. The best times to film in Africa are the so-called golden hours, just after dawn and just before sunset, when the light is soft and mellow and the grassy veld and tawny coats of the lions really do look like they're made of precious, molten metal. I had to be up at four in the morning to get the lions ready for the day's filming, and in the middle of the day I would spend time with little Meg and Ami, and load the others onto vehicles and prepare them for the afternoon shoot.

I couldn't stay mad at Maditau—I'd known her as long as I had Tau and Napoleon. She was a great mom and was really looking after her cubs.

She was in a separate enclosure with her cubs, in order to simulate the eight-week period that occurs in the wild when new mothers take their offspring away from the rest of the pride. The theory was that male lions might not recognize newborn cubs as their own and would kill them, or that tiny cubs were simply not strong enough to endure the rest of the pride's rough play.

When I approached her, Maditau would come to the fence as she always did, and start talking to me. "*Wuh-ooow, wuh-ooow.*"

"*Wuh-ooow,*" I'd say back to her. "How's my girl today?"

I would tickle her through the gate and it seemed as though nothing had changed between us. The next time I stopped by, Maditau was out in the open with her cubs in tow and they trotted over to the gate on their tiny little legs to see who their mother was talking to. Cubs are curious, and soon they were weaving in between Maditau's legs to try and get closer to the fence and see what all the fuss was about.

I knelt to look at the cubs. Where the sliding security gate met the fence there was a small gap, and as I was chatting to them all one of the cubs pushed its way to the front of the litter and fell through the gap.

"Shit!" I thought Maditau would have a fit. I scooped up the little squealing cub in the cupped palms of my hands. Maditau lowered her big face to the wayward cub and looked up at me. She was totally relaxed and looked at me as if to say, "Thanks, Kev," as I pushed the tiny bundle back through the gap to her.

Helga and I were doing the rounds a couple of days later and

Maditau was still in her night pen with her cubs. "I'm going to go in with them," I said.

"Kev, you're crazy. It's one thing to check the cubs through the fence, but are you sure you want to go inside with a lioness and young cubs?"

"I'm going in," I said to Helga. "But I want you here, just in case something happens. I wouldn't want to try this by myself."

I opened the gate, closed it behind me, and went to the night pen. I opened the door, but instead of leaving I waited in the open area of the enclosure. Maditau came running out and gave me her greeting the same way she would have if I had been on the other side of the fence. The cubs came out of their house a few seconds later and started to explore. I sensed no enmity from Maditau at all. Helga was looking on anxiously from outside and I started to think that we humans were making a bigger deal out of this whole interaction than the lioness was.

The cubs came up to me and I started to pet one. Maditau could see what was going on, but she seemed fine with the interaction. It might have been different if I had walked over to the cubs and tried to pick one up in front of her. It's kind of like when a human mother has a baby. It's okay if she says, "Here, Kev, hold the baby", but if you go "Come on, let me hold it," or just grab the kid without permission, some moms can be a bit nervous.

I'd been accepted by the males of this pride, Tau and Napoleon, and Maditau was happy for me to be in the same enclosure as her and her young. When the cubs came over to me and Maditau showed no sign of aggression, I knew something big had happened. If I had been accepted in this way, how much closer could I get to this family? People have said to me that lions tolerate people, and that is the extent of their relationship with humans. It's like the old saying, dogs have owners and cats have servants. I don't believe that about lions. Some lions only tolerate me—just as some people only tolerate me—but that day I knew I'd been accepted by Maditau.

I knew that I was part of the pride.

Filming began a couple of weeks after the two lionesses had given birth and Maditau still seemed comfortable with me being around her own cubs. As a result, we were able to let the French film crew get some shots of her picking her cubs up, moving them around and feeding them.

As usual, the crew was behind bars in a cage within the enclosure, but Maditau was happy for me to work with her in the open. The filmmakers were ecstatic, as they had planned on filming hand-reared cubs separately and superimposing them on film of lionesses. Conventional wisdom had it that lionesses with cubs would be incredibly protective and very aggressive towards outsiders, and that we would not be able to get close enough to her to film her interacting with her cubs. Maditau was happy to move her cubs around when I wanted her to, and it was an honor and a privilege for me to work with her on that film.

We were already doing ground-breaking stuff with Maditau, so I took another chance and introduced Tau and Napoleon to their young offspring. Conventional wisdom, of course, had it that the males would kill the cubs because they were less than eight weeks old. With me standing by expectantly, we let Tau and Napoleon in to see Maditau and her three cubs.

Tau and Napoleon were on edge, Maditau was on edge, and I was on edge. I didn't know how the lioness was going to react—if she was going to be more aggressive now because of the males. It was Tau who broke the ice. He walked up to the little cubs and gave them a good lick, as if to say that he really wanted to be part of their lives.

Napoleon, however, was acting really strange. He was like a cat on a hot tin roof, or Tigger in *Winnie the Pooh*—all wound up and bouncing around the enclosure. Occasionally he would stop and sniff the cubs, and they were just lapping up the attention, calling, "*Wa-OW, wa-OW.*" Of course, it wasn't all fun for the cubs. When lion cubs are first released they're nervous, on edge. Sometimes they even urinate and defecate out of sheer stress.

It was amazing, all the interaction that was going on, and none of it violent or aggressive. Maditau was greeting all the other lionesses for the first time since she'd gone off to give birth; Tau was greeting the cubs; and Napoleon was bouncing around with excitement, all at once. And I was there at the center of it. It felt like another moment or milestone of pure acceptance and I was privileged to be a part of that special day.

Tau and Napoleon and Maditau and the cubs were all fine, and no one killed or ate anyone. Perhaps my boys were just exceptional dads, or perhaps conventional wisdom needs to be challenged a little more often.

Pelokghale was a huge lioness.

She must have weighed in at around four hundred pounds, and was as big as some adult males I've seen. She could be monstrous and vicious, and I wondered what sort of a mom she would make—whether having cubs would make her even more foul-tempered.

When Pelo had her cubs she started coming up and talking to me when I passed her enclosure, but then she would trot back to her night pen, where her young were denned.

Eventually I thought I would go in with her. I'd always had a very close relationship with Maditau, but I could see no reason why Pelokghale should act weird with me if I entered her enclosure, as she had been just as communicative with me through the wire of the fence as Maditau had been after she gave birth.

I went into Pelo's enclosure and called her. This enormous lioness came bounding up to me, then paused. She turned back towards her night area, where her cubs were, and then looked back at me. Next she closed the distance between us and started nudging me.

"Come, come. Check this out, Kev," she seemed to be saying to me. She led me towards the den.

I took my cue, and walked steadily behind her towards the pen. Pelo walked inside. I'm not completely stupid, so I waited at the entrance to the night enclosure. I knew that if I crawled inside, I would be confined and have no means of a quick getaway.

I peered inside, letting my eyes adjust to the gloom. Pelokghale had walked to the other side of the den where her cubs were sitting in a nest of straw. She picked one tiny bundle up in her mouth, brought it across to my side of the pen, and set it gently down on the concrete floor for me to look at. I was close enough to touch it, but I didn't. One after another she repeated the process, depositing each of her cubs, which were only a few days old, in front of me.

At the time we were filming the documentary *Dangerous Companions*, about my relationships with the various animals at the Lion Park. The next time I went to visit Pelo and her cubs I arranged for the cameraman to come along, and I took a small digital camcorder with me in case Pelo repeated her offering of the cubs to me.

While the camera was rolling, I went in and Pelo again led me to the night area. I kneeled down at the doorway and once again she picked up one of her cubs and plonked it down in front of me. She was standing there licking the cub and talking, and the next thing I knew she was pushing the cub into my hands.

I knelt there, hands outstretched, with this tiny cub in my palms, holding it while its mother licked and cleaned it.

What happened with Maditau and her first litter, and Pelokghale and her cubs, doesn't happen with every lioness, or even with those two every time they give birth.

At the time when I was so fully accepted by Maditau and Pelok-ghale, I had no hidden agenda and no intentions about why I was going in with them and their cubs, other than to see if it was possible. I wasn't trying to strengthen our relationship so I could film a lioness and her cubs, or get pictures of me holding a cub. I did it because I wanted to, and because the lionesses were happy for me to be there. In Pelo's case, she trusted my innocence enough to deliver her offspring into my hands.

Relationships change, however, in both the human world and in the animal world. One day I might go in with Tau and Napoleon and one of them will say, "Don't come any farther, Kev." At that point, I'd have to say, "Thanks for a great ten years, guys." I'm not going to push our friendship. That would be hard, but I would have to respect the fact that change happens, and perhaps look at myself a little closer.

One of the scariest moments I've ever had with a lion—including my encounter with Tsavo—happened while I was working on this book, and it involved Maditau. I had been in Johannesburg at the recording of the soundtrack for our forthcoming feature film, *White Lion*. It had been a busy couple of weeks working with the production team, putting the finishing touches on the movie, and I was conscious that I hadn't spent time with the lions for quite a while. Tabby had given birth to three cubs a week earlier—again an unexpected though pleasant surprise—and I was eager to get back to the Kingdom of the White Lion and see how the youngsters were doing.

The Sunday afternoon we finished recording, I rushed home. "Do you want to come see the lions with me?" I asked Mandy.

"No, thanks. I'm going to put dinner on," she said.

It's hard to explain, but the feeling that I needed to spend some time with the lions had been nagging away at me. I got into my Land Cruiser Prado, and on the short but winding and scenic drive through the Kingdom I was still feeling uncomfortable, even though I was on my way to see the pride.

I went straight to Tau and Napoleon's enclosure because I wanted to see Tabby's cubs, but when I got out of the vehicle I saw the big males were in the far corner and Tabby was obviously distressed. "*Wuh-aaah, wuh-aaaah,*" she moaned, almost as if she were calling her cubs.

"What's wrong, my girl?" I said to her. I thought it was strange that she would be calling for her cubs when they were most likely in the night pen, where the lionesses usually den their newly arrived cubs.

Suddenly I noticed a flurry of activity in the middle of the enclosure. I saw Maditau and her three latest cubs, which at fifteen weeks were much older than Tabby's and already proving to be a handful. Two of Maditau's older daughters—each about three-and-a-half years old—were also with her, and mom and all her children were huddled together, totally engrossed in something.

I went closer to Tabby, and it was plain she was definitely very distressed. I checked the night pen and saw, with a sense of growing dread, that only two of her three cubs were in there.

Maditau and the others had managed to drag one of Tabby's cubs out of the pen into the wider enclosure, and as I strode closer to them I saw that the lions were all fixated on the missing cub. They were in the process of almost pulling the little one to pieces. It was then that I heard the cub's terrible wailing, a tortured, raspy *raaarrr, raaarrrr* noise. The plucky little thing was fighting for its life.

I ran at Maditau. It wasn't the first time I've acted before engaging my brain, but I couldn't stand by and let them torture the cub to death. Maditau turned on me when I got to within five meters of her, and in the nine-and-a-half years I've known that lioness I have never seen such aggression in her eyes. She had the cub in her mouth. She could have killed it immediately if she had wanted to, but instead she was taunting her own offspring with it, letting them bite and bully it, but also challenging them by taking possession of the hapless baby.

I could see the cub was badly lacerated and would probably die soon if I didn't get hold of it. It wailed away in pain and pure fear for its life. Maditau stooped low to the ground and curled her tail, her eyes as wild as a snake's. She charged me.

It's common knowledge that one shouldn't run from a charging lion, and I have honed my senses over the years to try and ensure that I say calm in potentially dangerous situations. This time, however, I wasn't sure that my base human instinct to flee wouldn't overpower me. As it happened, my legs froze on me. If, for some reason, I'd decided I had to run, I couldn't have.

Maditau stopped half a meter from me. She was huffing and puffing and staring at me, while I stayed there, rooted to the spot. She looked back at the fracas she had left behind her and to the injured cub she had dropped. Maditau wanted to regain possession of the cub so she turned and ran back to it. But she wasn't finished with me.

Three more times she left the pack and the cub to charge me, over and over again. After the second charge I picked up a rock and threw it at her. It bounced off her harmlessly, but seemed to make her even angrier, so I realized that probably wasn't the smartest move I'd ever made. With each successive mock attack she seemed to get more aggressive. I knew that if I took a step backwards from the spot where my feet remained planted, or if I ran, she would come for me again.

I thought if she charged a fifth time, this book might end up being called *Part of the Pride—in Memoriam of Kevin Richardson*.

Maditau returned to the others and the stricken cub and I sat down. We eyed each other off in a tense standoff for a few minutes, though it seemed like an hour at the time. She backed down, but when she left the other lions, she took the mangled, screaming cub in her jaws and ran off into the bush.

"Screw this," I thought. I wasn't going to let her get away with killing one of her nephews or nieces, and showing her own kids how to torture a cub in the process. I ran to the gate, opened it, and got into the Land Cruiser. I turned the key and rammed the truck into gear and drove it back into the lions' enclosure.

"Maditau! Maditau!" I roared, my arm out of the driver's side window and banging on the Cruiser's door as I drove slowly over the rocky ground in search of the recalcitrant lioness.

I found her eventually at the top end of the enclosure, with the cub still in her jaws. When she saw me, she dropped the cub. I thought that when she saw me in the vehicle she would realize that it was "game over." I was wrong. It was game on. She charged the Land Cruiser, and for a moment I thought she was going to come crashing through the driver's side window, which was open.

The Prado has electric windows, and I was stabbing the button with all my might trying to get the damned motor to move faster. She wanted to kill me, but like before, she still wanted to continually regain possession of the injured cub. She raced back to the cub then decided to come and charge me again.

When she came at me, I saw my chance to outmaneuver her. I drove around her and straight at the cub. It was so tiny that I was able to drive over the top of it—the wheels on either side of it—so that for a moment the four-by-four was providing the little one with an umbrella of steel.

Unable to reach the cub, Maditau stormed off and started running around the enclosure. Frustrated at losing the cub, she took her anger out on one of her older daughters, sinking her teeth into the other lion's backside with a sound that made me wince.

By now, Tau and Napoleon had caught on to the madness that was unfolding in their enclosure. The two males ran to Maditau and one of them—I can't remember which—gave her a beating. Thankfully, during that commotion I was able to get out of the car and pick up the cub.

As I drove toward the gate, Maditau escaped her dressing-down from the males and followed me. She circled me for a while, not letting me out of the vehicle to open the gate, but mercifully she eventually moved off.

My heart was racing, but inside the Toyota with me was a torn and shredded cub at death's door, with severe lacerations and puncture marks on its throat and side. Strange as it might sound, I knew from experience that taking such a young cub away from its mother to the vet was probably the worst thing I could do for it right then. It was a feisty little thing and having survived so much torture, I thought it might pull through if I gave it some emergency first aid and then returned it to the care of its mother, sooner rather than later.

I carry an extensive first aid kit in the car. I pulled out antiseptic cream and a special type of powder we use which slows bleeding. I ran my fingers over the squealing cub, parting its fur to check its wounds in more detail. Where the others had bitten into the cub, they had punctured two layers of its stomach muscles, so that only a thin membrane of skin was stopping its internal organs from falling out. If they had managed to disembowel it, the cub would have died. It needed stitching, but I still believed that it would be better for me to hand the cub straight back to Tabby and have her care for it and feed it overnight. I would take it to the vet the next day, once the commotion in the enclosure had finally subsided. I returned it to Tabby, and while she received it graciously, once the cub was safe Tabby turned on me and threatened to eat me. She must have thought I was the one who had taken it from her in the first place! I couldn't win.

I got home to Mandy shaken, and I was a very worried man. Not only did I think that I had just wrecked my nine-and-a-half-year relationship with Maditau, I was also worried about how it would affect my bonds with Tau and Napoleon, as we had all been getting on so well together as a family. I started cutting myself up mentally. I should have let Maditau kill the cub, I thought. Why had I intervened? No way, I countered myself. I couldn't have lived with myself if I had stood there and watched Maditau kill Tabby's cub.

Of course, nothing like this ever happens without complications: ABC News from the United States was coming to film me with the lions two days later, on Tuesday. The ABC anchor was fascinated with the way I had integrated myself into the pride and how the lionesses allowed me free access to their cubs. Great. Here was the problem: now one of those mother lions wanted to kill me! On Monday we had to record the audio dub for the actors' voices for *White Lion*. We also had to take the cub to the vet. And there was that final thing on my mind: the looming prospect of my death being recorded by ABC Prime Time the next day.

Monday evening I went back to the enclosure and I was, quite frankly, shitting myself. I opened the gate and went in. Maditau didn't charge me, but she wasn't particularly charmed to see me. She glared at me and flared her lip. I went on, talking to the other lions and interacting with them like nothing had happened. Tau and Napoleon rubbed heads with me in the traditional form of lion greeting, and Maditau's cubs came up to me to say hello, as well. While Maditau remained surly, she didn't eat me, which was about the only good thing I had to report to Mandy.

I was still fretting when the television crew from ABC arrived on Tuesday. I considered calling off the shoot right up to the last minute, but when we got to the lions I saw Tau and Napoleon were away from Maditau. The little cub was back from the vet and was doing well; we were able to present him to Tabby with no aggression on her part, which the TV guys loved. However, the crew really wanted to see me interacting with the males, so I went in to Tau and Napoleon's enclosure and they greeted me. Maditau kept her distance, which was just fine by me.

I went up to Tau and he was fine. Next, some of the cubs came to join us and soon we all moved to where Napoleon was. We all sat down in the grass and it was great. The TV crew had three cameras, and they were loving the vision they were getting of the whole pride together—or so it seemed. Maditau was still off by herself.

Right then, an amazing thing happened. Maditau decided she didn't want to be on her own anymore, so she came straight over to me, singling me out from the rest of the pride, and gave me the most friendly head rub I can recall receiving from her in many years, right in front of the cameras. I was lying down at the time, very vulnerable, and after she finished rubbing me, she plonked herself down between Tau and me. So there we were, all of us lazing there in grass in the shade of a tree, one big pride once more.

Humans are so used to wronging other people that we try to project these failings of ours onto lions and other animals. When you wrong another human, the victim can end up holding a grudge against you and we think the same thing is true with animals. Maybe Maditau did want to kill me because I intervened over the cub, but she didn't do it. Maybe she was just having a bad day. I was so worried that she was holding a grudge against me, yet she was able to lose the baggage and get back to normal quicker than I was. It's what I really love about lions, this ability to forgive and forget so quickly.

Sometimes I go to bed at night and wonder if I am getting too cocky. Am I thinking that I can conquer the world? Do I think I can go to America and tame rattlesnakes for another documentary? It's at times like this that I take a deep breath and try and appreciate what I already have and what I've achieved, and simply to be thankful for the day I've just spent.

Every once in a while—sometimes it's every two weeks, and at others it's every couple of months—I get an overwhelmingly emotional feeling and start talking like a bit of a blithering idiot.

We'll be in bed and I'll say to Mandy, "Do you know how lucky I am?"

"You've told me, Kev," Mandy will say. She is also a great leveler.

"No, you don't understand how amazing it is for me to be accepted by these lions. They're incredible. You're incredible. I can't believe how lucky I am."

"Yes, Kev."

I'm conscious of the fact that it's human nature to only fully appreciate what you've had when it's gone. I make a point of realizing how privileged I am, because I like to appreciate what I have. I make an effort not to take what I have for granted and I try to humble myself. The fact is, it is easy for a human being to go beyond himself and think that everything he does is special.

What is special, in my case, is that my wife and my animals have let me into their lives.

When Meg and Ami come to greet me they run at me like they're trying to take down a zebra.

They were boisterous as cubs when I was hand-raising them, and now, as lionesses weighing in at nearly four hundred pounds each, they can knock me to the ground when we play. It freaks Mandy out. She is far more concerned about me playing with the lionesses than with old Tau and Napoleon, who are past the age of jumping on my back and knocking me to the ground. Mandy is not jealous of Meg and Ami at all, but she is worried about how rough we all play together. To me, however, Meg and Ami are the most gentle lions I know, in terms of their characters, if not their strength. Fortunately, too, Mandy only comes to see the lions a couple of times a week, so she doesn't get to see everything that goes on when I play with the lions on a day-to-day basis.

When I was raising them, and Tau and Napoleon, people would always tell me that at some point I would have to stop letting the lions jump all over me. The thinking was that when a lion reached a certain age, it would decide to kill me rather than just play with me. I thought this was nonsense. Sure, I learned the hard way to be wary around some lions in their teenage years—between two and three years—but the lions I hand-raised have never wanted to kill me. When Meg and Ami reached about two years old, they became too heavy for me to piggyback around their enclosure. They still wanted to jump on me, only now when they did so they would push me to the ground. Having reached that level of maturity did not mean they would kill me once they could knock me down.

The only danger I face with Meg and Ami is being squashed to death, and in fact that has almost happened to me. One day the girls and I were lazing about, and first one then the other decided to lie casually across my body. I couldn't move, and every time I breathed out their combined weight compressed my chest a little more. I couldn't draw a breath as Meg and Ami were crushing my lungs. I wasn't strong enough to lift them. Plenty of people have predicted I would be killed by my lions, but not like this! I was panicking, laughing and crying from the ridiculousness of it all at once. Fortunately, they shifted just in time.

Occasionally when we are lying around, one of them will accidentally punch me in the face with a huge paw when she is trying to get up again. I do suffer cuts and bruises and scratches, but it's all part of the play. These girls are special lions and special friends of mine, and I am as intimate with them as a human can be with a lion.

There is a difference, I think, in how I am perceived by the different lions in my family. Tau and Napoleon treat me as an adopted brother, but they know I am not a lion, so something in them makes them hold back a little when we play. I jumped on their backs once to see how they would handle it. They left me there for a while then shook me off.

Meg and Ami think I am another lion, and that's the way they play with me—rough. From an early age I used to carry the two sisters on my back and people thought I was crazy, piggybacking lions. Now if I jump on their backs, they jump on mine—and flatten me. They hold nothing back with me, but just as when I had Meg clinging to my back when she swam with me, she knows not to claw me, because that wouldn't be play.

If I pushed the boundaries of relating to lions with Tau and Napoleon, then I broke every single rule relating to what one can and cannot do with a lion with Meg and Ami. I imprinted myself on them from the day of their birth, when I saved them from drowning by Maditau.

I was at the vet's one day and someone brought in a South American jaguar. It was a stunning animal. When I got back to the Lion Park I told the guys what I'd seen, and unwittingly set the wheels in motion for the animal to be purchased for the park.

Personally, I'd always thought we should stick to African animals, but other people thought it should be a predator park, so we soon found ourselves with a jaguar named Jade, after Rodney Fuhr's stepdaughter. The jaguar was beautiful, with a richly colored coat, similar to that of a leopard's but with larger, more vivid rosettes. Beautiful . . . and bad.

Jade was a terror—in fact, she was a witch. At seven months she was attacking people. Helga was the only one of us who had some success with Jade, who otherwise wanted to murder everyone and everything that got in her way. She had a thing about jackets and attacked many a staff member in order to get her claws on their clothes. Once she got hold of something, she claimed it. She was very possessive.

One morning I was doing the rounds and when I stopped by Jade's enclosure, she wasn't there. "Oh, no!"

I moved on to Meg and Ami, who were living next door with a mixed bunch of other brown and white lionesses. To my surprise I saw that Jade was in with them. She had scaled the high fence of her enclosure, paw over paw, and landed in with two exuberant lionesses who dwarfed her. Something had happened—Jade had finally met her match. The lionesses had obviously sorted her out during the night, but she was still in one piece, and sitting in there with them quite placidly.

Meg and Ami and Jade all still live together, and while the girls put Jade in her place, they are still wary of her. She's still a witch, though the lionesses keep her in check.

I've been criticized for deliberately putting different species in together, but I've only ever done it when I thought it was in the animal's best interest. Jade would have been a solitary animal in the wild, but she needed a mature female—or two—to sort her out and teach her some discipline. I've also put hyena cubs in with lions and they've gotten on fine. Lions and hyenas are sociable animals that live in a hierarchical society. They like company, and despite good old conventional wisdom, they are not natural born enemies. At the moment I have a hyena called Spannies who is living with some feisty six-month-old lion cubs. They're all the same age, and while the lions already dwarf Spannies, there is no doubt that the little hyena thinks he rules his mixed clan. I'll separate them eventually and put Spannies back with the hyenas—an extremely complicated process—but for now they're all learning about relationships.

I might have become part of the pride of lions and an honorary member of Uno's hyena clan, but at the Lion Park I was still an employee. I had formed relationships with the animals I worked with, but I had no real control over their destinies.

Mandy and I went on leave for a beach holiday at Knysna on the Garden Route, about 1,500 kilometers from Johannesburg. Some people think I never take leave, but I do. I'm a normal person in that respect, though Mandy will tell you that after three weeks away from my lions I'm like a bear with a sore head.

When I got back to work on a Monday morning I was walking around saying hi to all my animal companions. When I got to Meg and Ami's enclosure, I called them but they weren't there.

"Where're the girls?" I asked Ian, the park manager.

"We sold them."

"You *what?* Fuck! No way. How can you sell my lions?"

"Kev," Ian explained patiently, "they're not actually your lions."

"You sold my soul mates." It turned out Meg and Ami had been purchased by a guy who wanted some new females to ensure genetic diversity among the lions on his private game reserve. It was like having two of my children sold into slavery.

I had a lot of respect for Ian, but he was busy making business decisions while I was busy making relationships. I was still furious. I knew Ian was right, that it wasn't my call to make, but I still couldn't believe that anyone would have sold those two lionesses in particular without consultation. It wasn't like we didn't have lionesses to spare. We had plenty of other "wild" lions—those that hadn't been tamed or grown up around humans—who would have been perfect for the game reserve's needs. I didn't imagine the owner had especially asked for two tame lionesses.

I went to Rodney Fuhr and asked if we could get Meg and Ami back.

"And just how are we going to do that?" Rodney asked.

Rodney was the park's owner—and by now like a father to me—but I couldn't abandon Meg and Ami. "I'll call the reserve. We'll give them two other lionesses."

"All right, Kev," Rodney said.

Ian, to his credit, called the reserve and they agreed to the exchange. The reserve's owner drove to the park with two lionesses on the back of his truck.

"Here are your lions," he said, opening one of the boxes. The first lioness jumped out and looked around her. She clearly had no idea where she was.

"That's not one of my lions," I said. I checked the other box, but neither Meg nor Ami had been brought back.

"*Ag,* all lions look the same. How do you know the difference?" the man asked.

"How do you recognize your dog?" I spat back at him. "How do you know your sons? That's how I know these lions."

The man scoffed, but we put the lions back in their boxes and I told the man I was going to his place to bring back Meg and Ami. He shrugged and got back into his vehicle.

We loaded two crates onto the back of the Toyota pickup and took Helga with me for the drive to the game reserve. It was about an hour and a half deeper into the rolling hills and farming country of North West Province, and I broke all the speed limits on the way. I was still seething. I'd learned that Meg and Ami had been put into a pride of fifteen lionesses and they had been with them for two weeks already. I was sure I would know them as soon as I saw them and was equally sure they would remember me.

When we got to the reserve, the owner and his wife offered us drinks and muffins, but I was impatient to see my girls again. In his own good time he led us to where he was keeping the lions, and I was sure he was quietly sniggering at me on the way. The lions were in a temporary enclosure, where the man was building up the pride prior to releasing them into the reserve. They had no shade; just bare earth with a man-made mound in the middle of their yard.

"So how are you going to recognize them from this distance?" the man asked me. "Or are you going to walk in there with all those lions?" He was clearly still very skeptical.

"I'll call them."

The owner just shook his head, as if I was a madman.

"Meg! Ami!"

Two lionesses lifted their heads and stood. They bounded over to the fence to me. The other cats ignored them, and the humans outside.

"Hello, my girlies!" They started talking back to me and rubbing themselves against the fence.

"Jeez, man," the reserve's owner said in his thick Afrikaans accent, "I can't believe those things know you, and know their own names. So now how do you get them out of there and into the boxes? I had to drug the other two to move them."

"Watch," I said.

I had the two boxes brought over and when I opened the gate a little, just wide enough for a lioness to squeeze through, I called Meg. She walked over and straight into the box. Once she was secured and the other box was in place, Ami did the same thing. We put them on the truck and we all went home. The guy was dumbstruck.

That incident was one of the defining moments of my life. It was the point at which I realized that I didn't have any control over these animals' lives. They could be sold at any time. Would I have to play favorites next time the park had to sell a lion? I didn't have the means at the time to buy up all the animals I had developed relationships with. I'd started at the Lion Park as a visitor, then moved on to become a part-time and eventually full-time employee. My job was initially to enrich the lives of the animals under my care, but what use was there in getting them to trust a human if they could be sold off?

The future of animals in my care remains a predicament for me to this day. I had to face the fact that I simply couldn't keep every animal I was close to, especially once they bred and produced cubs. Even now, space and money are issues. It takes both to enclose predators properly.

What use, I wondered back then, was being part of a pride of lions, with equal ranking to the two senior males—my brothers—if I couldn't protect them?

ELEVEN

Lights, Camera, Action . . . Sometimes

I learned the hard way where the theatrical expression "break a leg" comes from.

We had made a few television commercials at the Lion Park and were getting involved with documentary making when the French production company came to Africa in search of lions, locations, and wranglers to help them make their feature film, *The Lion*.

I helped put together the pitch on behalf of the Lion Park, and realized pretty soon that this was going to be very different from any filming work we had done in the past. For a commercial, we might need to work one or two lions for half a day, but filming *The Lion* was going to take about four weeks of shooting, using our animals every day. I had to put together a schedule and work out if we could supply enough lions and how we would share the workload among them. The most exciting part of the whole thing was that my boys, Tau and Napoleon, were going to be the stars of the show if we won the business.

The weekend before we were due to start shooting, I went to watch a friend of mine racing motorcycles at Kyalami. After the race my buddy showed me one of the new Big Boy 100cc motorized scooters that he had started bringing into South Africa. This wasn't your garden variety commuter scooter, it was a big boy.

"Take it for a spin, Kev," my mate said. "It goes like the clappers."

I climbed on, pressed the starter, and revved it. When I took off I realized he wasn't kidding. The scooter was a fantastic little machine and it had some serious power. As I was putting the scooter through its paces, a guy pulled his car out of a parking space in front of me without checking his rearview mirror. I hit the anchors and the scooter screeched to a halt, but as it stopped, the rear end swung round. I had put a leg out and the back of the bike smashed into my ankle. I cursed and groaned with pain.

"Shit, Kev, are you all right?" my friend asked as he ran up to the scene of the accident.

"*Ja,* I'm sure it's fine," I said, hobbling to one side of the street. "I'm sure it's just sprained."

I limped around for the rest of the day, and tried to kill the pain with a few beers when I got home, but as the evening wore on I realized that this was the worst sprained ankle I had ever suffered. Next morning it was swollen like a balloon and the pain wasn't abating. I asked Mandy to take me to the doctor.

"Lion or hyena," the admissions nurse asked, as usual, when she saw me limp in.

"Scooter." I blushed a little, I think.

The doctor ordered an X-ray and later confirmed the bone was broken. "We're going to have to put you in a plaster cast," he said.

"No way. I'm filming for the next month."

"Kev, you can't put pressure on your ankle. You've got to rest up and take it easy."

"Doc, you don't understand. I have to put pressure on it and a cast is just no good. I'll be walking through dirt and mud for the next four weeks working with my lions."

The doctor shook his head at my stubbornness or stupidity—I

don't know which—and then decided to try me out with a new device, a plastic "moon boot." He slipped the boot over my broken ankle and then inflated it with air. The pressure kept the bones in place and provided a cushion under the foot, which would hopefully allow me to walk.

I hobbled out of Sunninghill on crutches, but when I got home and tried to walk without them, it was too bloody sore. "Shit," I thought to myself. How was I going to wrangle lions on film sets in the outdoors and in studios if I couldn't walk? What an ass I was, getting myself into this situation. I saw my film career vanishing before it had even taken off the ground.

When I arrived at the Lion Park on crutches on Monday morning, I was greeted by a show of shaking heads and negative comments.

"There's no way you can go in with the lions like that, Kev," one of my colleagues said.

"You know the old story, man," another said. "Lions always look for the injured and lame. Your buddies will think you're prey—they're going to eat you."

"Bull," I said to them all. I had spent half my life in the doctor's surgery and the other half doing things people told me I shouldn't or couldn't do.

Angry at myself, and determined to prove everyone wrong, I set off slowly for Tau and Napoleon's enclosure. When I opened the gate, resting awkwardly on my crutches, and closed it, the two big lions wandered towards me through the grass. Immediately, they sensed that something was different with me.

They paused and seemed wary, their inquisitive stares saying to me, "Kev, why are you holding those two sticks, dude? You never use sticks with us."

They closed the gap between us and I greeted them. "Hello, my boys." I put down the crutches and they relaxed. I took a deep breath, tried to ignore the pain, and started limping away from Tau and Napoleon on my moon boot. If the so-called experts were right then this would be the moment my relationship with my lions changed—for the rest of my short life.

They followed me. When I stopped, both of them, first Napoleon and then Tau, lowered their massive heads to inspect the moon boot. They started sniffing and curling their top lips up over their teeth in the way lions do when they are trying to scent new smells. I think they were intrigued by the hospital odor still on the moon boot, but what was encouraging was that they clearly didn't see me as a different person, and certainly not as prey. Fortunately, too, they didn't take a bite of my boot and let the air out of my filming career for good.

My lions had accepted me, but the problem was I still had to work for the next month on my moon boot.

"I don't care about the money, we'll cancel the shoot," Rodney Fuhr said to me after I explained what had happened.

"You can't just cancel a feature film, Rod," I said to him.

The next hurdle was explaining to the French production company what had happened. When I told them, they couldn't believe it, and I'm sure they thought I was a complete bloody idiot. I felt like I had screwed up a huge opportunity for Rodney and the Lion Park, so I told them I would be fine.

Working with lions is hard physical work at the best of times for someone in good shape, and this shoot was going to involve me doing a lot of running and jumping, leading the lions with a piece of meat to make them do what the crew wanted. I convinced Rodney and the French team that everything would be fine. On the first day I was cautious, using my crutches, and the lions performed like the stars they were. By the second day I had ditched the sticks and I was hopping around doing a kind of two-step to try and favor my injured ankle. By the end of each day of filming I was tired and sore, but my ankle held up and my lions didn't eat me.

Even though they had to work hard, Tau and Napoleon did me

proud and performed even better than I had dared dream. The days were long, starting before dawn and continuing till after dusk, and I was able to spend a lot of time with my lions, which was great. We would laze about and sleep together in the hot hours of the day, giving them time to digest the meat I had been feeding them as rewards for their performances. Tau and Napoleon must have eaten about seventeen dead horses between them during those four weeks, and by the end of shooting they were so full they were refusing to take the treats. However, they kept on working even without their rewards, and I felt they were doing what I wanted, not only just for me, but because they wanted to, which was fantastic.

Big Boy was quite an easy lion to work with, considering he was wild, but he had a temper and I had seen him go crazy in the past. He hadn't had close human contact all his life, and he could be a ferocious beast when he wanted to be.

The French film crew wanted a scene of a lion being aggressive towards an African warrior and I thought Big Boy would fit the bill. We weren't going to have an actor in the shot, for obvious safety reasons, so the plan was to film Big Boy against a blue screen and then add in the footage of the warrior actor later. The screen was set up in one of the spare enclosures at the Lion Park.

I parked a cage next to Big Boy's night pen in Camp Three, where he was living at the time, and he moved into it without any problems. Next, we loaded him onto the vehicle for his trip to the set for a dress rehearsal, and so far everything was going well. Big Boy was growling nicely and when I opened the door and coaxed him into the filming enclosure, he went ballistic. The cameras weren't rolling, but the director and crew were there, safely on the other side of the bars as Big Boy roared and growled and swiped at the slightest sign of movement. This was our ferocious lion at his best.

"Is that what you were looking for?" I asked the director.

"*C'est magnifique!* This lion, he is the champion. This is beautiful—exactly what we want. Tomorrow, we come with the cameras and we film this scene."

Big Boy slept outside the set in a big cage adjacent to the filming enclosure, and the next morning we brought in the crew. Having seen Big Boy in action, everyone was paranoid about safety. No one not directly involved in filming was allowed within fifty meters of Big Boy, who had already gained a reputation as the meanest beast around.

"Okay, we are ready," said the director. "Release the lion."

I opened the cage door and Big Boy came striding out into the filming enclosure. He turned and fixed the camera crew with his golden eyes, no doubt sending a chill of pure terror down their spines.

He paced to the corner of the set . . . and lay down. I tried everything ethically possible to get Big Boy to be the big ferocious lion he had been the day before, but he wouldn't budge. He yawned and did what lions do most of the time, slept.

In the end, we used Tau for the part of the ferocious lion, not because he was a particularly mean lion, but he did have a dislike for one particular person who worked at the park. I don't know what it was between them, but this guy couldn't go near Tau's enclosure without the lion showing his extreme displeasure. I made sure the man in question was on the blue-screen set the next day and Tau acted like he wanted to kill him, which the director loved.

A guy by the name of Mike Rosenberg, who had run Partridge Films, a UK company specializing in documentaries, came to the Lion Park one day. He was a friend of Rodney Fuhr's and I was asked to show him around. Mike saw me doing my thing with the animals. He was amazed.

"I've seen lion tamers in circuses, and animal wranglers interacting with animals, but nothing like what I've seen you doing," he said to me.

"These are just my friends. I go in with them to enrich their lives and we all get something out of it."

"But it's not just lions. I've seen you go from a lion to a spotted hyena, to a jaguar and a leopard and then a brown hyena, and you're doing the same thing with all of them. How do you do it?"

"It's easy. I have a relationship with each of them."

He started asking people around the Lion Park: "Have any documentaries been made about this guy Kevin?" Of course, one's colleagues are always supportive and said, "No, why would anyone want to make a film about Kevin?" Thanks, guys.

The documentary he wanted to make about me would later be called *Dangerous Companions*, and we worked on that film for two years, which was a long time. These days, documentaries are shot in six months. Some of the filming was quite amateurish, and on occasions I even used a digital camcorder because that was all that I could use. For example, when I filmed Pelo's cubs in their night enclosure, it wasn't possible to take a full-sized camera and cameraman with me—the lioness would have killed the cameraman. In the end, I think the different formats and approaches are what made *Dangerous Companions* special. It wasn't the quality of the video that was important, it was the scenes people were seeing—for the first time.

Some documentaries have a shot list and a director who says, once the lighting is exactly right, "Kevin, get the lion to walk from left to right, will you? Cut!" Our documentary was more like a home movie with me walking around with my camcorder saying, "Oh, look, here we have some little cubs. Here's mom and . . . oops, here comes dad"—the 550-pound lion—"to check us out."

People were seeing unique stuff, such as Meg running into the water and swimming for the first time. We had been filming some scenes for *Dangerous Companions* on the day I was walking with her, and while I didn't encourage her to go swimming for the documentary, it made for a great visual because it was seen to be unique.

I always wonder if filmmakers really know what the public wants. They think that to be successful a documentary has to be perfectly lit, well stage-managed, and expertly filmed. While all of that is important, I think that people want to be entertained, to see new content, and to feel like they're part of the story. All the fan mail I received from *Dangerous Companions* was about the relationships I had with the various animals, not the type of digital videotape we were using. While I appreciate how wonderful the film looks, the mail I was getting suggested that people were amazed at the bonds between me and my friends at the Lion Park. I wonder if someday both the look and the content of a documentary can be melded so that one can present astonishing footage that's also beautifully photographed.

Around about the time we were making *Dangerous Companions*, I was approached by a producer from Natural History New Zealand, an organization which had been funding a series of documentaries about the formative years of various animals, all entitled *Growing Up*.

They wanted to make a *Growing Up Hyena* documentary and had found out about the Lion Park and the work we were doing raising hyena cubs and forming our hyena clans. I was excited about getting involved, as I've always felt that hyenas have never received the recognition they deserve as fascinating, intelligent animals. Hollywood, documentary-makers, and even Disney have tended to portray hyenas as sinister scavengers, feeding off the efforts of other animals and stealing from them. In reality, hyenas are efficient hunters who live in highly organized and structured clans, as I'd learned firsthand.

I've also found that some people think they will hate being around hyenas or getting close to one, but when they are introduced to them in the right way they fall in love with them immediately. I've seen volunteers come to the park who are itching to start working with lions, yet after their first introduction to the hyenas they come away wishing they could spend more time with them instead. It's the same when you are forced to confront any prejudice, preconception, or phobia you may have head-on. Mandy, for example, always considered herself a cat person until she moved in with me and we acquired two dogs, Valentino and Dakota, and now she loves them to bits, especially the Staffie, Valentino.

In contrast to the way we were filming *Dangerous Companions*, the director and crew of *Growing Up Hyena* arrived with a plan and a shot list. They wanted to capture the life of a hyena cub at various key points of its life and I had the perfect animal for their story. Homer was one of two cubs that Uno, our supremely dominant wild hyena, had just given birth to. Homer had a sister, Marge, and in the way that Mother Nature ordains, Marge started picking on Homer as soon as the pair of them was born. In her bid to assert her dominance as the firstborn female cub of the leader of the clan, Marge was determined to ensure that Homer lived as short a life as possible. She would bite and scratch him and do her best to ensure that her brother did not get his fair share of Uno's milk.

I knew that if I didn't rescue little Homer—his sister was already outgrowing him—he would die. I thought that I could hand-raise him and then, when he was big and strong enough, introduce him back into his clan where hopefully he would be accepted.

There was something about Homer that touched me in a way that few other animals have. I have special relationships with Tau, Napoleon, Meg, Ami, and many others, and I knew from the moment I first picked him up that Homer and I would be great mates. When the director, who flew from New Zealand, and the local film crew arrived and started work on *Growing Up Hyena*, they too soon sensed that Homer would be a star.

Photograph by Mark Hildyard, courtesy of The South African Lion Park

Brothers in arms—a younger Kevin and Napoleon around
fifteen months old

Photograph by Mandy Richardson

Moving a brown hyena named Shy, Kevin style. No drugs, no fuss, no stress!

Photograph by Mandy Richardson

Kevin enjoying some exfoliation from Bongo the spotted hyena

Photograph by Helga Jordaan, courtesy of
The South African Lion Park

Baby homer.
No spots yet!

Photograph by Mandy Richardson

Kevin, Valentino, and baby Homer. A proud moment.

Photograph by Kevin Richardson, courtesy of The South African Lion Park

This is what acting's about! Trelli snoozes between takes
on the backseat of a brand-new station wagon!

Photograph by Rodney Nombekana, courtesy of The Kingdom of the White Lion

Kevin and Meg cool off in the Crocodile River.

Photograph by Rodney Nombekana, courtesy of The Kingdom of the White Lion

Swimming 101: First learn to blow bubbles, Meg.

Photograph by Mandy Richardson

I only kiss lionesses on the lips! Kevin and Suja share an intimate moment.

Photograph by Rodney Nombekana, courtesy of Peru Productions

Waiting to be picked up after a long, hard day of filming aerials with Thor at Nash's farm

Photograph courtesy of Peru Productions

Letsatsi and me at Nash's farm shooting the movie *White Lion*— his first and last appearance in front of the camera. Moments later he went walkabout for four hours.

Photograph by Rodney Nombekana, courtesy of The Kingdom of the White Lion

Contemplating swimming across with Thor, the lead actor in *White Lion*

Photograph by Michael Swan, courtesy of Peru Productions

Now seriously, whose teeth are whiter? Kevin and Thor.

Photograph by Kevin Richardson, courtesy of The South African Lion Park

Putting to rest the rumors that I work with only declawed lions. Thunder shows off his weaponry.

Homer was a loveable but odd little guy, and for a while I thought he would go down in history as the world's first vegetarian hyena. He was bottle-fed, but when it came time to wean him onto meat he wasn't interested. Try as I might I couldn't get Homer interested in flesh. I would place succulent cuts and bowls of different meats in front of him, but Homer would turn up his nose. He kept feeding from the bottle, but like the overindulged spoiled child he was, he didn't want to give up the milk. My mom told me that I had the same problem as a kid and stayed on the bottle far longer than most kids did at the time.

In desperation I decided to make a game out of feeding. Homer liked to chase things, so one day I bundled my mountain bike and Homer into my vehicle—like Trelli, he loved riding in cars—and drove out to the airstrip at the park. Also in the back of my truck was a leg from a dead cow which had been donated to the park. I took a length of rope and tied the leg to the back of my bike and got on.

"Come, Homer!" I called, as I got on the bike and started peddling. It was hard work, but Homer immediately wanted to play. As I pedaled furiously, the leg of meat raising a mini dust cloud in my wake, Homer the hyena bounded happily after the foreign object. Up and down we went, with me getting increasingly exhausted, but Homer becoming more and more interested in the dust-encrusted lump I was dragging through the dust and grass. At some point a switch tripped in Homer's little brain, and when he pounced on the cow's leg that time he sunk his teeth into it and started eating. He was happy, I was happy, and finally I was able to stop pedaling.

As Homer started to feed and put on weight, I began the experimental process of introducing him to his old clan. His sister Marge was already much bigger than Homer, loving her position as the matriarch's daughter. When I first drove him into their enclosure, she eyed Homer warily. Little did I know that this was a sign of things to come.

"Kevin, come quick, Homer's desperately ill." Rodney Nombekana had called me on my cell phone while I was driving and my first thought was that he was overreacting.

I thought, no way. Hyenas are tough, they never get sick.

"No," Rodney insisted when I told him my thoughts. "He's at the vet. You have to come, this is serious."

I tuned the wheel to change course and planted my foot on the accelerator. When I got to the surgery, Homer was catatonic, passed out with his eyeballs rolled back in his skull.

"I think he's been poisoned by something," the vet said when I arrived.

While the vet monitored Homer's deteriorating condition I paced up and down, wracking my brain to work out what could have happened to him. The *Growing Up Hyena* film crew was already at the vet's surgery, and they filmed my arrival and my concern. I couldn't blame them for being intrusive. It was their job to film the whole story, but when Homer died, I cried.

The autopsy showed that the vet's initial suspicions were correct. Homer had died from poisoning by an unknown heavy metal, though there was no indication of how it had been administered. There was nothing in his enclosure he could have eaten or licked, and to this day I still don't know what happened to him. I wondered if someone could have poisoned him, but why would anyone do it? He was such a cute little ambassador for the world of hyenas that I couldn't figure why anyone would want him to die. I remembered, though, the look on Marge's face when I brought him back to the clan and it sent a little shiver down my spine.

Homer's death hit me hard and got me thinking about how I would react when all my other beloveds passed away. I'm not a fool—I know animals come and go, but this was a tragedy and it made me realize that forming so many relationships with my animals, rather than just "working" them, meant I had invested a piece of my heart in each of them. Homer was really the child whose life was ripped away before he got to make his true mark. His short time on earth, however, had more impact on the way people think of hyenas than any other documentary ever made. He was just one in a million. You don't get dogs like Homer, never mind hyenas. I always felt, and still do, like a proud father when I speak of him, and I inevitably get all teary and emotional. Losing him and thinking about the others I might lose was as wrenching as losing a close friend or family member. These aren't simply pets. They've become part of my family and I've become part of theirs.

What made it worse with Homer was that he was only three months old. To all intents and purposes I had been his father, hand-raising him and even teaching him to eat. I had lived, slept, and breathed with him for virtually all of his short life. It made me think about the pain people must feel when they lose a child. If Tau and Napoleon had to die tomorrow, I would be very, very sad, but I'd know that they've led great lives—better than any lion in the wild. Homer, however, had been poisoned at the start of what I thought might be a great life. He would have had me as a friend and I would have had him. But it was not to be.

The documentary makers, of course, loved it, from a professional perspective. They and their viewers were seeing real, raw emotion when Homer died in the vet's surgery. At the time, however, the producers were very compassionate and said to me, "Let's leave it," and it looked like that would be the end of *Growing Up Hyena*. Later, they phoned me and asked if I would consider carrying on the story, perhaps with two other hyena cubs we had just acquired, Bongo and Tika. They hadn't been part of the program, but they became the main game when I agreed to carry on with the filming.

It was an emotional time for me, getting over Homer's death, and while I probably wouldn't have been involved in raising Bongo and Tika, the filming forced me into their pen, along with Helga, who had been working with them. I needed to get over Homer, and while I may have been reluctant at first, Bongo and Tika worked their way into my heart, as well. We were able to complete filming the documentary showing the pair's development, and in the process I made two new friends. Several years on, Bongo and Tika are still with me and we are great mates, but I'll never forget Homer. I'm not a crier generally, but I cried all over again when I saw *Growing Up Hyena* on television for the first time.

TWELVE

Life Away from the Lions

I'm like a lion. If I'm not sleeping, I'm up and doing something active. However, unlike a lion I have more than four hours of waking time per day to occupy, so I am a real busy body.

If I am not interacting with the lions or the hyenas or the other animals, I'm either working on a documentary or other filming project, or in my spare time pursuing one of a number of hobbies. The making of the feature film, *White Lion,* has consumed much of my time in the last few years, but when I can, I get out and ride my vintage Triumph motorcycle; I fly; I hike; and I ride superbikes on the racetrack.

When people meet me for the first time I think some of them are surprised. I don't wear khaki safari clothes or *veldskoen* shoes; I don't have a big bushy beard and long hair; and my whole life does not revolve around animals only.

I do have a life away from my lions, hyenas, leopards, and other predators. My passion for bikes as an adult was nurtured by my ex-girlfriend Lisa's brother-in-law, a guy called Clayton, better known as Gopher, who remained a good friend of mine after Lisa and I broke off.

Gopher and I would sit for hours drinking ice cold Windhoek lagers and talking about bikes. When Mandy met him, I'm sure she thought Gopher might have been a bad influence in my life, but I assured her I had matured from my teen years, which I had already told her all about. Nonetheless, I knew she was concerned about what we got up to on Saturday afternoons, when Gopher and I would set off on our motorcycles together.

There is a great chain of outdoors shops in South Africa called Cape Union Mart, and the big store in Sandton Mall has its own indoor climbing wall. Gopher and I used to like going there on a Saturday and competing against each other to see who could reach the top of the wall first.

It was a good place to hang out, literally, and the shop also had a separate "climate room" with the air-conditioning set way down low. The idea was that rich suburbanites could try on some winter clothing for their next ski strip and go into the climate room to see how their gear performed in sub-zero temperatures. Gopher and I saw the possibility for a new competition immediately. We decided to go in dressed in shorts and T-shirts and see who could stand the cold for the longest time before freezing his nuts off. It was such good fun the first time that it became a regular game for us. Sadly for me, Gopher has now emigrated to Australia.

"What do you and Clayton get up to on Saturday afternoons when you disappear together?" Mandy asked suspiciously one evening early on in our relationship, after I'd returned home on the bike.

"We hang out in Cape Union Mart and then see who can last the longest in the cold room," I told her honestly.

She looked at me and shook her head. "Is that the best story you could come up with?"

People also think that when I go into the bush I'm going to be serious and sonorous like the great BBC commentator David At-tenborough. Others think I'd be chasing every dangerous animal I can find, just like Steve Irwin. The truth is a lot more boring: when I get away I mostly just like to have fun. When I get to a national park or game reserve, I don't go out looking especially for lions or hyenas or other predators. I don't need to see big cats in the wild or see a predator make a kill to think I've had a worthwhile time. I like to simply be in the bush and appreciate everything around me in nature, even the little things—especially the little things.

Rodney Fuhr sponsors a wildlife research base in the Okavango Delta in Botswana, on the edge of the Moremi Game Reserve. I get up there when I can, as I love the bush, and one day, if I get the time, I would like to pursue some research ideas of my own, particularly in relation to wild hyenas.

The camp, called Squacco Heron Projects, is in a beautiful set-ting, overlooking a permanent waterhole not too far from the Gomoti River. Rodney's funding provides researchers with accommodation and an office where they can work on their reports. Most of the per-manent staff at the camp are from the local community, the tradi-tional owners of the land. Rodney leases the land the research base is on, and the rights to a photographic safari operation nearby, called Moremi Tented Camp (MTC).

The area abounds with game, such as buffalo, elephants, zebra, giraffe, kudu, and impala, and all the major African predators can be found around, and sometimes in the camp. When you visit, the nightly lullaby is usually the whoop of spotted hyenas, and your alarm is the low, mournful call of a lion in the predawn darkness. There are few places in Africa I've been to where you can see as many animals in one place as the rich verdant floodplains around the Gomoti at the end of the dry season.

Mandy and I were visiting the camp during a break and went

out for a game drive with Guy Lobjoit, the research camp manager, and Rodney Fuhr. We loaded the Land Cruiser with drinks and *padkos*, which means food for the road.

The delta is beautiful. Moremi's landscape ranges from forests of tall trees fed by a high water table beneath the Kalahari sandveld, to vast areas of marshes bisected by shallow clear water channels as the Okavango River trickles its way from Angola and Namibia to the north into the dry heart of Botswana.

Guy stopped the vehicle at a nice pan, a waterhole set in an open sandy area where we had good visibility. As we got out of the vehicle and started unloading our food and drinks for sundowners and dinner, Guy spotted movement in the bush at the edge of the pan. Before we knew it we found ourselves among a pack of about a dozen wild dogs.

The African wild dog is the most efficient predator on the continent. These highly organized professional killers bring down a higher percentage of the prey they chase than any other carnivore. They can rip an impala or wildebeest to shreds and devour it in a matter of minutes, yet there has never been a recorded incident of them attacking a human being in the wild. They have also been one of the most endangered mammals in Africa, which makes any sighting of them a rare treat.

"Kevin, get back in the vehicle," Mandy hissed. She was already perched back inside the Land Cruiser.

Guy and I stayed on the ground. The dogs had seen us, and while they paused for a moment, their big ears rotating towards us and noses sniffing the air, they did not turn and run from us simply because they saw two humans standing by a vehicle. Guy has lived a lot of his life in the bush, and worked as a section ranger in the Umbabat private game reserve on the border of the Kruger National Park. He has a good knowledge of the bush, and we're both the kind of guys who are sometimes more comfortable around wild animals than people. We held our ground and the dogs started moving slowly towards us.

Wild dogs are also known as painted hunting dogs because of their intricately patterned coats, which are decorated with blotches of yellow, white, brown, and black. They're the size of a small Alsatian and have overly large ears, which help them sense prey and danger, and long, spindly legs. Like all dogs they're curious, and this pack was no different.

"Kevin!"

I ignored my wife's command and stayed put with my friend and my dinner. Rodney was in the vehicle, having his dinner and enjoying the show. One by one the dogs closed the gap between us and them. I'm no different than how I was as a kid. I can't just look at things. I wanted to see how the dogs would react to me when I was on foot, as opposed to being in the vehicle. I don't feed wild animals—no one should—but one of the dogs in the pack was curious about what I was eating. It came close enough to me to smell my fingers. Mandy was having a heart attack but I knew the law of averages was on my side. The dogs had made a conscious decision to approach the humans and they satisfied themselves we were no threat to them.

As the dogs sniffed and played around us I realized, once again, how lucky I am to be able to have such an experience and to live on this continent. Like I said, I don't go looking for close encounters with wildlife in the bush, but sometimes things find me.

I love to fly and I took Rodney Fuhr's Cessna 182 up to Liuwa Plains in Zambia when he made the decision to close his research camp there and move it to Botswana. I had helped with some of the logistics at Liuwa camp and while I was excited about his new venture in Botswana, it was a little sad to be going back to close things down.

My regular safari tent was still set up in the camp, and I made myself at home again. I helped dismantle the camp during the days and each night, after a couple of beers, I lowered myself onto the camping bed on which I slept.

On the third night I brushed against the canvas wall of the tent and heard a rustling noise, followed by a low, guttural, almost ghostly noise: "*Hoaaaaaaaaarrrrrrrrrrr.*" Odd sound, I thought, so I deliberately hit the wall again. Up beside me reared a fully grown black cobra. This snake was probably one-and-a-half times my size, and as I don't have any snake-wrangling experience, I beat it out of that tent in quick time.

It's interesting how man and nature can live side by side in harmony until something disturbs the balance. That snake had probably made its home in the tent for some time and had been quite happy to tolerate me for two nights until I bumped the canvas. If I hadn't disturbed or alarmed him, we might never have confronted each other.

I like to look after my machines and I keep all of my cars, my Triumph motorcycle, and a 1957 Series I Land Rover I own in pristine condition.

Rodney's 182 was being kept at Lanseria Airport, and while that is not far from where I live, I wanted to move the aircraft to the Lion Park's airstrip so that I could better care for the aircraft.

The park's airstrip is only four hundred and fifty meters long, which is not huge. At the time I was a relatively novice pilot, but I read the spec sheets for the Cessna and found that it could be landed on an airstrip the length of ours, though there was a note that said only experienced pilots should attempt landing on strips less than a certain length. I had about a hundred hours at the time and I was bold enough to consider myself experienced enough.

I'm not a recluse, but I love flying by myself and having time to myself. The only person I have to talk to in the air is the air traffic controller, and for the rest of the time I can think and just enjoy the freedom of being airborne and as free as a bird. As well as the 182, I fly a Thunderbird fixed-wing microlight, and a Zenair Sky Jeep. We use the aircraft at the research camps and to keep an eye on our game at the Kingdom. Recreationally, I catch up for breakfast with a bunch of other pilots at different airstrips from time to time.

When I took off from Lanseria it was a very short hop across to the Lion Park. As I brought her down it didn't feel right. The airstrip seemed to rush up at me and it looked impossibly short. The aircraft seemed to have a mind of its own and it didn't want to come down there. I finally touched the grass, but the aircraft bounced, then bounced again. I was nervous, and some power lines that run through the bush at the far end of the strip seemed to be rushing towards me too fast. I decided to go around, so I pushed the throttle to full power to take off again.

I could feel the speed building, but the electricity cables still seemed to be hurtling towards me rather than the other way around. I pulled back on the stick to try and coax the aircraft up, but I was sacrificing airspeed for altitude. I crossed the power lines by the skin of my teeth, but in doing so stalled the aircraft. The Cessna smacked down on the far side of a road which runs the other side of the cables, onto open ground. By this stage I had lost control completely.

There was a jarring thud as the nose wheel hit the ground and bent forwards, causing it to brush the propeller. The tail bashed into the dirt and she bounced again. The ground started to fall away below me. Amazingly, the jolt allowed the Cessna to gain enough speed and height to unstall the wings and start flying again.

I managed to regain control of the aircraft and my pounding heart and flew around in a low circle. I didn't know the extent of the damage to the plane, although many of the instruments had fallen out of the cockpit control panel. I pushed them back in as best as I could and found, miraculously, that the radio was still working.

I looked out of my side window and saw that part of the rear tail of the plane was flapping around in the slipstream. I was shitting bricks by this time and wondered when the plane would start to break up. When I looked out the other side window I noticed the tip of the wing was missing. I didn't even know if I still had a nose wheel.

As a trainee pilot you are taught two distress calls you can make to declare an emergency. It you are in dire straits and about to crash you call, "Mayday, mayday, mayday." If, however, you need to make an emergency landing you call, "Pan, pan . . . pan, pan . . . pan, pan."

What should I say, I thought to myself as the aircraft shuddered around me. Do I call pan pan or do I call mayday mayday? As well as stressing about my predicament I was also trying to think through all of the implications if I made the wrong call over the radio!

I took a deep breath and keyed the radio. "Lanseria, this is Foxtrot Uniform Golf."

"Foxtrot Uniform Golf, this is Lanseria, go ahead," replied the air traffic controller in a calm voice.

"Um . . . Lanseria, this is Foxtrot Uniform Golf . . . pan, pan, pan . . . I mean, mayday mayday . . . Actually, I have an emergency!"

I babbled on for a bit longer, explaining that I'd balked a landing at the Lion Park. The park is in Lanseria's airspace and I should have reported to them by now that I was safe on the ground. I told them I didn't think I had a tail left on my airplane. I was a nervous, gibbering wreck.

The controller was very calm, and I'm sure he knew that my tail hadn't fallen off—especially as I was still flying.

"Foxtrot Uniform Golf, you are cleared to land two-four right." They had given me the long runway at Lanseria. "Foxtrot Uniform Golf, are you declaring an emergency?"

"Um, yes, I mean . . . like, yes, I am." They were so calm and I'd forgotten all my procedures for communicating over the radio. I just wanted to get on the ground. Through my headphones I could hear the controllers diverting all the other air traffic, from small private planes to commercial jets, away from the area while they allowed this idiot—me—to land his plane.

I could have flown past the tower and asked them to check if I still had a nose wheel, or simply put the aircraft down. Without a wheel the prop would hit the runway, curl up, and destroy the engine. I made the decision that with other bits flapping away there was no time for a flypast.

I tightened my safety harness, coaxed the wounded Cessna down, and, as it happened, made one of the best landings of my life. I braced myself as she touched and the nose came down, expecting to hear the agonized shriek of the propeller blades connecting with tarmac.

But I was safe, and the prop was still spinning as I followed the special taxi route off the runway that the controllers had arranged for me. I climbed down out of the aircraft and I started shaking. Taking an unsteady walk around the aircraft, I saw the full extent of the damage for the first time. The nose wheel assembly had been pushed forward into the firewall when I'd first hit the ground, lowering the clearance to the extent that the tips of the propeller's blades had been spinning less than half an inch from the surface of the runway.

I have been in bike crashes, rolled my sister's car, been bitten by hyenas, and mauled by Tsavo the lion, but for the first time in my life I really thought I had been about to die. I learned a lot about pushing boundaries, trusting one's instincts, and the toughness of the Cessna 182 that day.

THIRTEEN

White Lion

Ian and I had just finished our morning coffee when the phone rang. We were about to leave the Lion Park to look at some white lions that we hoped would be suitable for a new feature film we were about to embark on.

"Mister Kevin, come quickly. Sly has got in with the others and he is killing them!" It was a breathless Sam, one of the park's African camp staff.

"Who's he killing, Sam? Where?"

"I don't know. You must come quick!"

"Shit." Ian and I piled into the *bakkie* and I tore through the park, ignoring all the animals I normally would have stopped and chatted to. When we arrived at the enclosure where we kept our white lions, we were greeted by a scene of gory havoc. Lying motionless in the grass was a white lion, his beautiful coat stained red.

Sly, a big, wild brown lion, had somehow escaped from his own enclosure and got into the yard where we kept Graham, our sixteen-month-old white lion, and some young lionesses. Sly had always had a bad temperament. I had never formed a relationship with him and didn't even consider him an acquaintance lion. Here was the prime example of a grown male who was in the process of taking over a pride. However, not content with just killing the young upcoming pride male, Graham, Sly now had his massive jaws around the head of one of the lionesses. Others had joined me at the fence to see what all the commotion was about. I fumbled for my keys and unlocked the padlock.

"Kevin, what do you think you're doing?" Ian asked. I didn't stop to answer him. I slid open the gate and ran in, reaching for the pepper spray in the holster on my belt. Sly was growling as he chomped down on the lioness's head and she thrashed in vain against his merciless strength.

Graham, whose body I passed, had been a magnificent white lion, and aside from being a marvelous animal, he was going to be one of the stars of our new feature film, *White Lion*. I wasn't thinking about money or filming schedules, though, when I saw him lying there. I was simply in a state of rage. What made things worse was that I had named Graham after my brother-in-law's late brother, who died of cancer. Graham was born very shortly after his namesake died, so I told my brother-in-law that I had christened the cub so his name could live on. He was quite touched and it enraged me that this lion was now dead.

This bastard Sly had killed my mate, and now he was trying to murder one of my girls. I raced up to him and squirted the spray into the face of this fully grown predator. The pepper spray was enough to make Sly gasp—that was all—but it gave the lioness a chance to shake herself free. She had puncture marks on the back of her head and neck, and the enormous pressure of Sly's jaws had caused one of her eyeballs to pop. Bloodied and in pain, she slunk away.

"Get back! Get out of there, Kevin, you're bloody mad!" Ian was shouting at me from outside the fence.

Blinded by rage, I hadn't thought twice about running into an enclosure to take on a lion in the midst of a killing frenzy. I paused, and in that brief quiet second, I thought, "Uh . . . maybe Ian has a point here." I'd found myself in a bad situation.

Sly shook his head and snorted to clear the stinging residue of the pepper spray. As a defensive weapon it had saved the researcher from Rain's fury, and it had given this lioness a chance to get away. I doubted it would stop Sly from finishing me off, though.

He looked at me. He didn't know what I had done or why I had done it. I was asking myself the same question at the time. The gate slid open and a *bakkie* roared into the enclosure. The arrival of the vehicle diffused the situation, and we allowed all of the young lions to run out into the "no-man's-land" passage that runs between the various enclosures. This corridor is still gated at each end, so there was no risk of the lions escaping the park. We locked Sly in Graham's enclosure until a vet could come and dart him and treat the injured lioness.

Rodney Fuhr thought I had acted carelessly, to put it mildly. "It was just a lion, Kevin," he said. He was right, but I'd seen Graham's body, and the lioness being crushed to death between those huge canines. I'd seen the other lionesses huddled, traumatized, at the far end of the yard and I'd become enraged. "You are not going to murder her," I had thought to myself. This was personal. Sly was on a killing spree and would have finished off all of the animals if no one had intervened.

People do strange things under stress and, believe me, having someone hand you the equivalent of several million dollars and say, "Here, Kev, go and make me a movie," is a stressful experience. That's basically what happened to me.

Rodney has for a long time wanted to make a feature film about a white lion who gets kicked out of his pride, meets some other animals, and has some adventures. The young lion grows up alone, but eventually takes over a pride of his own after narrowly escaping a trophy hunter's bullet. In the beginning we thought we would cruise around with our cameras filming a lion walking around and being put in a few different situations; in the end we would put it all together and have ourselves a feature film. It was the same plan we had initially when filming *Dangerous Companions*. What we soon learned, of course, was that making a full-length feature film was much more complicated than shooting a documentary.

We put a team of guys together, some of whom I'd met on film shoots where I had supplied lions, who I knew were used to working around animals, and who were good at their jobs.

I think everyone who talked to me in those early years thought, "What's this lion wrangler up to, trying to put together a multi-million-dollar feature film?" Some people in the industry laughed me off or didn't even bother calling me back. Every time someone rejected me or came up with a reason why I couldn't make a film, it made me more determined, even though I didn't really know what I was doing back then. I learned fast.

We auditioned potential scriptwriters, asking them for ideas about how they would write a script based on Rodney's basic idea for the story. The writers we subsequently worked with were under a lot of stress, because although the idea for the story sounded simple, they were under very stringent direction from Rodney about what could and couldn't be in the script. Some of the writers wanted to overcomplicate the story and work in some mythical elements. For example, the Shangaan people believe that a white lion is born when a shooting star falls from the heavens, but Rodney didn't want the audience to think the film was a fable. He wanted to show the real Africa, not a mythological one. In many respects the writers weren't given much creative freedom because Rodney wanted to be true to the real Africa; however, he became more flexible over time as he realized the ins and outs of compelling storytelling.

We wanted to shoot the movie in much the same way as we would a documentary, such as *Dangerous Companions,* getting the lions to do things as naturally as possible, rather than trying to stage-manage them. I had to make it clear to the people who worked on the film that we couldn't plan on making the lions and other animals do exactly what they wanted at exactly the right time. It wasn't like shooting a commercial where all the lion had to do was walk from left to right, look at the camera, shake its head, and walk off. I needed to find people who had experience working with animals.

One of the questions I was constantly asked by people who knew the film industry was this: "Will your lions be able to continue working for the long periods required for a feature film?" I needed to start thinking about how many lions I would need for the various scenes. In the end, we used thirty different white lions to play the lead character, Letsatsi, throughout the various ages of his life, and over the course of what stretched from months into years of filming. Lions grow very quickly so I needed to preplan in advance to make sure we had enough lions of the right age to play Letsatsi at the right times of his life. This on its own presented a huge challenge.

Letsatsi, which means "the sun," was the first white lion born at the Lion Park and we used his name as that of the lead character. Our plan was that Letsatsi would do most of the filming as his adult self in the movie, but you can only really learn how a lion is going to behave during filming by putting him in front of a large group of people.

Rodney wanted the film to be set against the backdrop of the wilds of Africa, and by that he meant that we wanted wide-open vista shots of lions set in endless expanses of Africa. That wasn't so much of a problem for me, I thought, as my methods were already very different from those of other lion wranglers who worked on television and films. All the lion wranglers I know of want their lions to be fenced—they won't take a chance of letting them roam free. That means if you want to set up a wide shot, then somewhere out there in the not-too-distant distance there needs to be a fence. I was happy, however, to work my lions in large expanses, on huge farms. I was confident that they would not feel the need to go wandering off to the other side of the farm. The film crew, however, would be behind fences, while the lions walked free, with me. It's far quicker, cheaper, and easier to cage the people in a five-meter by five-meter cage, than setting up a huge perimeter fence for the lions.

I was aware of the risks, such as a lion running off and chasing some game on whatever farm we were using, but I was confident in my animals' abilities, and the relationship I had with my lions.

One of the other strict criteria Rodney had for his film was that it would show Africa like it had never been shown before.

"What do you mean by that, Rod?" I asked him early on.

"I don't want to show Africa in the winter, I want to show Africa in the summer, when the grass is green and the bush is thick and lush."

There is, as I had learned during the making of the French film, *The Lion*, a good reason why nearly every documentary or film you see made in Africa shows the grass long and dry and golden, and the bush in shades of dull khaki and brown. It is because most filming is done in the long, dry, relatively cool African winter, which is ideal for filming, as opposed to the hot, wet summer months. In the winter dry season, the ground is firm and you are virtually assured of clear blue skies every day for months on end. Sunrises and sunsets are spectacular and the golden hours, just after dawn and just before dusk, are perfect for filming. The sun is lower in the sky and you get more hours of light to film in. Also, the cool temperatures are ideal for working animals

By contrast, in summer it rains nearly every day. It is hot and humid, and the dust and dirt turn to thick, cloying mud. Sunrises and sunsets are often obscured by towering cloud banks, and you can have three or four dark, dingy days at a time when the cloud and mist and even fog take hold. You can have thundershowers in the morning and you're virtually guaranteed to have them every afternoon. To make a feature film in the South African Highveld in summer, you have to be crazy. You guessed it. We were.

December 2005, when we began filming, was particularly bad. It rained, and it rained, and it rained. We changed from day shoots to night shoots to try and escape the rain, but then it started pouring at night. We changed from night back to day, but the rain stayed ahead of our plans and played havoc with crew turnaround times, as people needed appropriate breaks between shoots.

Everything around us was luscious and green, but that was the only thing going according to plan. Every week we were delayed added another week to the age of the lions we were using, which created problems with continuity. We couldn't stop our white lion cubs from growing. We simply weren't getting the footage we needed and we battled to make progress during that first summer season of filming.

We had vehicles stuck in the mud, and spent money we hadn't budgeted to hire special eight-wheel recovery vehicles to tow our other trucks out of the thick, cloying muck. Eventually, even the tow vehicles and the Lion Park's trusty tractor got stuck in the mud. I remember spending a whole night pulling and digging vehicle after vehicle out of the mud for the end result of not a second's worth of filming. I wanted to cry that night.

Many of the sets and locations we chose were ruined by vehicles and people churning the grass into mud, and even when we could film, the lions quickly got wet and dirty. The white lions, in particular, had to be cleaned on a regular basis. Twice a day I would have to phone Rodney and give him an update. He would be sitting at home, in his living room in Johannesburg, watching the rain patter his windowpanes, and I would have to call him and confirm his worst nightmares, that for the cost of between 40,000 and 120,000 Rand per day we were achieving absolutely nothing. To make things worse, the rain always seemed to come on the days we had hired the most expensive equipment.

Thinking back on it now, as the final edits of *White Lion* are locked away, I realize our earlier schedules were too ambitious. We were trying to cram too much into a short time, during the worst season of the year to be filming. The whole thing was a learning process, partly because this was the first time anyone had tried to film a full-length feature film using lions as the stars, in as natural a setting as possible, in the African summer.

I promise you, I now know why Disney's *The Lion King* was animated. During that first season of shooting I was starting to think that it was just not possible to make a movie about lions using real lions without spending hundreds of millions of dollars. Rodney was also probably starting to wonder what he had got himself into. There was, though, a ray of light: when we were able to film, and later sit down and go through the rushes, the footage we were getting was absolutely amazing. It was, as Rodney had desired, Africa like we had never seen it on film before. Here we had these beautiful snow white lions set against the lush emerald greens of the grass and bush in full bloom. It really was striking and Rodney's wish was coming true. This was something different, something special.

Early on, before shooting even began, I started getting Letsatsi, our only adult male lion, used to the idea of playing himself in a movie.

To start with I had to get him accustomed to being loaded into a vehicle and unloaded, so that we could transport him easily around the park and to the various farms and other locations we would be using in the film. Half of the job of getting a lion to work on a film is just getting him to the set safely, and unstressed. A stressed lion is dangerous to both himself and humans. I've seen lions bash their heads until they bleed and break teeth off when they're upset.

To make it easy on ourselves, we built a new fifteen-hectare enclosure off the back of the Lion Park where we would be able to film some of our story. We also used our current property, the Kingdom of the White Lion, which Rodney had bought in 2000. For the shots that required truly wide-open spaces and panoramic vistas, we used a place called Nash's Farm that totals about 22,000 hectares. It is, I believe, the single largest freehold game farm in the province of Gauteng. The farm held wildebeest, giraffe, impala, and other species of game.

"Hey, *boet*, you're taking big chances with these lions," said a guy called Hennie, who managed the farm, when I told him about our plans for filming.

"Don't you worry," I told him confidently. "It'll be fine."

By the end of our first rainy season of filming in early 2006, we had enough of an idea of what our story would be, and almost enough good footage, to go to the Cannes Film Festival in France to promote our project. What we needed, though, was a promotional clip—a promo—including some footage of our big adult white lion, the majestic Letsatsi, our star, striding through a wide-open expanse of lush, green Africa in her summer finery. I had worked with Letsatsi on other shoots, although he had yet to play himself in the filming of the motion picture in which he would star. His first appearance before the camera, and his future public, for *White Lion* would be the filming of the promo.

We drove Letsatsi out to Nash's farm to shoot the scenes for the promo, which would also be used in the film. We also decided to use the day to promote the film to the local media, so we had an assortment of press people, photographers, TV, and even the big boss, Rodney Fuhr, penned in a temporary cage in the middle of the veld, along with our own film crew. We had been setting up since three-thirty in the morning and there was an air of excited expectancy as the truck carrying the star lion rolled to a stop in the thick green grass.

As soon as we let Letsatsi out of the truck and I looked into his eyes, I started getting that sinking feeling. In a vain attempt to get Letsatsi back on the truck, I started shouting, "Load him, load him," to Rodney Nombekana, Alex, and Helga, who had all come from the Lion Park to help wrangle Letsatsi. But we were out of luck. Letsatsi looked out over those twenty-two thousand hectares of Africa and didn't look back at the truck. Despite my assurances to Hennie that everything would be all right, Letsatsi decided that he had had enough of the film world, and of captivity. He started walking.

"Load him!"

Rodney Nombekana shook his head. "He's going, Kev."

I started walking with Letsatsi, as though this was all part of the plan, and the cameras started rolling. "Get what you can," I hissed.

"Kev, Kev, get out of the shot," the cameraman was calling back to me. I was walking beside Letsatsi, although my confident stride was an illusion as by now I had no control over what he was doing or where he was going. I had to continually lie down in the grass or duck behind a mound so the crew could get something—anything—of Letsatsi in action before he disappeared into the wilds of Nash's farm. If it hadn't been such a disaster it might have been comical. I would drop out of sight for a few seconds, then get up and frantically run to catch up with Letsatsi, appear to wrangle him, then duck for cover once more. The same thing was happening to Rodney and Helga, who were also having to run and dive.

Initially, Letsatsi wasn't aggressive. He just didn't want to do what anyone told him; not me, not Rodney, not Helga, and not Alex. Letsatsi usually lived for treats—pieces of meat given as a reward—but on that day, in front of all those cameras, not even the morsels I was pulling out of my pocket were enough to make him behave. Also, he started to tire of us running in front of him and trying to corral him and began growling all the time.

I think Letsatsi had been overawed by the sight of all the people waiting to see him and I believe he suffered stage fright. He was just not interested in performing in front of that crowd of people. As with Tsavo in front of my family, and Ricksey the cheetah in front of my wife-to-be Mandy, here was an animal that had sensed a different vibe and decided to behave differently around strangers.

In the park, Letsatsi was a fat, lazy lump of lard. He lived in a medium-sized camp and was always happy in it. He never needed a lot of space, and in true adult male lion fashion all he ever wanted to do was eat, sleep, and make love. I loved him to bits, but our relationship took a big strain that day, when all of a sudden he decided he wanted to roam free. In fact, my five-year relationship with him went down the toilet at that point. He sensed our anxiety the first time he stepped out of that truck. I had lost his respect, and he was telling me, simply and without aggression, that it was over between us. My relationships with Helga, Rodney Nombekana, and Alex were also strained that day, because I was accountable for Letsatsi's lack of behavior.

It wasn't just that day that caused the relationship to go sour with Letsatsi. Some lions are brilliant filming lions; some are more relaxed than others around tourists, or with me when I go in with them. Letsatsi wasn't a filming lion, and I think despite trying to convince ourselves that everything would be all right on the big day, Rodney Nombekana and I had already seen the writing on the wall. We'd already had many discussions about Letsatsi prior to the filming day. Letsatsi had never enjoyed being loaded and driven around on the trucks, unlike Tau and Napoleon, who love that sort of thing. However, he was our only adult white lion at the time and we just had to hope that it would work out. It didn't.

I am not exaggerating when I say that Rodney, Helga, and I followed that lion on his walk across Nash's farm for five hours. Eventually we decided it was safe for the film crew to get out of their enclosure, pack up, and move location, leaving us to get Letsatsi back to the park. Letsatsi hadn't turned wild and decided he wanted to kill people, though after five kilometers of strolling across the open plains, he caught scent of Hennie the farm manager's horses.

"Guys, this is starting to get out of control," I said, delivering one of the great understatements of my career as a lion caregiver and filmmaker. "Get the dart gun."

I was still walking behind Letsatsi, but now every time I closed within about four meters of him he would turn, flare his lip at me, and growl. He was giving me some very clear signals and he was a very big lion.

Alex went back and fetched the tranquilizing drugs and a dart gun that we always kept with us on shoots, just in case. He drove back to where we were, still following Letsatsi en route to Hennie's horses.

"What's going to happen?" Hennie asked me. "Is he going to eat my bloody horses?"

"It'll be fine," I said, in my most confident voice. I neglected to tell Hennie that Letsatsi often ate horse meat at the Lion Park, although I was praying Letsatsi didn't know what a whole horse looked like!

We might have been making a movie, but darting a lion is not as easy as it seems on TV. I worked faster than I ever have before, pressurizing the air-powered gun, lubricating the barrel, assembling the dart, mixing up a double concentration of Zoletil, drawing the drug, and attaching the rubber stopper on the end of the needle so the fluid wouldn't leak out. Zoletil is a good drug to use when tranquilizing lions; it is safe and even if the dosages are not spot on it does not have adverse side effects.

I had one shot at Letsatsi. If I missed, or if the dart just pricked him and fell out, he would be off like a shot and in amongst Hennie's horses before I had time to prepare another projectile and reload. I loaded the dart in the gun and stalked as close as I dared to Letsatsi. I raised the stock of the gun to my shoulder, took aim at his pristine white rump, and fired. The dart left the barrel with a *pfft* of compressed air.

"*Rooooaaaaaaaaaar*," bellowed Letsatsi. Man, was he pissed off.

He ran around in circles, and for a second I thought he would turn, charge me, and kill me. I stood my ground as Letsatsi calmed himself. Still angry, he walked to a patch of shade under a tree and lay down.

We humans sat down and waited for the drug to take effect, while reflecting on what had just happened to us all. The Zoletil took hold of him after about ten minutes and Letsatsi fell asleep. There were five of us there—me, Alex, Rodney Nombekana, Helga, and Hennie the worried farmer—but that wasn't enough people to lift Letsatsi. The ground at Nash's farm is seriously rocky and we had been following Letsatsi on foot. Alex had brought the vehicle back as close as he could, but there was no way we could pick Letsatsi up and carry him to the *bakkie*. It took about twenty minutes to drive the truck twenty yards over the rocks to where the lion lay.

In the meantime I gave Letsatsi a top-up of Zoletil. Finally we had the pickup parked next to him. The five of us, grunting and cursing under the strain of more than six hundred pounds of dead weight of lion, just managed to lift Letsatsi high enough to slide him into the rear carrying compartment of the vehicle.

"We're completely stuffed," I said to Rodney Nombekana as we drove Letsatsi back to the park. Rodney nodded. We still had plenty more filming to do, but our star had quit on us, and, though we tried again in vain, he never worked on the film shoot again.

My relationship with Letsatsi had deteriorated not only because of peer pressure, but because of money pressure. I had been pushing him harder and harder in the weeks that led up to his spectacular walkout, not because I wanted to prove to the crew and other on-lookers that Letsatsi would follow my every command, no matter how tired he was, but because I was working to a budget.

"You shouldn't feel responsible for things going wrong. It's not your fault," Rodney Fuhr said to me.

But I did feel responsible. I was involved in every aspect of this film's production, from the animal wrangling to the writing, from the catering to the artistic direction. I was feeling pulled in every direction. Someone had to be responsible when things didn't go according to plan, and it was usually me.

It would have been different if I had just been involved in one part of the film. In the past, when I was working as an animal wrangler on commercial shoots, I had pulled lions when I sensed they were in danger of being overworked. I would happily say to other film crews, "Guys, look, you've got one more take and then this lion is going to bed," and they would always respect that. My job had been not only to ensure that the lions delivered, but to look after their welfare, as well. If I had been simply the wrangler on the set of *White Lion*, I probably wouldn't have unloaded Letsatsi from the truck in the first place, as I would have been able to sense—and obey that feeling—that everything was not right with this lion. In fact, I would have sensed all was not right much sooner and pulled the plug months before the shoot, as the signs of Letsatsi not working were there for all to see.

As the animal wrangler *and* producer, I was wearing two hats. If a lion performed the same action five times, I might still want him to do it again for a sixth, to ensure we got the best possible shot. As a wrangler I would have called a halt after four or five—more than a crew would experience on most film or television shoots—but as producer I would go to bed at night worrying that we had ended up with a second-rate shot.

I was pushing the lions—all the white lions that played Letsatsi at various ages, and his brown lion companions. In the first two seasons of filming, summer 2005–2006, and again in the wet season of 2006–2007, I learned a lot more than I ever had about lions and their limits. Poor Letsatsi had cracked before he even got started on *White Lion*.

It's important for me to point out that I would never allow any animal cruelty during the filming of *White Lion*, no matter how far behind schedule we were. In South Africa, as happens around the world, animal welfare experts are always present on film shoots to ensure no improper or cruel practices are employed when working with animals, and that no animal is harmed during the course of the production. I have had a very good relationship with the Animal Anti Cruelty League (AACL) over a number of years. I have really come to respect their welfare officers. They have a tricky and difficult job, ensuring the rights of animals are protected in the high-pressure environment of a film set. Film people always want to get the best possible shot and they're being paid a lot of money to be there.

One very experienced guy from AACL, Rulof Jackson, had a way about him that engendered respect. I see the anti-cruelty people as friends and a backup on set, not as adversaries. When things are not going right with an animal and the pressure is increasing to make the shoot go according to plan, it's the AACL person who will step in and say things are becoming dangerous. As a producer on *White Lion*, it was sometimes difficult for me to walk the line between getting the job done and watching out for the animals' interests. It was at times like that that I really appreciated Rulof being there. He did a great job, and I think it's fair to say we came out of the project with a great deal of respect for each other.

We never broke the rules, but I don't think that it is necessarily a bad thing to put an animal under a little bit of stress when working with it. Animals need to be challenged and kept active and interested in what is going on around them—it breaks the monotony of captivity—but in my heart of hearts I knew that I was sometimes pushing too much. When Letsatsi walked out on me at Nash's farm it wasn't because I had hurt him, it was because he was sick of me and the lead-up work we had been doing together.

The pressure to make a perfect film did not lessen, particularly as shooting stretched over the following two years. In all, we filmed over three summer seasons, from 2005 through 2008. However, I knew that sometimes, from that point onwards, I would have to settle for a "good enough" shot of a lion rather than the best that money could buy.

As it turned out, people in the know who have seen parts of the film were amazed at some of the shots we did get. We were pioneering techniques, working animals in wide-open, unfenced spaces. Other filmmakers might have used locked-off cameras, keeping the frame still so that footage of a lion walking could be cut and pasted in later. We were doing it live, often in one take, so shots that I thought could have been done better were wowing people. Our philosophy was to get as much that was "real" action on film as we could, in order to save time and money on post production. Of course, for some scenes we still had to use blue screens and split screens, where different people or animals are filmed on the same set, but at different times, especially when safety was an issue.

Rodney Nombekana helped keep me true to the principles that I had applied when working with lions before the film, and that I had tried to instill in him. He became my conscience, and he was very good at it.

"Kev, I think we maybe need to give this lion a rest now if we want to work him tomorrow," Rodney would say to me gently, on occasions after Letsatsi freaked out. In essence, he was doing for me what I had done for directors and producers on shoots in the past.

The downside of the way I work with lions is that when a relationship breaks down, as mine did with Letsatsi, there is sometimes no going back if you pass that point of no return.

A lion tamer or wrangler who works with a shock stick, or a stick, or a whip, will probably always be able to get his lion to jump up on a chair or through a hoop whether the animal hates him or tolerates him. For me, I couldn't change methods in midstream.

Following the debacle at Nash's Farm, the other production team members started to convince themselves that perhaps Letsatsi's walkout was a one-off. "Maybe he was just wowed by the wide open spaces, or put off by the number of people on the set that day," one of the guys said to me during a production meeting. "Maybe we should give him another chance. What do you think, Kev?"

I could hardly say to them that no, our one big white male lion would never work again, even though that was what I believed in my heart of hearts. "Okay, let's give it a try," I said, bowing to the pressure again.

We thought that if we put Letsatsi in the fifteen-hectare enclosure at the back of the Lion Park, we might be able to get some footage of him doing things at his own pace. There was another pride living in the big enclosure, two males named Jamu and Mogli, and their four lionesses, one of whom, Ice, was heavily pregnant. We relocated them without difficulty, but it was a different matter altogether when it came to moving our temperamental star white lion to his new home. Letsatsi was onto our game and did not want to play. It was a mission just to load him into the truck to move him to the bigger enclosure, but eventually we managed to get him there.

Letsatsi became progressively more aggressive and he started to learn, like a disobedient child, that we were intimidated by his behavior, and that we would back off from him when he showed his anger. It was a case of stimulus and response, and he kept upping the ante. He would see me and growl, and I had to say to the other executives on the film, "This has gone beyond a lion refusing to work—this is about a lion becoming dangerous."

We had moved Jamu and Mogli and their girls out on a Friday, and Letsatsi into the big enclosure on the same day. On that Saturday morning the film crew arrived and we tried to work with Letsatsi. He was impossible. He refused to respond to food or any other stimulus and just sat around doing absolutely nothing. His urge to explore, which had been so strong on Nash's farm, was nowhere to be seen. It was a complete waste of time, so we finished work at lunchtime.

"Should we move him back to his small enclosure, Kev?" Rodney Nombekana asked me.

I shook my head. "It was so bloody difficult getting him here I doubt he'd load again. Look at him," I said, gesturing over to Letsatsi, who was sitting under a tree glaring at me. "He's not going to get in a truck or do anything we want him to do. Let's give him some time and space, Rod, and see how he's doing on Monday." With that, Rodney and I went home for the rest of the weekend, and the film crew left with diddly squat.

I was tired and depressed and frustrated and, as usual, Mandy had to bear the brunt of me unloading my woes when I got home. She, more than anyone, knows what I went through during the filming of *White Lion*. She saw the relationships with lions and people erode, and was always there to let me vent when I needed to.

On Monday morning Rodney and I turned up to the big enclosure to check on Letsatsi. I called him, but couldn't see him. We began walking along the fence line, but there was no sign of him. He's a very big, very white lion, and the bush was very green at that time of the year, so he normally stood out a mile off.

"Letsatsi!" I called.

Rodney looked at me and shrugged his shoulders. Neither of us could see him, so we decided we would go in and look for him. Fifteen hectares is a sizeable area, and this enclosure contained a good deal of natural vegetation, which we had hoped would look good in the film.

We started working a search grid, moving slowly from left to right through the long grass and bush of the enclosure, calling his name as we went, and keeping each other in sight for safety. We couldn't find him. "This is crazy. He can't have disappeared," I said.

"Escaped?"

I shook my head, not even wanting to consider the possibility of this cranky male lion being somewhere on the loose. It had been bad enough when Bonny and Chucky the Houdini hyenas had got out and chewed up the guy's lounge suite. In the mood he was in, Letsatsi might prefer people to furniture. To be sure, I checked the fencing and searched for spoor, but there were no gaps in the wire and no tracks or other signs that Letsatsi had got through, under, or over either one of the two fences that surrounded the big enclosure.

"Let's try again on the Polaris," I said to Rodney. We hopped in the four-wheel all-terrain vehicle to try the search again. I was hoping that the noise of the engine might make him stick his head up, or stand, in case we had somehow missed him while he was hiding under a thick bush. "Here boy! Letsatsi!" we cried as I drove the vehicle over the uneven ground.

"*Wa-OWWW,*" came a high-pitched, squeaky noise from off to our right.

I pulled on the brakes, cut the engine, and cocked my head.

"What is it?" Rodney asked.

"Shush. Listen, Rod." I held my hand up and waited for the noise again.

"*Wa-OWWW,*" something squealed again.

"Wa-OWWW?" I parroted. "That sounds like a bloody lion cub. Did you hear that?"

Rodney turned to look in the direction I was pointing, concentration plain on his face. "No, no, no, Kev. There are no cubs here."

Rodney is part deaf at the best of times. I knew what I had heard. "Listen, man."

"*Wa-OWWW.*"

"There it is again! You must have heard it that time."

Rodney's eyes widened. "Yes, I heard it that time. What is that? That's not Letsatsi."

"Shit," I said. We got off the Polaris nervously, because now we were wondering if there was a lioness in there with cubs.

Rodney and I recounted the events of the previous Friday in

whispers as we walked. We had counted Jamu, Mogli, and the four lionesses into the truck. It was only six lions, so it wasn't like we could have missed one.

"*Wa-OWWW. Wa-OWWW.*"

Rodney and I paced quickly towards the sound, which was getting louder. I grabbed a fistful of thorn bush and pulled it aside. There in the grass were two tiny little lion cubs, alive but badly dehydrated, still stumbling about, squawking for their mother. Lion cubs are blind for about the first week of their lives and particularly vulnerable.

"Ice?" Rodney said, reading my mind as realization dawned on his face.

"Bloody hell," I said. We knew Ice, one of Jamu and Mogli's lionesses, was pregnant and due to give birth, but she had still looked pregnant when we had loaded her on to the truck three days previously. I remembered her bounding up onto the back of the vehicle—there had been no snarling or reluctance on her part to leave the tiny cubs that she must have only just given birth to.

I felt sick to my stomach. We had moved Letsatsi—an unrelated adult male lion with a worsening attitude—into another pride's enclosure that contained newborn cubs. By all the laws of the wild and captivity, Letsatsi would have been driven by instinct to kill Ice's cubs as soon as he encountered them. Yet here were two babies that had miraculously survived a weekend caged with a killer. Was it possible that Letsatsi, who was still nowhere to be seen, had missed these two, or had Letsatsi escaped from the big enclosure? All the possibilities were too scary to consider.

"*Wa-OWWW!*" This time the cry came not from the two little weaklings that Rodney and I cupped in our hands, but from another bush, ten yards farther on.

"More of them?" Rod said.

My heart was pounding in my throat as we moved forward. This day was getting weirder by the second and Letsatsi could still be waiting behind the next tree, preparing to ambush the humans he had grown to distrust. The bush was thick in this part of the enclosure and I brushed a sapling aside.

There was Letsatsi. He turned his big white face and looked at me, from the thicket where he had been hiding from us. I froze. One more tiny cub was nuzzling Letsatsi's snowy stomach while a fourth was plonked on its bottom, nestled between the male's two huge paws. Letsatsi opened his mouth, revealing his wickedly gleaming teeth, and rolled out his long, studded tongue. He gave the little cub a lick and looked back up at me. He gave a low, friendly greeting: "*Wuh-ooow.*"

Here he was, not killing, but protecting; playing with and caring for another pride female's cubs that had been sired by one of two unrelated brown male lions. I had thought Letsatsi was becoming a danger, but here he was treating the strange cubs like his own. Even if they had been his own, conventional wisdom had it that cubs couldn't be introduced to their father until they were eight weeks old, and Ice's babies were far younger than that.

The cubs clearly hadn't had a drop of milk since they had been born, and Letsatsi, for all his kind intentions, could not suckle them, so now Rodney and I had to get the two other cubs away from him. Incredibly, Letsatsi didn't bat an eyelid as we approached him and picked up the cubs. We left him there, loaded the cubs and ourselves into the Polaris, and drove quickly back out of the big enclosure, off to where Jamu, Mogli, Ice, and the others were now living.

Other Park employees started gathering around us, checking out the cubs and asking what had happened. If Rodney hadn't seen what I had, and been able to back me up, I doubt anyone would have believed the tale we breathlessly recounted. As humans, we have no clue how complicated and intelligent these majestic animals can be. When they kill their own kind or do something we find unspeakable, we think they are being mindlessly cruel, but there is always some unknown reason for their behavior.

"There's no way Ice will take the cubs back now," someone said.

"She's not stupid," I said back. Conventional wisdom was dead in this Lion Park.

Rod and I carried the cubs over to the new pen and I called to Ice. She came bounding over to us.

"Wow! Look at her vulva, Rod," I said. We both noticed for the first time that there were blood stains on her. Mentally we both kicked ourselves for not noticing on Friday, although Ice had given us no other clues that she had left a litter of helpless cubs behind her in the big enclosure.

"*Wuh-oooh, wuh-oooh,*" Ice said when she saw her babies. I knew that call well and I smiled. It was the noise lionesses made when talking to their cubs, a different sound from all others.

Quickly, we transferred Ice to a segregated night pen away from Jamu and Mogli and the rest of the pride—I didn't want to chance anything else going wrong for these cubs—and let the tiny dehydrated youngsters in with her. Within ten minutes they were happily and greedily suckling from their mom.

Ice looked up at Rodney and me as if to say, "Thanks guys." I can't deny that there is an unspoken language that the lions and I communicate with. Sometimes people ask me, how do you know what he or she is actually telling you? I answer back, "I just know."

Rodney and I were like a couple of joyous new fathers. We hugged and slapped each other and laughed and danced on the spot.

FOURTEEN

The Show Must Go On

I always thought that Letsatsi was a super lion. After seeing the way he behaved with Ice's cubs, we all knew that he was not the monster that we feared we had created. However, while he had let us take the cubs back, he refused to move from under the bush where he had been denning the babies, and refused, again, all our efforts to load him onto a truck.

Ultimately, we were able to lure him with food into the big enclosure's night pen, and from there into a smaller temporary fenced yard, and eventually into a cage. We then had to lift the cage onto the truck to move him out. I didn't want to dart him, as I felt he had been through enough already. Whereas Ice had given us a look of thanks and contentment, Letsatsi's stare from the back of the truck said to Rodney Nombekana and me: "You guys are the ones who have given me so much grief in my life, and our relationship will never be the same."

Nowadays when I drive through the camp I say hi to Letsatsi and he says hi back to me, through the car window, but that's about as far as it goes between him and me. As well as losing our relationship with Letsatsi, Rodney and I from then on also had to give up any relationships we had enjoyed with Letsatsi's future pride females, as it wasn't worth the risk of approaching the girls that belonged to Letsatsi. He was just too protective of them around us. It was probably my confidence that had been shattered and both Letsatsi and I had responded to that realization. It was sad, but we had to move on.

But there was another problem: making *White Lion* was just starting to get me down. Both the people and the lions involved were not exactly behaving according to the plan. I had met a lot of fantastic people from the film industry, including Mike Swan, who started as our director of photography and ended up, after we lost out first two, our general director. Our focus-puller, Houston Haddon, was a great guy; but there are others I would be happy never to see again as long as I live. Apart from Mike and Houston, Rodney Nombekana and Rodney Fuhr are the only other people apart from me who have been with the film from its beginning to its end. Helga, as always, was brilliant, though she left to have and raise her first child during filming, otherwise I am sure she would have been with us all the way.

Usually when I have problems with people, lions take up the slack and rarely disappoint me, but this time, there was no such luck. Our star adult white lion, Letsatsi, was on permanent strike, and Graham, a promising understudy, had been killed by Sly in his murderous rampage. I had only one other biggish white male, a wonderful lion named Thor, who would eventually grow big enough to be used as a stand-in for some scenes as the adult Letsatsi, but we needed another full-sized white lion to replace the real Letsatsi, and we needed him quickly. Having Thor maturing in the wings would also relieve the pressure on the newcomer in the following season of filming.

Some of the other production people and I hit the phones and the Internet, literally scouring the world for a full-sized white male lion.

We spoke to people in the States, Europe, and Australia, and it looked like we might have to bring a wrangler into South Africa as no one wanted us to work their lions by ourselves. That was a fair enough point, as I wouldn't have a relationship with the new lion and didn't particularly want to strike up a new one, either. However, employing both lion and handler and shipping them from overseas was going to cost us a fortune. One American-based animal handler told us that we would not find a workable white lion, but he would dye one of his brown lions white for us! I said no thanks.

Closer to home we checked up on other white lions that we had raised at the park and subsequently sold to other operators, to see how they were doing. One of these was Snowy, who was living on a farm in the Eastern Cape where he was being used for display. We went to the farm to have a look at him, but as our luck would have it he was mating at the time. As you can imagine, when Snowy was faced with the prospect of mating with his new lioness or befriending two humans he didn't know from Adam, he took one look at Rod and me and growled. We got the message and backed away from Snowy's enclosure. I don't need to be told twice when a lion is in no mood to become a film star.

People e-mailed us pictures of their white lions but we couldn't find one that was even worth following up. Some were young males with little Mohawks, but we needed a fully grown lion with a luxuriant mane. We thought we had exhausted all our leads. We went back through our old records at the park one more time and found one we had missed—Sphinx.

Sphinx had been sold by the Lion Park to another tourist operation near the giant Sun City casino and hotel complex northwest of Johannesburg. We worked out that by now he would be the right age to act as a possible replacement for Letsatsi. Ian got on the phone to them.

I had helped raise Sphinx and remembered him as a very good lion, but I had no way of knowing if we would be able to work with

him. His new owners agreed to hire Sphinx to us and I asked Rodney to go and pick him up. As Rodney was leaving to go and get
Sphinx, I said to him, "Look, Rod, if he shows the right signs—
coming up to you through the fence and talking to you—then at
least see if you can load him. If you can get him onto the truck,
maybe we'll just bring him here, put him in the big enclosure, and
try and film him through the fence." I was so desperate to keep the
project rolling I didn't want to push my luck with a lion I hadn't
seen in years.

When Rodney returned with Sphinx he was excited, and his
enthusiasm was contagious. I wanted to get a good close look at
Sphinx myself by now.

"He was fine, Kev," Rodney said, when I met him at the enclosure. "He recognized my voice as soon as I talked to him and he
loaded with no problem."

I didn't want to get my hopes up. Sphinx was about three-and-
a-half years old, but he was a little smaller than I had expected.
This, however, wasn't a major problem as it was wintertime and
the grass was still dry and yellow. It would be four or five months
before the rains came again and Mother Nature allowed us to pick
up where we had left off filming with Letsatsi, against the lush
green backdrop of an African summer. I was sure that in that time
Sphinx would grow to the right size, but the important question
lingered—could I even go into the enclosure with a lion I hadn't
seen for many years, let alone work him?

We unloaded Sphinx into a small pen which fed into the big
fifteen-hectare filming enclosure. He seemed pretty relaxed and was
responding to the sound of our voices, but even if Sphinx remembered me, we had nothing like the relationship that I shared with
Tau and Napoleon, or Meg and Ami.

"You don't have to go in with him," Rodney Fuhr said to me.
"You can film him from outside the fence."

It sounded good in theory, and even though I had suggested that approach, I didn't really think it would be possible to get everything we needed from outside an enclosure. Rodney Nombekana, Helga, and I were standing outside the enclosure. I called to Sphinx.

He trotted up to the fence and started greeting us: "*Wuh-ooow, wuh-ooow.*"

"Come," I said to the other two. "Let's go in."

"Kev, I'm not sure," Helga said.

I looked at Rodney Nombekana. He just shrugged.

I knew we had to cross the barrier, and even though my two friends might not have been convinced, I was sure that with three of us, we would be safe. None of us carried sticks, as I didn't want Sphinx to think of us in that way, though we each had a pepper spray canister on our belts.

"Come," I said to the others again, trying to sound more confident than perhaps I really was. I unlocked and slid open the gate and we walked in.

Sphinx was like a teddy bear. It was if we had never been apart. He rubbed his head against me and I did the same back to him. We gave him water and scratched and groomed him, and spent, all in all, about an hour with him. It had been two years since we had seen him and he had been quite small then, but even as a maturing adult he remembered the three of us.

We now knew we had a lion who was tame, but would he work on a film set? Letsatsi had been fine on other jobs prior to the disastrous day of filming the promo. In the months we had before filming was due to begin again in earnest, we went through the process of loading and unloading Sphinx from trucks, getting him used to following us around, and responding to offers of meat from the hand. He seemed to enjoy the theatrics of getting on and off the vehicle and he also enjoyed going for rides and exploring progressively larger areas. He was fantastic, and our relationship just got stronger and stronger. Sphinx played the part of Letsatsi like a pro in a couple of sequences until we could work with our own older white lion, Thor, who eventually came of age. Though he was only really a stand-in, it was hard to say good-bye to Sphinx when I eventually had to take him back to his owners.

Though at times I felt that filming *White Lion* was one disaster after another, I must admit that we had some fun moments, some really great times, and overcame a few challenging situations that told us we were doing ground-breaking stuff for a motion picture.

We had a scene in mind where the young Letsatsi is snapped at by a crocodile, falls into a river, and has to swim across to the other side. During the filming of *Dangerous Companions* I had shown Meg, and later Ami, how to swim with me, and they had loved it, but I didn't know if I could get Gandalf, one of five lions who played the teenage Letsatsi, to do the same thing.

Over time, Rodney, Helga and I were able to teach Gandalf to swim with us, first in a river and later in the dam we wanted to use for filming. Gandy was reluctant to swim unaccompanied; he preferred it when we were in the water with him and he had someone to chase and play with. The problem with this was that unless we humans ducked underwater—which none of us could do for long—then one of us would end up in the shot. Also, Gandy, unlike Meg and Ami, couldn't learn to keep his claws in while he swam, so I was getting nicely sliced every time we went for a dip.

We solved both of these problems in an ingenious way. We rigged a cable from poles on either side of the dam and fitted me into a very thick wetsuit and a harness with a line and pulley attaching me to the cable. I also had a long rope tied to me, which was held on the far side of the dam by a couple of guys. I would run into the water, holding a piece of meat in my hand to entice Gandalf into the shallows. Once we were both in and swimming, the guys on the far side of the dam would pull on the rope, dragging me through the water, in front of Gandalf but out of the camera's view. As a result we got this fantastic footage of Gandalf furiously paddling through the water trying to keep up with me while I was sliding safely out of reach and out of frame. I was the human bait for the swimming lion, but Gandalf proved to be such a good swimmer that every now and then he would move faster than the guys on shore could pull, and Gandy would catch me and drag me under. Fortunately, the thick wetsuit protected me from the worst of Gandalf's claws. Even though I got a little sliced and diced by Gandy's claws and people will say I'm crazy, I still had a lot of fun getting Gandy from one shore to the other.

The truth about the life of a lion is that it can be pretty boring. A lion can sleep for twenty hours of the day, hunt the other four, and then start all over again. The main character in our film had to have some adventures and some drama during his life. Otherwise *White Lion* would have become one of those arthouse favorites of a lion doing nothing but sleeping for two hours. In the story, Letsatsi's brother, who is a brown lion, is killed as a cub, leaving little Letsatsi on his own. We decided that the brother would meet his tragic end at the point of a snake's fangs. The evil snake would be a snouted, or Egyptian, cobra, a reptile with a reputation for extreme aggressiveness.

We could hardly stage the death of a lion cub to make a movie, so we decided to use a stuffed one. We were using a camera that was locked off at a fixed focal length so that after the snake had hissed and reared and attacked the stuffed cub, we would remove it and the stunt cub and then film the real cubs—little Letsatsi and his brother—on the same set under the same lighting and then put it all together during post-production.

The snake wrangler arrived with his snouted cobra—four of them in fact—and I deposited the stuffed brown lion cub and moved a healthy distance back from where the action was going to take place. Like everyone else on the set, I had a healthy respect for this particular creature. We stood back and waited expectantly as the first of the cobras slithered out of its bag. It lay there like a grayish brown slug. This thing didn't want to rise; it didn't want to strike; and it sure as nuts didn't want to kill anything. The snake guy prodded it a bit with his snake hook, a golf club with the club end replaced with a hook, but this famously aggressive snake wasn't interested at all in a stuffed lion cub.

I moved closer. "Come on, kill!" I said to it. It just lay there.

The reptile wrangler eventually gave up on that particular snake and tried another. The same thing happened—snake two showed no aggression or signs of action. It would have been comical if it wasn't so frustrating, but the same thing happened—or didn't happen—again with cobra number three. Finally, cobra number four became annoyed enough to make one half-hearted peck at the long-dead lion cub. Great.

The real cubs proved almost as problematic as the sluggish snakes. The problem with the cubs was that they were acting like real cubs, which was also a pain in the butt. That is, they walked around going "*wa-OWWW*" and searching for the milk bottle. We would give one a drink and then start filming, only to have to stop again to wipe the milk off its mouth. They would then want to roll around and play, or fall asleep instead of dying dramatically. Now, I love cubs as much as anyone and it was all very cute, but we were getting nowhere. In the final film, thanks to hours of effort over an entire night's filming and lots of trickery, we ended up with a dramatic, realistic scene in which Letsatsi's brown brother dies a heart-wrenching death. In reality, it was a one-take shot of a very bored snake and some clever editing of cubs at play. Luckily it was good enough—just.

Over four summer seasons we probably filmed for about a hundred and fifty days to make *White Lion*. It wasn't unusual for us to spend three days to get five seconds of film for the final cut. The continuity issues were a nightmare, as well, as the sets we used changed from year to year. In some years there had been fires before the rains arrived so the grass was short in some scenes and longer in others. Because of the number of lions we used, we also had to be careful to make sure the various Letsatsis at different ages looked the same throughout the final film. The dry winter months were spent on hundreds of hours of post-production and editing.

As well has having encounters with a warthog, a porcupine, cheetahs, hyenas, and even chickens in the film, Letsatsi gets into a fight with a fully grown brown male lion. I couldn't put Thor or Sphinx into an enclosure with Tau or Napoleon and have them fight—possibly to the death—so we had to get an animatronic lion made. It was an expensive process, so we only had one robot lion made.

For some scenes we had a real brown lion fighting a white animatronic lion, and in others the situation was reversed. We had two skins—one brown and one white—which we would slip over the robotic head, arms, and body. An obstacle we had to overcome was the lack of white lion skins in South Africa. There was no shortage of brown lion skins available, but not one single white lion skin that we could find because these animals are so rare. Our solution was to dye a brown lion skin white. What we found, however, was that treating a brown lion skin with peroxide actually turned it yellow rather than white. We continually had to go back to the puppeteers and tell them to keep on dyeing until they got our white lion white.

The only thing more ridiculous than a yellowish animatronic white lion on the film set was the day a giant pink chicken made an appearance.

As a precursor to the fight scene between the white and the brown lions, we needed to get footage of the brown lion—Napoleon in this case—stalking and then charging his unsuspecting prey through the bush. If I crawled through the grass in front of Napoleon he wouldn't hunt me, but would instead think we were playing a game. He would just look at me and think, 'Oh, there goes Kev, my buddy, what are you doing crawling, *bru?*' I needed to get him excited and curious about something.

In order to get the desired reaction we hired a pink chicken suit from a fancy dress place. The production runner picked up the costume, but he didn't tell the people in the shop what it was for—if he had, I doubt they would have let it off the premises. I put on the chicken suit and, ignoring the smirks and remarks from the rest of the crew, prepared to meet my fate.

We had the film crew set up in a modular cage with three-meter-tall sides that all slotted together. Inside there was Mike Swan, our director of photography, a focus-puller and a couple of assistants—black African guys who made no secret of the fact that they were terrified every time they had to work around lions, no matter how tame the animals were. Napoleon was released from his truck about a hundred meters away.

"Okay, we're rolling," said Mike.

I had been keeping myself low and out of sight, but as soon as I heard the signal I opened a gate in the cage, leapt out, and started jumping up and down and flapping my pink wings.

"*Cluck, cluck, cluck*!" I screamed at the top of my voice, leaping and flapping away like I was trying to take off.

All Napoleon saw was a giant pink chicken—he couldn't recognize me—and he swung into action immediately. He stalked forwards a few paces then charged at full speed, every primal instinct in his body telling him to attack and bring down the first giant pink chicken he had seen in his life.

As Napoleon closed in on me, I scooted back inside the cage and slammed the gate shut, leaving the confused cat pacing up and down outside our filming enclosure.

"Brilliant," Mike said.

It had worked well and we got some great footage of Napoleon charging across the veld. To be safe, we did two more takes, and each time Napoleon rose to the bait of the giant pink chicken and I was able to duck safely back inside with the now slightly more relaxed assistants and camera crew.

"One more take, Kev, just to be sure?" Mike asked.

It was tiring work. Between takes I had to undress and then walk Napoleon back to the truck and load him, then return to the cage and put on my chicken suit again. However, like Mike I wanted to make sure we got the best possible shot.

"Sure, why not?" I was also having fun, and so was Napoleon.

When we were ready to roll again, Napoleon was released from the truck. I opened the gate of the filming cage. As I started to emerge I knew I didn't need to do the clucking act as Napoleon was already running, determined to catch the giant fowl this time for sure.

However, as I emerged my feathers caught on something. Instead of the gate swinging over, the whole three-meter front side of the cage toppled forward into the grass, exposing me, Mike, the focus-puller, and their two assistants to a lion in full flight. Before I could even find the words to tell everyone to stay still and remain calm, Napoleon had covered the gap between us and him. He paused at the open front of the cage while I furiously tore as much of the pink chicken suit from my body as quickly as I could. All of us humans were potentially in trouble now as our safety cage had become a three-sided pink chicken trap.

"Napoleon! It's me, boy. It's Kev, relax!" Napoleon looked disappointed.

I turned and searched for the rest of the crew. Mike and the focus-puller were sitting there, wide-mouthed and goggle-eyed in shock, but their two African assistants were perched at the very top of the swaying cage fence behind us.

Napoleon, as I've mentioned, is one of the few male lions I have encountered who will allow me to hang with him and carry on as normal while he is in the company of a lioness in estrus. This not only makes him easy to work with, but also a pleasure to be around all the time. Making what is possibly the biggest understatement of the year, I can definitely say it's best to stay away from a male lion while he's mating. Otherwise, he'll most likely rip your head off.

For the film we wanted a shot of Napoleon walking towards the camera with an intent look on his face. I knew he would be "intense" if he thought his current girlfriend, Tabby, was being taken away from him. Napoleon didn't mind me being in the enclosure with him and Tabby, but when I loaded her into a truck while she was in estrus, he followed her with a very intent look in his eye. By using Tabby as the lure, instead of the giant pink chicken, we were able to film Napoleon with a different expression on his face. We would drive Tabby to the far end of the airstrip and Napoleon would then come bounding down to meet her—and sometimes get his reward, though she would stay in the vehicle.

It worked a treat the first time we tried it. As Napoleon got closer to his girlfriend he would look around and sniff the air, catching her scent and giving us some more magic footage to work with in the film.

The second time we tried this technique, several months later, we loaded Tabby and Napoleon and drove them to the property we were working on. "This is going to work like a charm," I said out loud.

We unloaded Napoleon then drove off with Tabby. When Napoleon set off after Tabby, he didn't really walk the route we had planned for the cameras, so we decided to load him again and drive back to the start point to repeat the whole process.

On this particular day Rodney Fuhr had come out to the set,

along with his brother and some other people, to see the filming. I walked Napoleon over to the truck, and as I opened the cage door at the rear to let him in, Tabby elbowed past us and bounded out into the grass.

With everyone looking on, I now had two lions out roaming free and, even worse, one of them was in estrus. It was the story of my life and a lesson I had clearly not learned yet: lions act up in front of visitors. Tabby walked off in the direction of the farm's perimeter fence. Napoleon followed her.

"Quick, let's load Napoleon before we lose them both," I said to Rodney as we drove down the track in pursuit of the lions. Fortunately, Napoleon was more interested in the offer of a handful of meat that day than he was in his girlfriend. I was able to load him, but Tabby refused to come when called, or even to change direction with the promise of meat. All I could do was follow Tabby patiently as she walked towards the distant fence. To make matters worse, and even more embarrassing, she would sit down every two hundred meters and have a little rest. She would gobble up a chunk of meat if I set it down in front of her, but she would not be persuaded to walk in any direction other than the one she had set for herself.

We walked like that, stopping and starting, for more than three hours, until it was after dark. At some point late in the afternoon, Tabby changed her course and took the long route back to her enclosure, over the rocky spur that runs through Rodney's property. She wasn't aggressive or angry, just determined to do her own thing, and as she looked at me from time to time, I swear she was sniggering at me. It was the unspoken language again, and this time she was telling me she would go home in her own sweet time.

"Shit, we lost a whole afternoon of filming, right in front of the boss. What a disaster," I said to Rodney Nombekana when I finally locked the gate on Tabby's enclosure. I wondered aloud if Tabby had acted as she did because she was mad at me.

"No," Rodney Nombekana said to me. "I think Tabby picked up

on the stress you've been under and wanted to give you a break from filming. I think she saw you needed to chill and spend an afternoon doing nothing."

Maybe he was right.

In one scene in the film, Letsatsi is harassed by a pack of hyenas. One of the hyenas I chose to star in the film was Chucky, the same one who, with Bonnie, had once escaped from the park. He had mellowed in his maturity.

We were filming at the Kingdom of the White Lion, where I now live with Mandy and my animals, but Chucky lived at the Lion Park at Muldersdrift, about half an hour's drive away, down the R512, a notoriously busy stretch of road that leads from Johannesburg out past Lanseria Airport to the Hartbeespoort Dam. Increasing numbers of people have moved to estates near the dam to escape Johannesburg's crime, so what was once a fairly quiet rural road has now become a popular commuter route. When people used to ask me if I was ever worried about working with so-called "dangerous" animals at the park, I used to tell them that the biggest risk I faced in life was driving to work each day on the R512.

Normally we would transport animals in a special caged truck, but that was being used elsewhere on the day Helga and I needed to fetch Chucky, so we took a normal *bakkie*, a pickup with a fiberglass canopy covering the load area in the rear. Chucky, despite his earlier escapades with his partner in crime, Bonnie, had become a well-behaved tame hyena, and like others of his kind I have known, he enjoyed riding in cars.

"You drive, Helga," I said, after we had loaded the obedient Chucky effortlessly into the vehicle. I closed the rear hatch of the canopy, locking Chucky securely inside. "I'll keep an eye on our passenger."

About three minutes after leaving the park, Chucky decided the rubber surround on one of the canopy's windows looked like a tasty treat. He began gnawing on the seal.

"Chucky! Stop that, boy. You'll ruin the *bakkie*." To make matters worse, it was a hired vehicle.

He kept chewing on the rubber strips like there was no tomorrow. Then, boom! The whole window fell out of the canopy and shattered on the road as Helga was driving.

"Helga, stop!"

She slowed and looked back over her shoulder, but even though the vehicle was still moving, Chucky leapt out of the gaping hole in the canopy onto the R512, just after the turn-off to the N14 Motorway, a major arterial traffic route.

"Slam on the brakes, Helga!"

Helga pulled off the road, but I jumped out before she had fully stopped. I was already having visions of headlines about a hyena on the loose near Lanseria Airport or, worse for me, a squashed hyena.

Chucky was on the road, bounding away, and I chased after him, arms and legs pumping as I ran down the broken white line that divided the two lanes of traffic.

"Chucky!"

A car swerved, narrowly missing me, while two others screeched to a halt, their tires squealing on the tar road. I gained on Chucky and leapt at him, bringing him down in the middle of the road with a flying rugby tackle. We rolled on the hot tar surface while more cars swerved and skidded around us.

Helga drove the *bakkie* up to where I was and I stood, picking Chucky up in my arms and admonishing him as I staggered to the side of the road. Horns blared behind me and other drivers and their passengers just gawped, open-mouthed, not believing what had just taken place in front of their eyes.

"Shit, we can't put him back in the canopy," I said to Helga, breathing heavily while I recovered from the chase.

The only place we could put Chucky, to make sure he didn't

make another run for it, was between us on the front seat of the pickup. Chucky was grinning from ear to ear as he peered out of the windscreen from his prime perch between Helga and me. God knows what people in the oncoming cars thought, but Chucky looked and acted like he rode to work on the R512 like that every day.

The rest of Chucky's day was relatively uneventful, but Mandy was studying marketing at night school at the time, and when she came home that evening she related a story one of her fellow students had told her.

"This guy in class says, 'Mandy, you won't believe what happened to me today. I was driving down the R512 behind this *bakkie* and the next thing this hyena jumps out, followed by this guy who runs after him, wrestles him to the ground, and loads him in the front seat.'"

"What did you say to him?" I asked Mandy.

"That's my boyfriend."

My cell phone rang. "Kev, the production vehicle's been hijacked and stolen."

I swore and braced myself for the news. No one had been injured in the attack, which was a blessing, but there were tapes from the filming of *White Lion* on board the car, and they were missing. Ironically, the footage was being taken to the production house for safe keeping. The driver had stopped outside the building where he was dropping the tapes, and hooted his horn to get the security people inside to let him in the gate. When no one appeared, he decided to leave the vehicle and go inside to find someone. He was gone for two minutes, and when he emerged the production car was being driven away. The driver tried to jump in front of the criminals and stop them, but they were too fast for him.

Crime is an unfortunate fact of life everywhere in the world, but it's particularly bad in Johannesburg. People are killed for their cars in this city, so our driver was lucky. "How many tapes are missing?" I asked. Perhaps it wasn't as bad as I feared.

"Thirty-two."

Now I started to panic. I'm a glass-half-full kind of person, so I organized production to go through the tape register so we could work out what was missing. It was bad.

Missing were hours of footage of the fight between our white and brown lions with the skin-clad animatronic lion; helicopter shots of wide-open expanses of Nash's farm, which had cost a fortune to shoot; and hours and hours of behavioral footage we had filmed with a camera inside an enclosure with a pride of lions. It was all gone.

We went through the usual channels, dealing with the police, and we went on air on the local radio stations and contacted the newspapers, offering a reward for the return of the stolen tapes. We didn't care about the vehicle, just the video. We received one call that led us to two of the missing tapes. It appeared the perpetrators had dumped the cargo as it was the vehicle they were interested in, but there was no trace of the remaining thirty tapes.

To make matters worse, there happened to be no useable footage on the two tapes we did recover. We had actually finished shooting by that point, but now I was faced with the task of organizing yet another season of filming. We were coming out of the rainy summer months at the time of the theft and the grass on the Highveld was drying to yellow, so we couldn't simply go out and start the cameras rolling again immediately. We had to wait until the summer of 2007–2008 to start again, and there was no way I could guarantee that we could recreate the amazing behavior we had captured on the missing tapes.

The extent of what we had lost was there for all of us to see, as all of the master tapes which had been stolen had been copied onto a lower resolution DV cam format. We did our first edit on DV cam, with the idea that we would later go back to the high-definition master tapes to do the final conform, but we couldn't use the DV cam dubs in the film as the quality wasn't good enough. It was heart-wrenching to lose all that film and the work we did, but in many ways the worst thing was that I was spending more time working on the film and dealing with all the problems than I was with the animals.

We had to reshoot the scenes with the animatronic lion, dressed in either its white or brown skin. It wasn't easy the first time around, and the second try took a lot of planning and preparation, as well.

The robot lion's paws, legs, jaw, neck, and body were hydraulically operated and electrically powered, with the juice coming from a generator. There was a lot of cable which had to be buried and the whole contraption had to be staked firmly into the ground so that when the fight began the real lion didn't totally destroy the fake one. Safety was a big issue, as well, as the real lion hopefully would be fighting the animatronic beast for real. We wanted to see real aggression on the set, so the crew was safely ensconced in a cage of wire and steel plate. I, of course, would be out with the lion, doing my best to keep things under control.

The plan was to have the brown lion fight the animatronic lion wearing the white skin, and then the reverse. After that we would edit the images together so that we had the best bits of the real and robotic action on film. The trick is to use less of the animatronic lion—whatever the color—and more of the real animals in action.

Different lions react in different ways, but generally they become possessive and defensive when it comes to food, so the idea was to show the real lion some food and then, just as it got interested in its meal, we would pull a cover off the animatronic lion and start it up.

With the crew safely locked in their cage, I walked Napoleon onto the set and showed him his meat, which caught his attention. When I uncovered the animatronic foe, he growled and lunged at it, sinking his fangs into the machine's neck. Unfortunately, at that point Napoleon, smart lion that he is, realized the thing was fake. He let go of it, sat down, and finished his meat.

The animatronics people had told me that they were concerned about their mechanical lion injuring one of my real lions. I think they wanted to make their worries known in advance, in case there were questions of liability.

"This thing is hydraulically powered and very strong. If it gets into a grip with your lion it could really hurt it—even break its back," one of the guys warned me.

"Dude, do you realize how strong a *real* lion is?" I countered. "These things are built to take down buffalo and giraffe."

We got into a debate about which would be stronger—real lion or animatronic lion, and despite my bravado the designer's words were starting to sink in. Maybe I was wrong.

I think we were all a bit relieved by Napoleon's first go at the animatronic lion, but more action was required, so we decided to unleash Thunder, the lion that had nailed the wildebeest during our ill-fated walk in the Lion Park with Rain.

I had high hopes for Thunder. He's not the biggest male lion I've ever seen, but he often became aggressive at feeding time. Well, when we let him loose and turned on the animatronic lion, he went for that thing like a lion possessed. Unlike Napoleon he didn't want to realize it was a mechanical dummy. He leapt on it and started clawing it to pieces.

"Lift it up, lift it up," I shouted at the animatronics guy.

"I'm trying, but it can't get up," the guy replied, flicking all his switches.

Thunder had pinned the pretend lion down, and the distribution of his weight and his sheer brute strength were preventing the hydraulics from working. Thunder was so enraged he broke the animatronics metal spine in three places and smashed its jaw and its arm. He snapped through welded metal and it took them a day and a half to fix their lion.

"I don't believe it," one of the animatronics guys said to me after the attack. "These lions are like gentle giants with you."

I nodded. "And now you understand how powerful they are compared to us puny humans."

We got some fantastic footage of Thunder annihilating the animatronic lion. He was a star, incredibly agile and blindingly quick, and he really seemed to enjoy hammering his opponent. The bar had been raised, and when it came to the white lions we had a similar mix of reactions. I tried Bravo and a couple of the younger white lions and they were pretty good, but what we really needed next was our big white male, Thor, one of the replacements for Letsatsi, to have a go.

I went through the by now usual sequence and Thor leapt across to the brown-coated mechanical king of beasts and grabbed it by the throat in his jaws. Thor stood there, holding on to the machine, but that was all he did. He seemed to see no need to fight it or rear up or jump on it. He simply took hold of the skin in his mouth and stood there. I really needed Thor to perform and I felt the pressure building on me to somehow make the animal do what we wanted him to do.

"Let's try again," I said to the crew. We switched the machine off and tried again.

Thor did exactly the same thing, again and again. Each time we set up the shot, he would take hold of the animatronic lion in his jaws and hang on to it.

"I'll try making the meat move while he's got hold of the animatronic lion," I said to the crew. "Maybe that'll make him angrier."

What I was doing, in effect, was trying to get my lion to do something he didn't want to do, and I should have known that it would end badly. I picked up a stick and while Thor was biting down on the robot I jiggled the meat about, teasing Thor into a reaction.

Thor let go of the machine and turned on me. He took my arm in his mouth and pushed me up against the filming cage. I held my ground against him as best as I could, staring at him. Thor glared back at me, flicked his tail, and released my arm. He turned and went back to his meat, which was definitely not jiggling anymore.

"I'm fine," I assured the breathless camera crew. When I checked my arm I saw there was not a single puncture mark, yet Thor had pinned me solidly against the wall of the cage.

"Enough is enough, Kev," Thor had said to me with that one lightning-fast reaction.

It taught me again, as if I needed to be reminded once more, that a lion is not like a light. They do not have an on-off switch in their brains that turns them from tame animal to frenzied killer in an instant. Thor, like Tsavo, had the ability to send me a message. He had probably been giving me other signs that I had either missed or ignored, but by grabbing me by the arm, he was able to tell me in no uncertain terms that he did not want to do what I wanted under any circumstance, and that he resented the way I was behaving.

I called an end to filming Thor with the animatronic lion, as he had set his boundaries and I did not want to push them. I could not afford to lose Thor's friendship, for the film's sake or for mine, and I didn't want a casualty on the set—especially not me. The footage was brilliant by most people's standards, but it was the push for perfection that had led me into trouble again. Perfection seems to be a vice of mine.

Fortunately, lions forgive faster than people do and I was able to start filming other scenes with Thor within a day or two. Like a lot of human actors, he had blown up when pushed, but the difference was, he didn't storm off the set.

On the set of the movie I broke both my rules. I often overruled my sixth sense to get a shot and I also succumbed to peer pressure. I just thank the good Lord that the animals were understanding. I was lucky that Thor sent me a warning as one friend to another, rather than killing me.

We were filming Thor again on Nash's farm, where everything that could go wrong with Letsatsi had gone wrong.

Once more, we wanted to get shots of an adult male white lion striding across a vast open area, this time from the air. We hired a helicopter for this day's filming and my idea was that I would leave Rodney Nombekana on the ground with Thor and I would keep an eye on things from the air. We wanted as few people on the ground as possible, as each of them would have to be "painted" out of the film. Rodney was wearing a camouflage poncho which he would use to cover himself and blend in with the grass whenever he paused. I had complete faith in Rodney; besides, I wanted a ride in the helicopter. However, once we started Rod radioed and asked if I would come down with them. Perhaps, like me, he still had the nightmares about Letsatsi on the day of the promo shoot.

As much as I was enjoying the helicopter ride I tapped the pilot on the arm and asked him to set me down. I chatted to Rodney and Thor, and the lion seemed fine. We set him on his way and he strode obediently, and calmly, across the veld. I also donned a poncho so I could hide from the camera. When Mike Swan, who was filming from the helicopter, radioed that he had shot enough footage, the aircraft took him away. I had decided to stay with Rodney Nombekana and help him load Thor onto the truck and ride back with them.

The driver had moved the vehicle about three kilometers—nearly two miles—away so that it would be out of the wide shots being filmed from the helicopter. As always, filming against the lush green background of summer grasses meant that mud was our constant companion.

"Kev," I heard the driver's voice say over the radio, "I'm afraid the truck's stuck."

I ran a hand through my hair in annoyance. "We can't walk this bloody lion three kilometers. He's been walking backwards and forwards all day and he's tired. We'll wait for you to get unstuck."

We had been shooting in the golden rays of the afternoon sun and now the light was fading. There was nothing else to do so Thor, Rodney, and I stopped and took in the view. As I looked out over the changing colors of the glorious African landscape, my mood calmed.

I shook my head. Who else in the world gets to walk freely through the most beautiful countryside in the world with an adult male lion and a glorious sunset on the horizon? It was a postcard picture laid out in front of us, rolling hills leading to mountains, and not another single human in sight. Thor made himself comfortable on the grass and Rodney sat on a rock beside him. I plonked myself down on Thor, which he loves, sitting on the lion's rump.

With all the stress and the crap I'd been through, I'd started to forget that I have a very good life. I was living a story anyone would be proud to tell their kids and grandkids later in life.

"All we need is a nice drink for sundowners, Rod," I said. He laughed, and we sat there in silence, happy for the truck to take its time finding us.

For a while we were alone in this incredible African landscape, three friends sharing a moment. A black guy, a white guy, and a lion. It was perfect.

EPILOGUE

A Pride of One's Own

When the truck finally freed itself from the mud about an hour later, it drove towards us, coming down the nearest road. When he heard the sound of the engine, Thor got up and led us to it. He didn't need to be ordered or bribed with meat, he just knew it was time to go home.

"How's your wife and child, Rod?" I asked as we walked along in the darkness behind Thor's guiding white coat.

"Fine, Kev. And you? Are you coping okay with all the hassles about the film?"

We chatted like that as we followed Thor. When he reached the vehicle, Thor climbed up of his own volition, got in, and we all drove home. To this day when Rodney and I have our business meetings it is often in the company of Thor on a long walk through the bush. Other people discuss the day's agenda around a table with their laptop computers open in front of them, but Rod and I walk with our lion.

I live and work at a different park these days, the Kingdom of the White Lion. Rodney Fuhr was concerned that the Johannesburg

Lion Park was too close to the city. In fact, human development has overtaken it so that instead of being in the countryside, as it was when I was a boy, it is now virtually part of suburbia.

I was involved in Rodney's search for a new piece of land and there was an extensive list of criteria that had to be met. It had to be farther out of Johannesburg, but still close enough for people to drive to for a day trip, with enough bush to provide shade and a natural habitat for the lions, but open enough to be accessible.

We eventually found the right property. It's beautiful country, a mix of open grasslands and rocky hills and valleys on the banks of the Crocodile River. We decided to film part of *White Lion* on the property, so I was able to design and build large enclosures which are ideal for filming. I had learned from my experience at the Lion Park about what works and what doesn't, and it was good to be starting from scratch.

At the Kingdom, we rotate our animals through the different enclosures, which helps keep them interested and engaged. When the lions move into an area formerly occupied by hyenas, they get busy sniffing and scent-marking and the same goes for the hyenas. We have retained as much of the natural bush as possible, and the enclosure where the hyenas now live has a natural stream running through it. They love bathing in it and they are always assured of fresh water.

It was tough for me, moving from my work at the Johannesburg Lion Park. While I was able to bring many of my animal friends with me, there was no way I could bring all of them. Although the process was expensive, at least I now have control over their destiny.

Rodney Nombekana and Helga moved to the new park with me. Volunteers from the Lion Park come to the Kingdom of the White Lion to spend time with me and to meet the animals many of them have seen on television. I will have school groups coming to visit, now that the film is finished, which I think is incredibly important in order to educate the next generation about predators, and explode some of the myths and misconceptions about African wildlife. I hope one day to open the Kingdom to the general public.

Looking to the future, I am in the process of setting up a not-for-profit company to ensure the future well-being of the animals in my care. I have been contacted by many people who have seen *Dangerous Companions*, *Growing Up Hyena*, and *Black Leopard* who want to donate money to support predators and predator research. I would like to be able to help raise money to ensure the valuable work the researchers do at Rodney Fuhr's research camp in Botswana can continue. I also want to ensure that if anything happens to me, my lions and other friends would be cared for.

There are more documentaries in the cards, though whether or not I venture into the world of feature filmmaking again will depend on the success or otherwise of *White Lion*.

I don't want to continue with animals in feature films in the way that I did on *White Lion*. I don't know if *White Lion* will be successful or not. If the movie is a huge success and we had, for example, an opportunity to make *White Lion II*, I would love to be involved, but I would wear only one cap. I do not want to be put in a position again where I am responsible for the welfare and performance of my lions on one hand, and under pressure as a producer to call on them to do take after take, until the animals are exhausted, in order to get a "perfect" shot. I don't want to put myself or my animals through that again. In fact, I would have to think twice about using my own animals in a feature film of that length again.

There were some things I did on the film simply because I knew that if I didn't do them, then they wouldn't get done. For example, I recorded sound effects up close with the lions that were later added to the film. I can go up to Napoleon and hold a small digital recorder next to his mouth when he roars, but a sound effects guy with a big microphone on a boom pole covered in a fluffy noise baffle can't do that, mainly because the lion will either try and eat the microphone or the sound guy. Rodney Fuhr had way more confidence in my own abilities than I did, which was how I ended up getting involved in everything from the script to the music score. I don't want to be in that position again.

I lost relationships during the making of *White Lion*, but others became stronger. I have a stronger relationship with Tau, Napoleon, and Thor because of the time we all spent together on the set, and because of the way I worked with them in the light of my experience with Letsatsi. Mandy and I always had a strong partnership, but she stood by me through the tough times and our love grew even stronger during the years I worked on the film.

Mandy was a martyr, putting up with all the crap I unloaded on her at the end of each day. We got married during the last season of filming, and no, there were no lions present at the ceremony or the reception.

I stopped working at the Lion Park once filming on *White Lion* began, and although I had a lot on my plate I had to work hard to keep up my relationships with the animals there—and with my wife. We would start filming early in the morning, before dawn, in order to be ready to film in the golden hours, and then spend hours packing up after the sun had set. The opposite held true for night shoots. I was spreading myself too thin, and it is only because of the good grace of Mandy and the animals I love that I retained my sanity and the love and friendship of those most dear to me.

Even though the film is finished now, my life is still busy, but I still take time to sit on my stoop, gaze out over the Crocodile River, and reflect on how lucky and blessed I have been in my life so far.

My relationships with the lions and other animals have changed and grown over the years. There have been hiccups, but we've become closer and we've learned from each other. It's the same, in many respects, as my relationship with Mandy. First there was the wow factor, the infatuation of meeting and being with someone new. Then came learning about each other, what we liked, what we didn't, what pleased us, what upset us. It continues, of course, as re-lationships are never stagnant.

Of course, sometimes with lions the adrenaline resurfaces, such as with Maditau's series of threatening charges at me when I rescued Tabby's cub from her. That may have had something to do with how her perceptions of me have changed. As I've said, I believe Tau and Napoleon treat me as a brother but know I am not a lion, so they hold back a little when we play. Meg and Ami think I am a lion and they treat me every bit as rough as they do each other. Perhaps Maditau, having been the first of the lionesses to welcome me into the pride, now thinks she can treat me like any other lion that wants to take possession of something she has claimed as her own. Being part of the pride means respecting and abiding by its rules, I suppose.

There are still plenty of people in South Africa, and now, thanks to the Internet and the documentaries and the film, around the world, who will look at the way I interact with the lions and shake their head. They will either choose to believe there is some form of trickery at play, or that there is no relationship between the animals and me. These are the people who tell me that one day one of my animals will "snap" and kill me.

As I said before, if I died in such an attack and the good Lord said he would give me a second chance—rewind the last ten years and do something different with my life—I wouldn't. Animals have always been a strong part of my life, since my dad rescued that first tiny stray kitten from the rubbish dump. They have helped me mature as a person and taught me so much about life and the way it should be lived. I like to think I have enriched their lives as they have mine.

Having raised so many lion and hyena cubs, and experienced the joys of watching Maditau and Tabby and Pelo bring their babies into the world, and of seeing Tau, Napoleon, Meg, and Ami and the many other animals in my care grow and mature, I am quite keen to start a pride of my own one day soon. So is Mandy.